The Death of "e" and the Birth of the *Real* New Economy

Other Books from the Authors

Enterprise E-Commerce
Peter Fingar, Harsha Kumar and Tarun Sharma
Meghan-Kiffer Press
Excellent companion to this book!

The Blueprint for Business Objects
Peter Fingar
Cambridge University Press

**Next Generation Computing:
Distributed Objects for Business**
Peter Fingar, Dennis Read and Jim Stikeleather
Prentice Hall

Forthcoming title ...
Peer-to-Peer Commerce
Email mkpress@tampabay.rr.com
to be notified of availability.

The Death of "e" and the Birth of the Real New Economy

Business Models, Technologies and Strategies for the 21st Century

Peter Fingar
Ronald Aronica
Foreword by Bryan Maizlish

Meghan-Kiffer Press Tampa, Florida, USA
Publishers of Advanced Technology Books for Competitive Advantage

Publisher's Cataloging-in-Publication Data

Fingar, Peter.
  The Death of "e" and the Birth of the *Real* New Economy : business models, technologies and strategies for the 21st century / Peter Fingar, Ronald Aronica - 1st ed.
    p. cm.
  Includes bibliographic references, appendices and index.
  ISBN 0-929652-20-7 (cloth : alk. paper)

  1. Electronic commerce. 2. Strategic planning. 3. Reengineering (Management) 4. Management information systems. 5. Information technology. 6. Internet (Computer network) 7. Object-Oriented methods (Computer science) 8. World Wide Web (Information retrieval system) 9. Computer software - Development. 10. CORBA (Computer architecture) 11. XML (Document markup language) 12. Information resources management. I. Fingar, Peter. II. Aronica, Ronald. III. Title.

HF5548.32.F464 2001   LC Control# 2001129113
658.8'00285–dc21   CIP

© 2001 Meghan-Kiffer Press. All rights reserved. Except as permitted under the United States Copyright Act of 1976, no part of this publication may be reproduced or distributed in any form or by any means, or stored in a data base or retrieval system, without the prior written permission of the publisher.

Published by Meghan-Kiffer Press
310 East Fern Street — Suite G
Tampa, FL 33604 USA

Any product mentioned in this book may be a trademark of its company.

Cover Art by Tad Fingar (tfingar@tampabay.rr.com).

Meghan-Kiffer books are available at special quantity discounts for corporate education and training use. For more information write Special Sales, Meghan-Kiffer Press, Suite G, 310 East Fern Street, Tampa, Florida 33604 or email mkpress@tampabay.rr.com

MK
Meghan-Kiffer Press
Tampa, Florida, USA
Publishers of Advanced Technology Books for Competitive Advantage

Printed in the United States of America.   SAN 249-7980
MK Printing 10 9 8 7 6 5 4 3 2 1

Dedicated to Jane Welch,
the "First Lady" of the *Real* New Economy.

GE's legendary CEO, Jack Welch, was introduced to the Internet by his wife, Jane. Welch launched his "Destroy your business.com before some upstart in a Silicon Valley garage does!" campaign in 1999 and challenged all of GE's line-of-business executives to "Grow your business.com" by reinventing every aspect —buy, make and sell— of their business units. Welch "got it," realizing that the Internet is about business transformation, not a Web site.

Companion Web Site

http://geocities.com/m_kpress

If you experience any difficulty with the Web site or require further information, please e-mail: mkpress@tampabay.rr.com

Table of Contents

Foreword

Part I: What's Really New in the Real Economy

Chapter 1- The E-clipse of 2000, *19*
The E-clipse of 2000
Lessons Learned, Myths Debunked

Chapter 2 The Rise of the *Real* New Economy, *33*
Technology Enables, Business Changes
The Business Technology Timeline
The Rise of the *Real* New Economy
  Stage 1. Brochureware
  Stage 2. E-Commerce
  Stage 3. E-Procurement
  Stage 4. Electronic Marketplaces
  Stage 5. The Digital Economy:
        Dynamic Business Ecosystems

Chapter 3 - The New Way of Competing:
       Value Chain Optimization, *51*
Value Chains: Arteries of the Economy
Industry Value Chains
Business Process Reengineering (BPR)
Industry Process Reengineering (IPR)
The Value Web: Structure of the 21st Century Economy
Value Chain Threads
Putting It All Together

Chapter 4 - The Art of Digital Business, *69*
The Art of Digital Business
Digital Marketplaces
E-Services: The Cathedral and the Bazaar
Knowledge Management
Customer Relationship Management:
  The Soul of Digital Commerce
Content, Commerce, Collaboration, and Context

Chapter 5 - The Commerce Resource Platform, *89*
21st Century Business Software: A Change in Kind
From ERP to CRP:
   Agile Software Powering the Agile Corporation
Building the Commerce Resource Platform

**Chapter 6 - The New Way of Competing Demands
             New Technology,** *101*
The Importance of Component-based Architectures
Peer-to-Peer: Commerce on the Edge of the Internet
Model Driven Architecture
The XML Factor and the Tower of Babel Challenge
Managing the Complexity with Software Agents

Chapter 7 - Digital Strategy, *129*
Business Strategy: People, Process and Technology
The Planning and Implementation Process
   Customer Value Analysis
   Business Strategy Formulation
   Value Chain Engineering
   Implementation
   Feedback and Measurement
Putting It All together

Part II: Thoughts from the Thought Leaders

Chapter 8 - Peer-to-Peer Commerce, *147*
        With Bob Anderson

Chapter 9 - Collaborative Commerce, *167*
        With Manoj Saxena, S.P. Rana and Tim Harmon

Chapter 10 - Portals: Business on the Network Edge, *185*
        With Barry Morris

Chapter 11 - Adaptive Strategies for B2B Marketplaces, *197*
        With Biri Singh

**Chapter 12 - B2B Integration:
              The Message is the Medium,** *219*
        With Scott Blackburn

**Chapter 13 - Bringing Visibility to the
Extended Supply Chain,** *231*
Justin Steinman And Chris Stone

**Appendix A - Prelude to the Digital Economy:
The Dot-Com Crash of 2000,** *251*

Appendix B - Pillars of Digital Commerce, *263*

**Appendix C - Business Fundamentals of the
21st Century Economy,** *281*

Appendix D - Understanding ebXML, UDDI and XML/edi, *297*
With Anthony Dutton and David RR Webber

Appendix E - Web Resources, *311*

Bibliography, *313*

Index, *339*

About the Authors and Contributors, *353*

Ordering Information for *Enterprise E-Commerce*

Foreword

"E" is dead, because e-business is no longer an option, rather every business *must* be an e-business. It forms the primary currency of our society, namely information, communication and documentation. It was the driver for the longest bull market in the history of the United States. Now that the "e" hype is over, the real work of business transformation has begun.

Digital business now comprises the fundamental fabric of business strategy and process execution, utilizing the Internet to integrate all aspects of business, connecting everyone, at anytime and in anyplace. The Internet is a new ecology, with many hidden interdependencies, unexpected events and multiple discontinuities. And, like a species that is part of an ecology, those that fail to embrace and adapt to the environment expose themselves to the risk of becoming extinct.

The Internet has revolutionized the way that companies, employees, customers, trading partners and suppliers communicate. It has caused a major paradigm shift, namely reengineering the value chain to eliminate waste and to drive value, much of it hidden. By assessing and reconstructing the variables in the value chain, the Internet ignites greater efficiency and flow, offers the customer enhanced value and control, decreases waste and costs, and provides a real-time feedback loop for improving performance.

Few executives have actually perfected the multifaceted skills needed for the road ahead; two-thirds of all major corporations have replaced their CEOs at least once since 1995 and more than 1,000 CEOs left office during the past year. Recent job cuts, excess capacity, and slowing technology spending have contributed to an over correction in the stock market (NASDAQ has declined by approximately 60% since March 2000). Notwithstanding these events, most agree that the productivity increases caused by the trajectory of "e" is a further validation for the rapid adoption of the Internet for process improvement to continue expansion through cost improvements, as opposed to top-line revenue growth during the current economic downturn. We are now witnessing the return to old, tried and true, sound financial business models in the world of e-business.

Successful companies now combine the experience and professionalism of established brands with the flexibility and adaptability of start-up firms. They have a deep understanding of how the elimination of time and geography change the way we work, communicate and live. Successful companies deconstruct their value chain, and create scenarios to dismantle and destroy their company in order to identify areas of vulnerability and exposure, and to take aggressive action against these weaknesses. They utilize decision frameworks such as six sigma and balanced scorecard to track meaningful metrics to address problems and issues early and anticipate trends.

The Death of "e" explores the stages of development of "e" from its beginnings as simple B2C front-office applications, to back-office and B2B applications, and on to e-marketplaces. E-marketplaces have been undergoing major consolidation, as the sheer number of sites outweighs the demand for these services. E-marketplaces, for the most part, have yet to demonstrate clear cost savings and acceptable returns on investment. They are very expensive to set up and operate; multiple ownership structures create confusion; they are complex and time consuming; and many are inefficient. *The Death of "e"* discusses that in order for e-marketplaces to survive, they must offer a real, sustainable and defensible value proposition, and must incorporate collaborative commerce, rather than simply combine buyers and sellers.

The book describes new peer-to-peer technologies that provide shared spaces for collaboration, communication and exchange of data in real-time. In these shared spaces, intelligent agents serve as facilitators, selecting the best resources to perform specific tasks and coordinating resources. Agents have the ability to alter business process execution in response to changing circumstances. The days of command and control, and the notion of end-to-end vertical integration within one entity are dead.

The Death of "e" points out the need for value added services, such as dynamic pricing, multiparty discovery, negotiation, supply and demand planning, joint product design, shared documents and workflow, change management and personalized offerings, which result in a collapsed, integrated supply chain among e-marketplace trading partners. Today, end-to-end value chain integration is critical but extremely difficult to achieve. Integrators face issues, such as firewalls prohibiting information distributed across the full value chain and the disparities in standards and architectures among the entities that comprise the ecosystem. *The Death of "e"* describes in detail the next generation technologies, pervasive e-services, that help cure these issues and alter the value chain. Participants in an e-services environment will be able to dynamically choose which partners they wish to utilize to satisfy the needs of a customer.

Digital business will continue to expand rapidly as new business models are developed and current business models continue to be refined to create greater value for customers. The cycle of rapid expansion, followed by integration, consolidation and restructuring will continue. Eventually, e-business systems and e-marketplaces will morph into architectures that enable the creation of modular and adaptive platforms assembled, disassembled and reassembled from components of multiple best-of breed applications. These "composite applications" render their capabilities as e-services that will work together as one solution.

As e-business grows more encompassing, companies are asking for one-stop software solutions that combine collaboration, analysis, operations and content and can securely integrate into existing back-end legacy systems. The commerce resource platform of tomorrow must allow its users to define only those features and functionalities that are needed in their business, provide the ability to easily migrate to more solutions as business models evolve, and to make it easy and instantaneous for any entity to join e-marketplaces. *The Death of "e"* provides the blueprint for the new commerce resource platforms and discusses specifications for B2B interoperation such as electronic business XML (ebXML), UDDI, SOAP, and the Common Warehouse Metamodel Interchange (CWMI).

In a few years, Internet-enabled mobile devices will outnumber PC's, further extending the collaborative community, enabling contextual, mobile and pervasive commerce. The convergence of these new technologies will deliver more choices, greater flexibility, and enhanced value to the most important entity, the customer.

The Death of "e" validates Darwin's theory of evolution. It shows that business fundamentals do matter. It challenges companies to be predictive, adaptive and flexible in unconventional ways. It lays the foundation for the networked economy operating according to the customers' rules of engagement. It demonstrates that if you are comfortable and believe your business is okay being status quo; if you do not understand that the demarcation between you and your competitors is becoming more ambiguous; if you are not willing to partner with your competitors; if you are not an innovative disrupter and think in terms of spaces instead of places, you are already in the danger zone and not moving fast enough to survive the death of "e."

Bryan Maizlish
Lockheed Martin Global Telecommunications
April 2001

Part I: What's Really New in the Real Economy

A Reader's Guide to Part I

From 1996 - 2000 the Internet took the business world by storm. The first books on the topic appeared in 1996 to meet the growing demand for information about the subject. By 2000 over 200 books covered various aspects, and today the number has soared to over 800. Some of these provide overall treatment of the topics from A-Z, while others address specific topics in detail.

This book does neither. Instead it provides an analysis of the business models, technologies and strategies *going forward* from where we are today. The authors make the assumption that readers will be at least somewhat informed, but not equally well read. Because of these differing backgrounds, we have included a number of *backgrounders* for optional reading. *We recommend skimming these to determine if the material will be helpful and fill in any gaps.* These backgrounders include:

- *Appendix A - Prelude to the Digital Economy: The Dot-Com Crash of 2000.* This backgrounder reviews the events of 2000 that saw market caps plummet for the dot-coms. The analysis places into perspective the fundamental reasons for the demise of the dot-coms deploying baseless business models that could not be sustained, and debunks the myths. If you have not yet taken time to digest the real meaning of the headlines of 2000, this backgrounder will be helpful and should be read first. Some of the reviewers of the book found this backgrounder to be a very informative summary of what happened in 2000.

- *Appendix B - Pillars of Digital Commerce.* Chances are you have read extensively about e-commerce and e-business. If not, this backgrounder is a "crash course" in digital commerce.

- *Appendix C - Business Fundamentals of the 21st Century Economy.* This backgrounder describes 15 ways that the Internet affects business fundamentals. We suggest that you skim the list to determine if you can benefit from a discussion of each point, or if you already have a working knowledge of the fundamentals.

- *Appendix D - Understanding ebXML, UDDI and XML/edi.* This backgrounder describes the emerging standards critical to business-to-business digital commerce. The authors invited David R. R. Weber and Anthony Dutton to develop the material for this chapter, as they are not only experts, they are deeply involved in the work of the standards organizations.

Part II:
In-Depth Analyses from the Thought Leaders

Part I of the book provides an overview analysis of Internet business models, technologies and strategies going forward. Part II provides in-depth treatments of the essential topics from the thought leaders who are taking us to the next level of digital commerce.

Chapter 1

The E-clipse of 2000

There is no "new" economy, but there is something very new in the real economy.

Y2K: The Real News

The year 2000 (Y2K) was supposed to be full of stories about the lack of a four-digit date field to accurately record the year in computer systems. Since most computer systems stored the year as only a two-digit number, pandemonium was forecast when the year became "00." In the years and months leading up to Y2K, consultants had a field day repairing computer programs, and the press spent vast amounts of ink and paper foretelling the worldwide chaos that was to come.

But the Y2K apocalypse did not happen. What did make headlines, however, was the crash of the dot-coms, those radical Internet commerce upstarts that were supposedly changing all the rules of business and ushering in a *new* economy.

Shock waves went throughout the business world as market caps came tumbling down throughout 2000. The public markets, led by the technology sector, wiped out about $2.5 trillion in market capitalization in 2000.[1] Many thought that the Internet was doomed as the new medium of business.

It is not. Deep business transformations are being driven by the Internet. But before moving on to the serious business of the 21st century economy, it is important to clear the air and get beyond the spectacular headlines, hype and myths.

The E-Clipse of 2000.

The new economy is dead. Long live the *real* economy, one where business fundamentals count. The Internet is not the economy, it's but a channel: you don't drive it, eat it or live in it; it's the information channel tracking what you eat, drive, and live in. You cannot even see it —its central nervous system is in cyperspace moving around in geosynchronous orbit. Today, only a small fraction of the transactions of the economy flow through it, yet, its force is reshaping the way buyers and sellers of economic goods do business. The news in Y2k signaled the end of the beginning of the Internet Revolution and marked start of real digital transformation in the economy.

The e-commerce, e-business, e-everything bubble had burst, and the shock wave is likely to extend through the next few years. What happened? Christmas 2000 witnessed an eclipse of the sun that temporarily blurred the light of day. After a few hours, there was again the full light of day. So it also was with e-commerce, e-business or e-whatever you want to call the 'e' phenomenon that briefly appeared in cyberspace and blurred the light of business fundamentals. After the e-clipse of Christmas 2000, the full light of business reality began to shine. The disbelief, fear, uncertainty doubt and overall blur created by the advent of the Internet as a business medium, had given way to full light of business principles. In the *real* new economy, business fundamentals —not the e-hype, astronomical market valuations and headliner IPOs for money losing dot-coms— count.

The magical change introduced by the first wave of the Internet in business has become demystified. The business community has made significant progress climbing the learning curve. Wall Street is now wise to the e-phenomenon and the dot-con game. Unrealistic market caps and wild IPOs no longer defy gravity.

E-business has become just business. E-commerce has become just commerce. The new economy has become just the economy.

Through the many lessons learned during the e-gold rush, the consolidations that follow the introduction of any disruptive business technology ensued. For example, consolidation in the automobile industry followed shortly after its introduction. In the early years there were hundreds of car makers. Today there is a handful. The economy takes time to move through the euphoria, alarm and control stages of any major technological innovation.

With the experience gained from "chapter one" of the business Internet, now is the time to chart a course using the business models, technologies and strategies that will most likely be the key to competitive advantage in the early 21st century.

Advertising and marketing specialist, Ashok Dongre, provides an apt summary, "All the people, who jumped on to the Internet bandwagon because it was fashionable, are now abandoning it. But that is simply good news for serious users. Now is the time to clear the debris and get on to the road ahead with a well thought out Internet strategy, that will really take you into the 21st Century."[2]

Lessons Learned, Myths Debunked.

***Myth 1.* There is a *new* economy.**
We still live in the *age of oil*, in an industrial economy, not a post-industrial, intangible, space-based information economy. When asked if we are in a post-industrial economy, Glenn Pascall, senior fellow at the Institute for Public Policy and Management at the University of Washington replied, "No, we live in a knowledge-based industrial economy. By the numbers, making and selling physical products remains the dominant activity. Manufacturing employment drifts down steadily but the value of output from this sector holds steady at 25 percent of gross domestic product. Some analysts believe business service inputs to manufacturing account for another 25 percent."[3]

There is no "new" economy, but there is something very new in the real economy. The Internet provides a powerful new business infrastructure, a universal information system, for handling the transactions of the economy, bringing radical new efficiencies to both buyers and sellers of goods and services.

The advent of e-commerce does not eliminate the business cycle nor will it create a *new* economy where the old rules are thrown out and productivity gains spiral only upward and upward. In almost all cases, the Internet does not change fundamentals of business: capital, innovation, profits, cost control, liquidity and quality. Nor does it change the basic demands of customers: delivering value.

The dot-com phenomenon was concerned with B2C retailing, and though it generated the e-hype, market frenzy and all the press, it is the business-to-business connections that make up the lifeblood of the economy that is at issue. Those B2B connections are a hundred fold larger than the B2C connections and are at the center of the search for economic transformation and hyper-efficiency —frictionless commerce where supply chains of inventory are replaced by value chains of information.

In remarks before the U.S. House Committee on Financial Services in March, 2001, Federal Reserve Chairman Alan Greenspan said the prospects for productivity growth in the U.S. economy remain bright, in part because of B2B e-commerce technology that has sped the reaction time of companies to ebbs and flows of supply and demand. "Extraordinary improvements in business-to-business communication have held unit costs in check, in part by greatly speeding up the flow of information," said the chairman. "New technologies for supply-chain management and flexible manufacturing imply that businesses can perceive imbalances in inventories at a very early stage —virtually in real time— and can cut production promptly in response to the developing signs of unintended inventory building.

"A couple of decades ago, inventory data would not have been available to most firms until weeks had elapsed, delaying a response and, hence, eventually requiring even deeper cuts in production. In addition, the foreshortening of lead times on delivery of capital equipment, a result of information and other newer technologies, has engendered a more rapid adjustment of capital goods production to shifts in demand that result from changes in firms' expectations of sales and profitability. A decade ago, extended backlogs on capital equipment meant a more stretched-out process of production adjustments."[4]

During the past few decades, manufacturing was globalized and the Western economies, once the manufacturing monopolists, were transformed. In the knowledge-based industrial economy, white collar work will likely be globalized because that too is now possible. Why would a New York corporation pay a quarter of a million dollars a year to a CFO in New York when the same services are available for thirty thousand bucks a year in South Africa? Same certifications, same quality. Already computer programming has moved to India, engineering design to Asian Tiger countries and basic research to Russia.

The fundamentals of business are still intact despite the pundits yelling "throw out the old rules" and "forget everything you know." Moving forward, B2B will mean "back to business", and B2C will see dot-com whiz kids going "back to college," hopefully to a good business school. We will need more work horses than show horses to build the Internet backbone for the hyper-efficient economy of the 21st century. It is going to be a lot of work and heavy lifting in the years ahead.

Myth 2. The Internet is a business fad that faded in 2000.

Despite the dot-com crash of 2000, the Internet still changes everything. Could a business work today without the telephone or fax? The Internet, too, is fundamentally reshaping businesses, the information systems that run them and the industries in which they compete.

This profound change has only begun and is so overwhelming that it will take several years for businesses and industries to learn, adapt and harness the most significant information medium of the 21st century. Unlike any information network before it, the Internet is pervasive, interactive, multidimensional and capable of delivering value chains of information never before possible.[5]

In an interview with *BusinessWeek Online*, GE's legendary Chairman and Chief Executive Officer, John F. (Jack) Welch said, "Where does the Internet rank on my priority list? It's number one, two, three, and four. I don't think there's been anything as important or more widespread in all my years at GE."[6]

His theme for GE's business unit executives has been "destroy your business." The idea is to study and discover how the Internet competitors wanted to destroy GE's business and change existing business models in response to these threats. The second part of the exercise, "grow your business," conceives how the Internet can be used to reassemble sustainable competitive advantage.

Why is Welch so excited about the Internet? The Internet exposes so many possibilities to so many facets of business, that the ultimate question any business must ask is "what can we now do to gain competitive advantage that we could not do before the Internet?"

What's the business impact on the business when the entire world can share one computer, one information system, one marketplace? What's possible when customers and suppliers —both their people and their computers— share the same information base? Answers to these questions will vary, industry by industry as leaders redesign and stress test end-to-end industry business processes, wringing out friction, inefficiencies and disconnects in the overall economy. *The Internet is an infrastructure for a whole new way of doing business.*

Myth 3. The foremost goal of a company is to deliver shareholder value.

In the era of too much cash in the public markets, it seemed that shareholder value (especially the stratospheric IPO) had replaced the customer as king. Not so. Thanks to the transparency the Internet introduces into markets, consumers have grabbed power from producers and transformed customers from kings to never satisfied dictators —demanding impeccable quality, the best price and excellent support.

Glenn Pascall paints the picture, "A basic reason shareholder returns can't give purpose to corporate life is the length of time a stock is held. The U.S. longevity champ is General Electric, where shares stay in the same hands an average of 3.5 years. For Microsoft, the average is 3.5 months and for Yahoo! Inc., it's 3.5 days.

"Even if a company embraces shareholder returns as its reason for being, what should it do if the average shareholder is gone before the impact of any strategy can play out? Moreover, what is behind the stock market surge, other than a vast pool of hot money floating around the globe and alighting for brief periods on targets of opportunity? Can such a "customer" serve as the proper focus for corporate strategy? The question answers itself."[7]

Myth 4. Clever ideas make new wealth.

"Why didn't I think of that? I could have been the next Internet billionaire." Actually, zillions of dot-com ideas amounted to nothing. The primary reason was baseless business models. Just because a business *can* be ported to the Internet, that does not mean it should be or that the venture will succeed. The new e-business had better add compelling value that is not available elsewhere.

Even with a sound business model, success can be difficult to achieve and requires ongoing effort just as any business venture. Success in using the Internet as a new business medium is all about *execution*.

Fresh ideas are *necessary* in light of the possibilities posed by the Internet, but only execution is *sufficient*. Ideas, plans, and strategies are one thing —implementation is something entirely different. CEO Jeff Bezos proclaimed that nothing Amazon.com does is very original —it just executes better than anyone else.

Strategy is nothing without execution, and execution requires firing on all cylinders: product planning, technology, marketing, promotion, fulfillment and customer care. Amazon began as an Internet pure play, but kept running hard until it too became a brick and mortar company with real warehouses and logistics systems. Furthering these moves, in March 2001, Britain's *Sunday Times* reported that Amazon, the best-known internet brand in the world, had begun talks to form a strategic alliance with Wal-Mart Stores Inc., the world's largest retailer. The alliance confirms the notion that the "click and mortar" business form will no doubt reign supreme in the 21st century economy.

Myth 5. B2B marketplaces should be the focus of e-business efforts.

During the business reengineering movement of the past decade or so, some companies downsized and outsourced themselves until they became anemic. Sure, the cost side of the business is vital, but the real prize of any business is to provide value to its customers and make a healthy profit in the process. B2B marketplaces and trading consortia will continue to be a moving force in the economy, but the danger is that, due to their popularity in the trade press, companies can commit too many resources on the buy-side of the business at the exclusion of the customer-facing initiatives. In this age of the customer, a company's differentiator will be pleasing never satisfied customers, not just squeezing costs.

Sam Nickless, associate principal at McKinsey & Company, says, "it is wrong for companies to view an online exchange as the exclusive focus of their e-business strategy, adding that the focus on online exchanges might be blinding them to better e-commerce opportunities elsewhere in their business.

Nickless estimates that a business can save 7-10% on purchasing costs by simply cleaning up its internal processes before joining an exchange, which might only achieve additional savings of 1-4%. Given that there is only a limited amount of time and energy that you can spend in the management of e-commerce, you may be better off focusing on e-commerce that is customer-facing rather than supply-facing."[8]

B2B is not the opposite of B2C, business-to-consumer. With the demise of the dot-com retailers, companies must not be distracted by crash and burn stories. They should keep their resources targeted at the *customer,* whether that customer is another business or the retail consumer.

Myth 6. B2C e-commerce is dead.

Ramin Marzbani, senior analyst at www.consult, says the only aspect of the B2C e-commerce market that should have been —and was— written off was the astronomical valuation given to pure-play Internet stocks. Looking beyond the United States, Marzbani says the growth of B2C retailing is evident in Australia, "It was about $920 million last year and is on course to do about

$2.9 billion this year in Australia. That figure is 1.5% of all retail consumer spending, so it's gone from being 0.5% to 1.5% in a year. It's still a small number, but its growth rate is huge, and it's very, very real, and will continue."

"The thing is that most of the B2C is going to be done by established businesses and established brands. Anyone who says that B2C is over is stupid. All that has happened is that we know how much Pets.com should have been worth, and it was not $10 billion."[9]

Myth 7. The need for *speed* is central to competitive advantage in the Internet Age.

The war cry for the past few years has been "speed." Time-to-market has been trumpeted as absolutely essential in the Internet marketplace. First-mover advantage is everything, goes the maxim. Black Christmas 1999, however, challenged that myth and the business world recognized that the ability to deliver was far more important to sustainable success. The ability to deliver depends on having a sound business design, depth of resources and proper positioning in a given industry. Total demand does not magically go up because businesses use the Internet, and companies must still earn their share of a given market. Only the best, not necessarily the first, can do that.

"Accepted business wisdom holds that the moment one company in a market comes up with a revolutionary new idea, its competitors will try to copy that idea as quickly as possible. E-commerce is no different. Although a 'first mover' may be able to achieve an initial advantage, and perhaps fatten its bottom line as a result, that benefit may be short-lived as its competitors race to introduce copycat strategies.

"Despite the multitude of e-commerce business plans that have been introduced over the past year or so, at a macro level most are remarkably similar (for example, online trading marketplaces). The real point of difference comes in the execution of those plans. The Asia-Pacific vice-president for the research company Gartner, Bob Hayward, describes the situation as a zero-sum game: at the end of the activity no one company is markedly better off than any other. He says the companies that have benefited most from the e-commerce revolution have been the suppliers of technology and consulting services for making it happen, although he rejects the theory that e-commerce is a conspiracy by technology companies to increase their profitability.

"Ramim Marzbani says that, regardless of the wonders of e-commerce, many companies are too reliant on sales in their domestic markets and have no way of increasing the demand for their products. If you were selling shoes or toothpaste yesterday, the demand for your products didn't change one bit as a result of e-commerce. Market demand does not change in the short term for anything, so if everyone else is doing this e-commerce stuff, the first thing that happens in the short term is that everyone's cost of doing it goes up. So profitability has got to get hurt."[10]

The zero-sum game does not eliminate the need for speed. That speed, however, must relate directly to the ability to sense and respond to changing customer demands and market conditions, not just to be the first off the starting block.

Myth 8. The Internet disintermediates.

Why use middlemen —wholesalers, distributors and resellers— when the Internet enables companies to sell directly to the end customer? Although some companies such as Dell bypass traditional channels and sell direct, intermediaries have added and continue to add value. They finance inventories, they warehouse, assemble and distribute products and they service and support customers.

Knowing the true value of middlemen, most companies are not the least bit interested in disintermediating them. Car manufacturers now let their customers customize and order online, but the sale is redirected to a local dealership. When intermediaries add value, the Internet can bring efficiencies to, but not dislocate the middleman.

If the middlemen do not add value, they will be eliminated as observed in the travel industry where the travel agents' primary value online would be to deliver a paper ticket. Only travel agents who act as travel consultants thrive in these times. Travelers who know where they are going, how to get there and where to stay when they arrive do not use travel agents, they use online booking services. Instead, thriving travel agents serve those who need the added value of advice and assistance. What happens to those that do not add such compelling value? They're gone.

These fundamentals apply to the pure net plays. Online e-marketplaces —MetalSite for steel, Transora for consumer product manufacturers, PlasticsNet for plastics— that only aggregate suppliers' products without significant value add will fail. After all, they are only Web sites and the conventional intermediary is so much more.

Myth 9. **Built it and they will come.**

Traditional marketing is still the key. Long time technology writer, Clinton Wilder, filed this report, "Once again, the theory is simple enough: The Web is the first communications channel that enables cost-effective one-to-one marketing on a huge scale. Marketing to a "segment of one" has long been the goal of database marketing, data mining, and telemarketing, but Web technology enables marketing of unprecedented exactitude and low cost. But how do companies get people to come to their Web sites in the first place?

"Customization and personalization are fine for customer retention but not so good for customer acquisition. In the global world of the Internet, what counts is brand. That's why Yahoo posted billboards at San Diego's Qualcomm Stadium during the World Series, and why Web shopping site Buy.com kicked off a $25 million mass marketing campaign with ads on Monday Night Football, and that won't happen with only targeted Web banner ads.

"Mass marketing is also a necessity for the captains of online industry. Dell isn't the largest online PC seller only because of execution; it also heavily markets its direct-selling approach —on prime-time TV and elsewhere. In E-commerce, branding and mass marketing are more important than ever. Ultimately, that's just common sense —at least for those who understand there's more to E-commerce than click-throughs. You can't just build it, because they will not come."[11]

Myth 10. **E-commerce is dead.**

E-business is certainly not dead. The e-myth, however, is dead. It crashed and burned in 2000.

Electronic forms of business and commerce have been deployed since the advent of the computer. With the introduction of the Internet, this trend takes a quantum leap forward, allowing even the smallest business to participate in electronic trading. Electronic forms of business have been embraced and evolved for over a half century, becoming increasingly powerful business tools.

The world's first global electronic network was capable of connecting a company to its customers and suppliers anywhere anytime, in real-time. A hundred years ago, however, the press did not rush all about calling it t-commerce, t-business, t-banking or t-whatever. For sure the telephone was a disruptive business technology and every business had to have one, but the t-hype did not emerge to confound public financial markets. Nor did the first ubiquitous document technology. Facsimile technology did not trigger a Wall Street stampede for f-commerce or f-business IPOs. As e-commerce and e-business emerge from the mystique of the IPO frenzy and become mainstream, the "e" will simply go away.

Don't Predict, Invent the Future

The e-hype was driven by irrational exuberance and wild predictions about the future of business. For those that insist on predictions to direct their behavior, here goes:

- "I predict the Internet...will go spectacularly supernova and in 1996 catastrophically collapse," Bob Metcalfe, inventor of Ethernet and 3Com founder, said in 1995.
- "640K ought to be enough for anybody," Bill Gates, chairman of Microsoft, said in 1981.
- "There is no reason anyone would want a computer in their home," Ken Olson, president, chairman and founder of Digital Equipment, said in 1977.
- "I think there is a world market for maybe five computers," Thomas Watson, chairman of IBM, said in 1943.[12]

Peter Drucker, father of modern management, summarizes the usefulness of predictions, "It is not so very difficult to predict the future. It is only pointless. But equally important, one cannot make a decision for the future. Decisions are commitments to action. And actions are always in the present, and in the present only. But actions in the present are also the one and only way to make the future."[13] The lesson is clear —winning companies will invent, not predict, their futures.

With the e-clipse of 2000 behind them, companies can now take a deeper look into how technology really changes business and the overall economy. The Internet did not just appear out of nowhere, and by understanding the march of technology from the beginning of business computing (the subject of Chapter 2), a valuable context can be gained. With such insight, companies can see the fundamental impact of Internet, and invent their futures. The journey continues.

References

[1] Catherine Tymkiw, Wall St. ends a tough year, CNNfN, December 29, 2000, http://cnnfn.cnn.com/2000/12/29/markets/markets_newyork/
[2] Ashok Dongre , "The Great Dot Com Crash," DQ Channels, India, November 15, 2000, http://www.dqchannelsindia.com/content/channeltech/100111501.asp
[3] Glenn Pascall , "New economy's myths fog analysts' crystal balls," Birmingham Business Journal, April 14, 2000,
http://www.bizjournals.com/birmingham/stories/2000/04/17/editorial2.html
[4] http://www.line56.com/articles/default.asp?NewsID=2217
[5] Term coined by Dave Hollander, co-inventor of XML.
[6] http://www.gegxs.com/geiscom/downloads/B2B_Integration_WP.pdf
[7] Glenn Pascall , "New economy's myths fog analysts' crystal balls," Birmingham Business Journal, April 14, 2000,
http://www.bizjournals.com/birmingham/stories/2000/04/17/editorial2.html
[8] Brad Howarth, " E-myths exploded," Australia's BRW, October 20, 2000
http://www.brw.com.au/newsadmin/stories/brw/20001020/7576.htm
[9] ibid. _____ (Howarth)
[10] ibid. _____ (Howarth)
[11] http://www.mgt.smsu.edu/mgt487/mgtissue/ecommerc/index.htm
[12] http://www.attrition.org/quotes/humor.html
[13] Peter F. Drucker, *Managing in a Time of Great Change,* Truman Talley Books, 1995.

Chapter 2

The Rise of the Real New Economy

"Revolutions never go backward."
—Wendell Philips, American abolitionist.

Technology Enables, Business Changes.

In the interlocked cycles of technology and business advances, the issues companies face are not just about business, not just about technology. They are inseparably about both. Technology enables, business changes. The Internet, although not the first change agent, may prove to be the technological capstone of economic structures for years to come.

Companies that may think that Internet is a fad, or at most the act of establishing a Web site, should read what one 90-year old senior citizen has to say, "The truly revolutionary impact of the Information Revolution is just beginning to be felt. But it is not 'information' that fuels this impact. It is not the effect of computers and data processing on decision-making, policymaking, or strategy. It is something that practically no one foresaw or, indeed, even talked about ten or fifteen years ago: e-commerce — that is, the explosive emergence of the Internet as a major, perhaps eventually the major, worldwide distribution channel for goods, for services, and, surprisingly, for managerial and professional jobs. This is profoundly changing economies, markets, and industry structures; products and services and their flow; consumer segmentation, consumer values, and consumer behavior; jobs and labor markets. But the impact may be even greater on societies and politics and, above all, on the way we see the world and ourselves in it."

That was written by the father of modern management, Peter Drucker, who went on to compare the steam engine to the computer. "The steam engine was to the first Industrial Revolution what the computer has been to the Information Revolution - its trigger, but above all its symbol." In 1776 the steam engine made it possible to mechanize the manufacturing process. By itself, the steam engine did not create the Industrial Revolution — it was necessary, but not sufficient. It was decades later that something totally unexpected happened. "Then, in 1829, came the railroad, a product without precedent, and it forever changes the economy, society and politics." With their ability to distribute mass produced goods, "the western world was engulfed by the biggest boom history had ever seen — the railroad boom. The railroad was the truly revolutionary element of the Industrial Revolution."

By itself, the computer has not created the Information Revolution. Since its introduction in the 1940s, the computer has only transformed processes that were here all along. Now, decades after the advent of the computer, Drucker describes the true meaning of Internet commerce, "E-Commerce is to the Information Revolution what the railroad was to the Industrial Revolution — a totally new, totally unprecedented, totally unexpected development. And like the railroad 170 years ago, e-commerce is creating a new and distinct boom, rapidly changing the economy, society, and politics."[1]

Powerful Internet technologies have let loose business change on a scale far greater than the computer itself. Historians will demark the Information Age not by the advent of the computer, but instead by the advent of the Internet and its ability to create a single, virtual computer for all to share, all the time, from anywhere. One world. One information system. One marketplace.

The issues that businesses now face have never been larger or more imposing than those posed by the Internet and its potential to restructure the whole economy to achieve heretofore unattainable efficiencies and efficacies. Traditional supply chains of the industrial economy are being transformed by Dave Hollander's "value chains of information" that take the friction out of the economy. The transformation is well under way —there is no turning back.

The Business Technology Timeline

It is important to know where we are if we want to chart any future course. Where are we today in using technology in business? How did we get here? With answers to these questions businesses can set meaningful goals and have a reasonable chance of reaching them. If we trace the watershed events in the technology and business co-evolution we can answer these questions and apply the appropriate business fundamentals to chart a course for the future. The Internet phenomenon did not appear out of nowhere. It is important to know from whence it came to fully understand what it portends for business and the economy as a whole.

The link between technology and business innovation goes back to the very beginning — it was a technology breakthrough that enabled trade and gave birth to commerce. The development of keeled hull ships by the Phoenicians in 2000 BC made it possible to sail against the winds and go beyond the shores to the high seas of the Mediterranean. By doing something never before possible, the Phoenicians broke the bonds of geography and developed a flourishing trade with other peoples.

Today, the Internet has broken the bonds of both time and distance and set the stage for profound, global change. Since the beginning of business computing, each introduction of a new technology caused a major change in business, which in turn drove the demand for yet further advances in technology. But there is not always a direct relationship between an invention and its ultimate use.

When Dr. John Vincent Atanasoff built the first electronic digital computer during 1939 - 1942, he did not even imagine the change that the computer would introduce, nor did he make a single dime from the invention. When Dr. Vint Cerf and his colleagues developed the Department of Defense's ARPA network in the 1960s, they made no predictions of electronic commerce. Nor did Drucker until he commented on the information revolution in October 1999, "The truly revolutionary impact of the Information Revolution is just beginning to be felt. It is something that practically no one foresaw or, indeed, even talked about ten or fifteen years ago: e-commerce."[2] Technology revolutions are not always apparent at their birth, and pioneers, like Atanasoff and Cerf, often do not reap the commercial payoff from their inventions. When it comes to the technology and business equation, pioneers innovate, while early business adopters and entrepreneurs exploit.

The use of computers to automate business has gone through both incremental change and major revolutions culminating in the convergence of computers and communication networks. *It is this convergence to the extent anyone anywhere can share a universal information system that makes the Internet the most disruptive information technology of the past 50 years.* It brings about the possibility for companies to actually change what they do, what it means to be a business, rather than just speed up what a company already does.

Some changes in information technology have been evolutionary while a few have been revolutionary. By reflecting on the business technology timeline, we can see that we are in the midst of a sixth era of major change as shown in Figure 1.

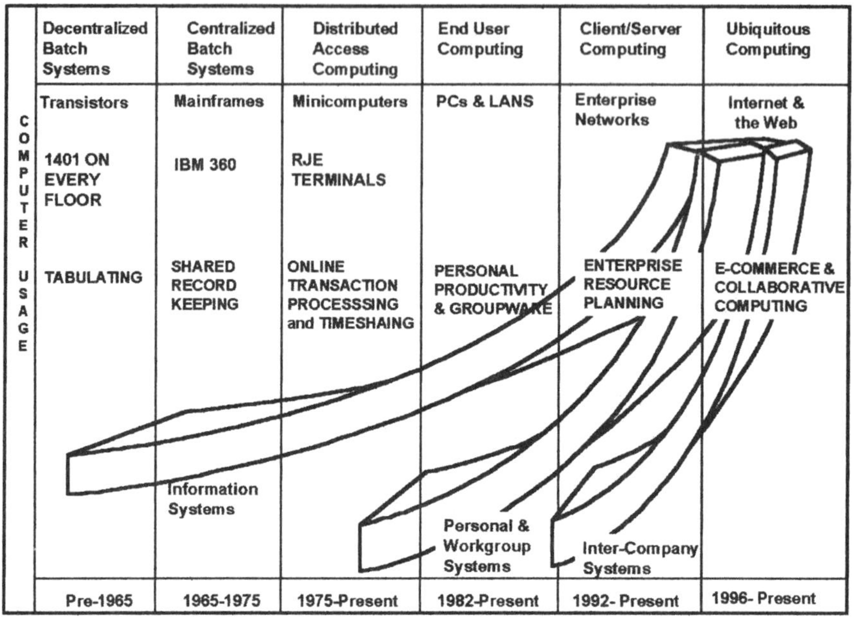

	Decentralized Batch Systems	Centralized Batch Systems	Distributed Access Computing	End User Computing	Client/Server Computing	Ubiquitous Computing
COMPUTER USAGE	Transistors 1401 ON EVERY FLOOR TABULATING	Mainframes IBM 360 SHARED RECORD KEEPING Information Systems	Minicomputers RJE TERMINALS ONLINE TRANSACTION PROCESSSING and TIMESHAING	PCs & LANS PERSONAL PRODUCTIVITY & GROUPWARE Personal & Workgroup Systems	Enterprise Networks ENTERPRISE RESOURCE PLANNING Inter-Company Systems	Internet & the Web E-COMMERCE & COLLABORATIVE COMPUTING
	Pre-1965	1965-1975	1975-Present	1982-Present	1992- Present	1996- Present

Figure 1. The Business Technology Timeline

Stage 1. In the early 1960s automation meant speeding up tabulating chores, and companies were able to increase efficiency of clerical tasks such as producing invoices, paychecks, and the like. The computer sped up what businesses did, but did not change the basic ways in which they went about doing their work. The super new electronic clerk did, however, allow companies to grow their business and keep up with their record keeping without hiring armies of clerks as they grew.

The transistor was the technology breakthrough driving the new approach to record keeping. A transistorized IBM 1401 computer provided speed and accuracy in manipulating very basic business data. It seemed that every department in a large corporation wanted one. When the payroll department saw the new computer in the billing department, they too found a business case for their own 1401. Soon there was a 1401 on every floor. The overall impact of the computer on the business, however, was

Chapter 2 - The Rise of the Real New Economy 39

limited to a single department. There was no automated information sharing and business processes did not change. All the new computers did was speed up the clerical work of an individual department.

Stage 2. In 1964, IBM introduced the solid-state IBM 360 mainframe computer —so named after the number of degrees in a complete circle. Instead of every department having its own system, the new mainframe could encircle all the computing needs of a corporation. The approach was called was "batch processing," where individual departments would gather up business transaction documents and send them in sequenced batches to a central "data processing" department to accomplish their record keeping. Shared record keeping became possible, and simple business functions such integrating order entry and inventory control processing could be automated with this new capability. That meant no more paper documents flowing from the order processing department to the inventory control department for reentry into separate systems.

Stage 3. While the mainframe became the stalwart of the large corporation, advances in electronics brought down the cost of computers and the minicomputer proliferated in small to medium sized enterprises in the 1970s. Minicomputers also were deployed in some departments of large corporations that could justify their own computer system in addition to using the mainframe.

In parallel with the minicomputer trend, telecommunications matured substantially through the mid-1970s. Remote access to centralized batch systems (remote job entry) became commonplace and computer terminals began appearing on back office desktops. Such distributed access became increasingly sophisticated and on-line transaction processing became the norm.

Timesharing made it possible for programming resources to be accessed remotely, and this era saw the emergence of commercially available computing services and products (not unlike the application service provider (ASP) movement of today). Corporate giants such as GTE got into the "computer utility" business with their subsidiary, GTE Data Services. IBM created its Service Bureau Corporation. Automatic Data Processing, Inc. (ADP) got into the payroll business and to this day processes the business world's payrolls.

Distributed access computing introduced considerable complexity and considerable business risk. As a result, early enterprise *architectures* were developed to design a cohesive approach to integrating computer hardware, software and information. Without such architectures, chaos would reign as many different departments and users shared a common asset, the information system. Corporate information systems (IS) shops grew in importance and became custodians of information resources and information systems architecture.

Stage 4. The era of the personal computer, the era of end-user computing would change the role of centralized IS shops. Just while enterprise architecture was beginning to influence central IS, PCs and local area networks (LANs) began to proliferate, delivering scattered point solutions to individual departments and business units, absorbing an increasing portion of corporate computing budgets. So much for enterprise-wide architecture and control by centralized IS departments. In many ways, individual lines of business went their own way with strong managers making the case for their own PC and LAN systems.

The business goal of personal or end-user computing (versus computer users in the centralized data processing department) was personal and departmental productivity versus the economies of scale of centralized departments. These systems may have optimized performance at the individual and departmental level, but what MIT's Robert Solow dubbed in an offhand pithy remark as the "productivity paradox" ("You can see the computer age everywhere but in the productivity statistics."[3]) taught companies that any real gain in productivity of the overall corporation could not be quantified. Where is the return on investment? Even without corporations being able to answer this question, the PC and the LAN are pervasive. What information worker in even the smallest of businesses does not have a PC? The PC and the telephone are two givens on information workers' desktops along with the notebook computer and cell phone for the sales force.

Stage 5. The next logical step was to connect the mainframes, minicomputers, PCs and LANs into an enterprise-wide network. The network made the need for an enterprise architecture greater than ever before, and the technical approach for making the connections resulted in client-server architectures. The enterprise-wide network laid the foundation for deep transformation within companies and the business process reengineering revolution ensued.

Companies tore down stovepipes of information contained in individual departments and connected these islands of information into end-to-end business processes that optimized not individual departments, but overall customer value. The era of downsizing and "rightsizing" had begun, and companies outsourced many business processes not identified as core competencies of the enterprise.

The business engineering revolution did not happen overnight and continuous process improvement continues to this day. Companies learned that the process was not simple and that integrating the software applications of individual departments or business units was an extremely complex proposition. This complexity gave rise to the enterprise-wide software platforms known as enterprise resource planning (ERP) systems, typically the most complex software systems ever adopted by business.

Because ERP systems were too complex to build in-house, new software giants such as SAP, Peoplesoft, J. D. Edwards, and Baan were born. However, configuring and installing ERP systems was so complicated that consulting firms and systems integrators had a field day with Global 2000 companies. The systems integration services could outstrip the cost of the ERP packages themselves. Yet large corporations had little choice. Streamline internal operations or lose the competitive edge to those who do.

Stage 6. The advent of a worldwide network of networks would change everything. No longer would there be just departmental local area and enterprise-wide networks, there would be one network for the entire world. Bang! The Internet.

The technologies of Internet itself have gone through several stages of development from the initial hard to use systems, to the breakthrough of the World Wide Web, and on to peer-to-peer technologies. The Web, although it was a breakthrough in navigating the Internet, still relied on client-server architectures with centralized resources being accessed by Web browsers. Peer-to-peer technologies began gaining attention in 2001 and are positioned to go beyond the centralized Web's client-server architecture. With peer-to-peer technologies, clients can be servers, servers can be clients and the Internet becomes a fully distributed computing environment.

Each stage in the advancement of business technology presented new competitive possibilities, caused irreversible change to the computing environment, and presented business and technology professionals with a new problem-solving paradigm.

Each paradigm shift pushed the envelope of what was being automated in the business. The business world saw new and far more reaching applications of technology in business. That which was being handed over to automation grew from simple tabulating of back office documents to real-time commerce. At each stage, the challenge to business was and is to extract competitive advantage from each technological breakthrough. If a company could not meet each new paradigm challenge, it would be at risk from competitors who could.

Connections are longer restricted to departments or a single enterprise; they are now possible inside and outside the enterprise, anywhere, anytime. The Internet has ushered in an age of ubiquitous computing and information system. While the focus of the ERP systems was to reinvent internal business design and operations, the Internet makes it possible to reinvent and streamline the business activities of entire industries, transforming paper flows to electronic interchanges between and among companies, their existing and future customers, suppliers and trading partners world wide.

Moreover, companies can share not just data and information but also know-how, inside and outside the corporation. Such qualitative changes in kind (from information processing to collaborative computing) fundamentally alter what a corporation is and what it does. That's the real business bang from the Net.

Shared knowledge can provide the foundation to optimize supply chains, eliminate inventory and its associated costs, design innovative products using real-time collaboration with trading partners to reach markets in record time. Knowledge management is the stuff of sustainable competitive advantage and removing waste and friction from the economy. *When competing on the Internet, knowledge bases containing digitally codified know-how become more important than data bases containing information about transactions.* Transaction data is necessary, but no longer sufficient for digital commerce.

When business know-how is migrated to the computer, the information system, in essence, becomes a digital simulation of work once done manually — the system acts much like people did in carrying out activities, processing information and solving problems. For example, Borders.com is a simulation of a real bookstore. Border's computers simulate all the activities of a real bookstore, letting customers browse the shelves, processing orders, and triggering movement of books from publisher to wholesaler to Borders to the ultimate customer. Computers allow customers to collaborate among themselves, sharing opinions, reviews and ratings of books — something not practical in a physical bookstore. As this approach to simulating the activities of business continues, the activities and processes of entire industries and, ultimately, the economy will migrate from places to spaces. The business of business will be increasingly digitized and migrate to cyberspace.

Of course, extending the traditional brick and mortar company to this new digital channel will not happen over night. The task is of great magnitude. Companies will guide their journey by asking very fundamental questions. *What does the Internet allow a business to do that was never before possible? How does the ability to connect any-to-any alter business fundamentals?*

The Rise of the *Real* New Economy

Venturing back to 1969 when the U.S. put man on the moon, Vint Cerf and Robert Kahn developed the TCP/IP protocols which make the modern Internet possible. From its humble beginnings as a Defense Department research project, the ARPA net, this network of networks has become the top telecommunications tool of our time and provides the common infrastructure of the future. Although half a billion people will use the Internet in the next few years, no one owns it and no one controls its destiny. *The Internet resembles an evolving biological ecosystem rather than a single invention.*

Because of its roots in research, the early Internet was limited to scientists and researchers. One would have to be a rocket scientist to use it back then as it was difficult to navigate. Not even the telephone companies embraced it as they did not see the technology affecting the masses. In fact, the Internet was a difficult tool even for researchers. This led to Tim Berners-Lee inventing the World Wide Web in 1989, an internet-based hypermedia initiative for global information sharing, while working at CERN, the European Particle Physics Laboratory in Switzerland.

It took one more step before the World Wide Web reached the masses, and it would not be Berners-Lee who capitalized on his invention. "Marc Andreessen was an undergraduate at the University of Illinois, writing code for $6.85 an hour at the National Center for Supercomputing Applications, when he and a fellow student, Eric Bina, became intrigued by the potential of the World Wide Web, a new technology for linking the resources of the Internet. But the Web lacked a rich graphical interface —an intuitive way for people to unearth the vast material it stored.

"In a wild burst of coding in the winter of 1993, Andreessen and Bina wrote the basics of a graphical Web browser called Mosaic. Almost singlehandedly, their work turned the Web into the business and pop-culture phenomenon it is today. They had created The Next Big Thing."[4]

Andreessen wanted to turn his next big thing into the next big business. At the end of the day of one of the most frenzied initial public offerings (IPO) in history, his new venture, Netscape, became the stuff of business legend in 1995. Young Andresseen was worth $58 million on paper and Netscape's Chairman James Clark's shares were worth over a half a billion after the first day of trading, instantly making him one of the richest people in the country. Wall Street valued the young company, with just $16 million in revenues, at more than $2 billion.

Netscape Communications Corporation had introduced two cornerstone Internet business models. First they made the Netscape browser free, hoping to gain an immense customer base so that they could sell other products and services. This model has been adopted widely: free e-mail, first introduced by Hot Mail, and free Internet access provided by companies such as NetZero. The race for building a huge customer base was on.

Second, Netscape was the first to introduce the gravity defying Internet IPO, a phenonemon that created a stable of twenty-something year old billionaires before the dot-com crash of 2000. Soon, talk of a "new economy" with new rules became commonplace. Who cared about old fashioned things like price/earnings ratios?

To analyze its growing impact, a quick reflection on the Internet business timeline provides useful context. The early years did not amount to much as businesses scratched their heads to figure out what if anything this new medium meant.

The real action started in the business-to-consumer (B2C) market space where radical new business models enabled first movers to grab market share as Amazon.com did in the book industry. In other cases, breakthroughs in reducing operating costs have resulted from companies automating their procurement processes. Each breakthrough has led to new possibilities and spawned yet additional business models. As shown in Figure 2, the use of the Internet by business has already evolved into what is now the fifth wave. Understanding the business consequences at each stage is useful to charting a course for the future.

Chapter 2 - The Rise of the Real New Economy

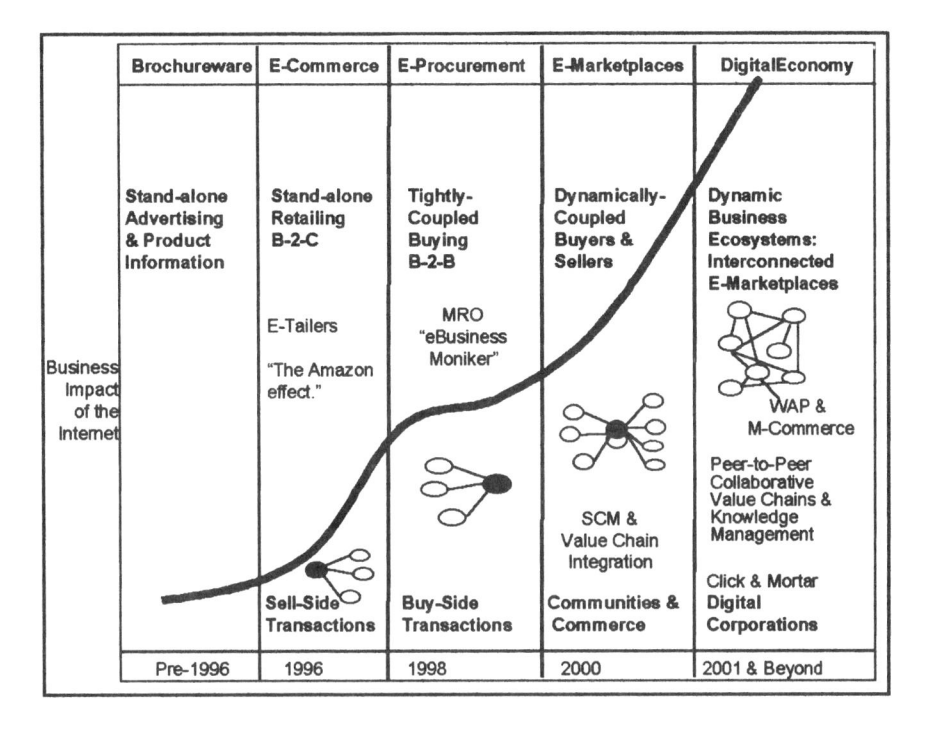

	Brochureware	E-Commerce	E-Procurement	E-Marketplaces	DigitalEconomy
Business Impact of the Internet	Stand-alone Advertising & Product Information	Stand-alone Retailing B-2-C E-Tailers "The Amazon effect."	Tightly-Coupled Buying B-2-B MRO "eBusiness Moniker" Sell-Side Transactions	Dynamically-Coupled Buyers & Sellers SCM & Value Chain Integration Communities & Commerce	Dynamic Business Ecosystems: Interconnected E-Marketplaces WAP & M-Commerce Peer-to-Peer Collaborative Value Chains & Knowledge Management Click & Mortar Digital Corporations
	Pre-1996	1996	1998	2000	2001 & Beyond

Figure 2. The Internet Business Timeline

1st Wave. Brochureware. The initial use of the Internet in business, circa 1993-1996, was to establish Web presence, publishing company and product information online. Electronic document publishing or "brochureware" was pretty much the extent of the first embrace of the Internet. Quickly companies learned that they could also share internal documents with one another as well as customers, trading partners and suppliers by using email and the Internet's file transfer protocol (FTP).

Forrester Research reported that by the end of 1996 about 80% of Fortune 500 had established Web presence compared to 34% in 1995.[5] Today, business Web presence is universal.

2nd Wave. E-Commerce. All was pretty much brochureware until something spectacular happened when the book industry was *Amazoned* in 1996. Amazon began "conducting business" on the Net, coming from nowhere to establish a global brand in book retailing. The company not only presented their catalog as brochureware, it accepted orders, took payments, triggered fulfilment, accepted returns, and provided customer tracking and support, all using the capability of processing business transactions on the Internet. Amazon initially outsourced logistics and warehousing and, through much publicity, launched the era of e-commerce by becoming a pure net play —electronic commerce is its only form of business, and the business resides on the Internet.

Amazon is an example of a private, enterprise marketplace. As shown in the figure, the business model is one-to-many, one seller, many customers. Other examples include traditional "brick and mortar" companies such as Dell, Lands End and Wal-Mart, and the slew of dot-coms that sprang up as e-tailers who used the Web to automate the sell-side of their business.

3rd Wave. E-Procurement: Tightly Coupled Buyers and Sellers. Indirect operating costs such as supplies, rent, business travel, repairs and maintenance are typically a company's greatest costs. Turning to the buy-side of their business operations, companies began using electronic procurement as they embraced the Internet to automate their indirect or Maintenance Repair and Operations (MRO) buying. Around 1998, early MRO software providers such as Ariba and Commerce One became the buzz on Wall Street. They supplied Fortune 500 companies with multimillion dollar procurement software packages, which, by the way, also required millions more for consultants and systems integrators to install.

Most of the early B2B procurement involved establishing tight links to a company's existing suppliers. They used their existing business practices and trading partners but lowered costs through automation. The savings resulted from dramatically reducing the transaction costs of the procurement life cycle, from requisitioning through receiving. The business model is many-to-one, many suppliers serving one company's buying needs.

General Electric pioneered B2B procurement, setting the stage for many followers. The buying modes supported include catalog-based buying, spot purchases, contract-based buying, and Requests For Quotes (RFQs). Usually, pricing is conventional: prenegotiated prices prior to creating custom catalogs, rather than pricing being determined in the market at the time of a transaction.

4th Wave. Electronic Marketplaces: Multiple Buyers and Sellers. E-procurement rose out of the far simpler business-to-consumer model which employs the *catalog-transact* metaphor of retail commerce where a customer browses an electronic catalog of, let's say office supplies, and clicks to buy the items of choice. This static catalog-transact model worked fine for B2C and early e-procurement systems, but does not unlock the real power of dynamic markets for competitive advantage. After all, companies are dealing electronically with existing suppliers and only the transaction costs, though substantial, are reduced.

The notion of MRO e-procurement went to the next level when multi-buyer, multi-seller e-marketplaces were introduced. The business model is many to many, many buyers and sellers. These early B2B marketplaces offered secure business document delivery services between marketplace participants. Business documents, such as purchase orders, order acknowledgments and invoices, could be sent between the marketplace and the systems of buyers and sellers.

But using e-marketplaces to acquire office supplies is not exactly a radical competitive breakthrough. Thus the next step in the evolution of B2B marketplace activities reached beyond operating resources to the supply chain. Large companies banded together to pool their buying power by establishing B2B exchanges. These "buyers' markets" deploy a many-to-few business model: a few large buyers purchasing from many suppliers. This business model was made famous by the Ford, DaimlerChrysler, GM buying consortium, Covisint, and has spread to other industries.

Some B2B marketplaces have a solid business model at their foundation and will no doubt become stalwarts in industries where commodities (e.g., electronic components, steel, aluminum, rubber, paper, plastics, electric power, oil and gas, bandwidth, and credit derivatives) are bought and sold. Examples include Altra Energies, Automated Credit Exchange and Enron. Online auctions for industrial parts, raw materials, and services are growing in importance. Spot buying for commodities with auction and negotiation facilities is offered by FreeMarkets, eBreviate and others. Auction services may include recurring auction events, price-only auctions, and multiparameter, multilingual and multicurrency auctions. Negotiation services may include requests for information, requests for proposals, requests for quotations and supplier profile surveys.

Independent market-makers, usually experts in a particular industry, began establishing multi-buyer and multi-seller electronic markets. The neutral market-maker is the central node, and buyers and sellers represent the wings of a butterfly market in a true many-to-many business model.

Although the business models of electronic marketplaces are intuitive and seem obvious ways of removing friction from the economy, the first generation of B2B e-marketplaces has not met expectations of either buyers or sellers. Simply aggregating supplier catalogs and facilitating sales transactions are not enough. The many conversations, negotiations and other business-to-business activities that surround a transaction are essential. In addition, businesses usually require total solutions when buying and selling goods and services. They need access to multiple industry marketplaces. It is too early to predict how electronic markets will evolve, but once experience is gained to learn what business models work the best, they are likely to be commonplace in the 21st century economy.

5th Wave. The Digital Economy: *Dynamic Business Ecosystems*. No industry is an island. Industries interact to form the overall economy. So it must be with electronic marketplaces. They must be interconnected as markets are in the real economy.

Typical activities in the real economy involve multiple industries simultaneously. To build a skyscraper in Manhattan, land, labor, financial and capital goods markets must be interwoven for the endeavor. In the emerging digital economy, stand alone industry markets will be woven into a dynamic business ecosystem of networked electronic markets, just like the real economy.

And, business people will need greater access to marketplaces than that afforded by desktop Web browsers. Going forward, wires will give way to wireless application protocols (WAP) and commerce will reach beyond the desktop as mobile commerce (m-commerce) takes transactions to the streets, shop floors, and shipping containers of the economy. Furthermore, peer-to-peer architectures will come into predominance as companies will need to interact directly with one another without mediation of central servers.

Complex? Absolutely. Intelligent software agents will be needed to manage the complexity and filter out the infoglut. Knowledge management will grow in importance as companies need to collaborate and share their know-how as well as their information.

Ruler of these emerging business ecosystems will be the almighty customer. The individual digital corporation and complete value chains will be totally customer-driven. The new competitive arena will be value chain versus value chain, not company versus company.

Business transformation to the digital economy is not a single event. Instead it is an ongoing journey with no guarantees and no silver bullets for success. Perhaps the only guarantee is that those that do not embark on the journey today will be severely diminished tomorrow. To get started, companies can turn their focus to something they have not had to do in the past, optimize their entire value chain, one that lives or dies in a business ecosystem made of interconnected digital marketplaces.

References

[1] Peter Drucker, "Beyond the Information Revolution," Atlantic Monthly, October 1999.
[2] _____ ibid.
[3] Brynjolfsson, Erik and Brian Kahin (Editors), "Understanding the Digital Economy," p50, MIT Press, 2000.
[4] Tom Steinert-Threlkeld, "Can You Work in Netscape Time?" Fast Company, November, 1995. http://www.fastcompany.com/online/01/netscape.html
[5] Economist, May 10, 1997

Chapter 3

The New Way of Competing: Value Chain Optimization

Chapter 3 - The New Way of Competing: Value Chain Optimization

In July, 1997, the White House released a document declaring a revolution, "... a revolution that is just as profound as the change in the economy that came with the Industrial Revolution."[1]

Value Chains: Arteries of the Economy

Value chains are the arteries of the economy. Through them flow the goods and services of our materially rich industrial society. In any industry, an enterprise is located in a *value chain* where it buys goods and services from suppliers, ads value, and sells to customers. These fundamentals apply to all kinds of businesses: manufacturing, distribution or services.

Value chain analysis was pioneered two decades ago by Harvard's competitive strategy authority, Michael Porter. Rather than outdate Porter's work[2], the Internet enables it and extends its scope from inside a given enterprise to end-to-end industry value chains.

Value chain analysis concerns the input and output of economic resources into a chain of value-adding business processes or activities. The result of these business processes is value delivered to customers, and the margin or "value" is the difference between the what customers are willing to pay and the cost of producing the value.

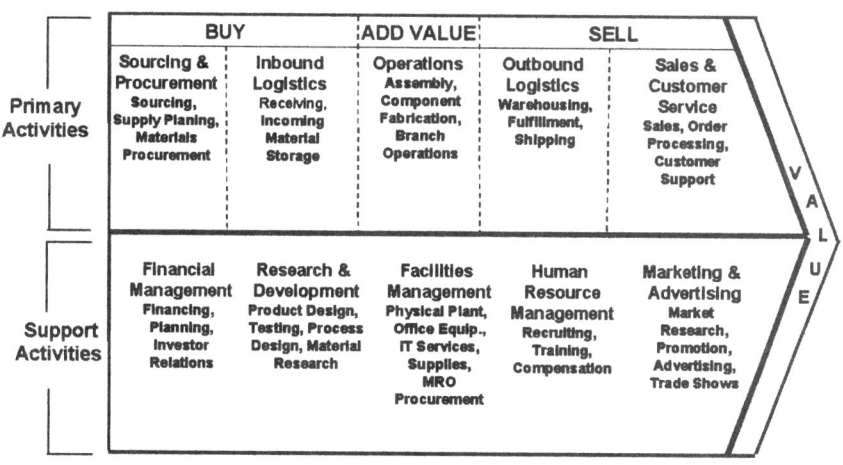

	BUY		ADD VALUE		SELL
Primary Activities	Sourcing & Procurement — Sourcing, Supply Planing, Materials Procurement	Inbound Logistics — Receiving, Incoming Material Storage	Operations — Assembly, Component Fabrication, Branch Operations	Outbound Logistics — Warehousing, Fulfillment, Shipping	Sales & Customer Service — Sales, Order Processing, Customer Support
Support Activities	Financial Management — Financing, Planning, Investor Relations	Research & Development — Product Design, Testing, Process Design, Material Research	Facilities Management — Physical Plant, Office Equip., IT Services, Supplies, MRO Procurement	Human Resource Management — Recruiting, Training, Compensation	Marketing & Advertising — Market Research, Promotion, Advertising, Trade Shows

Figure 1. Michael Porter's Value Chain Framework

Porter's approach asserts that by modeling the activities of an organization it is possible to distinguish *primary* activities, those that contribute to getting the product or service closer to the customer, from business processes that *support* primary activities. The model provides a framework to analyze the effectiveness of resource use and to evaluate the competitive capabilities of an organization.

Primary activities are directly involved in the creation of a product or service, its sale and transfer to the customer, and after sale support. As shown in Figure 1, these include sourcing and material procurement, inbound logistics, operations, outbound logistics, and sales and customer service. Support activities are those that, obviously, support primary activities by providing financial resources, research and development, facilities management, human resources and marketing and advertising.

Acquiring the materials and services that are used by the primary activities is termed *direct* procurement. The supporting business processes are those that keep the business operating and are often referred to as operating resources. Acquiring and maintaining the operating resources is termed *indirect* as these resources are not passed along to the customer for consumption.

Figure 1 is slightly modified from Porter's original model because the Internet makes customer-driven value chains a reality. Customer interaction can trigger sourcing and direct procurement in real-time. This new reality moves direct procurement business processes from Porter's support category to primary activities.

> The activities and business processes in Porter's value chain framework translate into e-commerce applications. A thorough discussion of these applications appears in the companion book, *Enterprise E-Commerce.*

The capability to add value is the very essence of being a successful business and constitutes an enterprise's core competencies. Adding value does not necessarily mean that the company itself carries out the activities of its core competencies. Dell Computer Corporation, for example, does not manufacture computers. Instead, it uses the Internet to trigger activities among its suppliers and trading partners that do make components and parts. Dell's core competency is managing the build-to-order process. Dell goes beyond the internal focus of Porter's value chain analysis and manages the end-to-end industry value chain.

Industry Value Chains

Figure 2 shows a top view of an industry value chain. Each participant in the chain from "my.company" to my.company's suppliers and their suppliers, to my.company's customers and their customers consists of primary and support business processes and resources as previously discussed. Two forces, the demand chain and the supply chain converge at the point of my.company. As can be seen in the figure, my.company does not act alone in obtaining materials and services from the supply side of the value chain. Neither does it act alone when facing the demand chain as it may sell direct or through marketplaces to reach wholesalers or distributors who, in turn, sell to ultimate consumers.

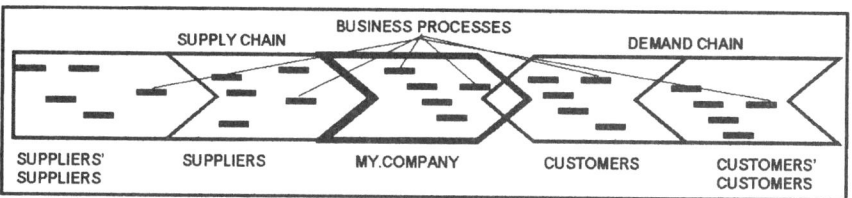

Figure 2. Top View of an Industry Value Chain

Business Process Reengineering (BPR)

Since the early nineties, companies have been focused on streamlining the business processes within their organization as a result of advances in technology. The introduction of client-server technologies meant that an enterprise could tie together islands of information contained across business units and individual departments. The enterprise-wide network laid the foundation for deep transformation within companies and the business process reengineering revolution (BPR) ensued.

Companies tore down stovepipes of information contained in individual departments. They connected these islands of information into end-to-end business processes that optimized not individual departments, but overall customer value.

The process of tying together islands of information with client-server technologies is shown in Figure 3. The lines connecting the individual business processes of departments resulted in enterprise-wide information systems and eliminated many unnecessary and duplicate activities. Business process reengineering provided the management framework, theories and methods for driving change.

Figure 3. Business Process Reengineering (BPR): Reengineering and Innovation Inside the Enterprise Using Client-Server Technologies

On the reverse side of the technology coin, a new business theory was needed to capitalize on the client-server technologies. Michael Hammer and James Champy obliged. In the very first line of their classic work, *Reengineering the Corporation,* Hammer and Champy declare "that American corporations must undertake nothing less than a radical reinvention of how they do their work."[3]

Their message was to tear down the stovepipes of functional management. They dispensed with the wisdom of Adam Smith's specialization of labor and hundreds of years of industrial management "best practice." Companies traditionally have sought to dominate their industries by using information technology to streamline their management structure and their internal operations. The goals have been to do things cheaper, better, and faster than the competition.

To achieve these goals, businesses traditionally organized themselves by pooling skills and knowledge into departments that performed specialized functions. The origins of specialization and functional management go back over two hundred years and were first articulated in Smith's classic, *The Wealth of Nations.*[4]

The principles Smith used to organize work are with us today. The focus has been on maximizing the efficiency of the functions performed by departments, not on the cross-functional processes that deliver benefit or value to customers. Hammer and Champy, on the other hand, tore apart organizations whose specialized departments optimized their individual tasks (often at the expense of the overall customer-facing process) and reunified those tasks

Chapter 3 - The New Way of Competing: Value Chain Optimization

into coherent, end-to-end business processes that delivered value to customers.

Their prescriptions were not based on magic, they were based on the enabling role of information technology. Herein lies the wisdom of their message. They recast the way a company must think about technology. They assert that a company that equates technology with automation cannot reengineer. A company that looks at and seeks to automate what they are doing cannot innovate, they simply reinforce and speed up old ways of doing things.

Hammer and Champy rephrased the technology question from how can we speed up what we are doing to: "How can we use technology to allow us to do things we are *not* already doing?" The introduction of client-server technologies did not speed up what companies were currently doing; it *fundamentally* altered what they did and provided an infrastructure for business process innovation and continuous process improvement. The focus of the business reengineering revolution was internal, on how the company must reorganize and streamline work.

Why has work been so specialized and fragmented? Traditional management instructs us to break large organizations down into smaller, specialized units that are more easily managed. This divide and conquer approach to organizational design has greatly influenced the ways businesses organize work. Specialized skills and activities are grouped into functional departments. Each department strives to optimize its specialty. However, such specialization has powerful side effects.

Within individual specialties, employees lose sight of the overall business. They are deprived of knowing the results of their individual actions on the customer. They do not get to see outcomes in cause and effect relationships. In many of today's corporations workers are locked up in their own departmental worlds.

Unfortunately, when people do not see the effects of their actions they stop learning. Feedback, specifically knowledge of results of our actions, is absolutely required for learning, innovation and improving performance.

The tough part in corporate reengineering is to understand the interconnections and the interactions of the business processes and sub-processes, the variables affecting processes, and the overall effects of decisions made by the organization. *General systems thinking* provides the basis for analyzing the business as a complex system. Systems thinking provides a new perspective for business process analysis and redesign. For example, can you imagine holding up your hand a foot in front of your face and blocking your view of the earth, the entire earth? Astronauts have been able to do that. The world looks drastically different from their perspective. They see the whole earth. Unfortunately, we only see bits and pieces of our company and industry in our earthly day to day work.

Today's businesses need an astronaut's perspective of whole, end-to-end business processes. Systems thinking is a formal discipline of management science that deals with whole systems and with the interconnections and interactions of the individual parts.

When Dr. W. Edwards Deming, father of total quality management, pronounced that the improvement of quality is 90% centered on the system, on processes, the bell tolled for the death of traditional business practices. Those who heard the tolling engaged in business process reengineering and the transformation from functional management to *process* management.

As a result of the BPR revolution, corporate hierarchies have been flattened. Cross-functional work teams are being charged with the complete management of customer-facing processes.

From BPR to Industry Process Reengineering (IPR)

Fast forward from client-server technology to the Internet. Companies that "get it" and are determined to thrive in the Internet era are redesigning business processes so that they cross enterprise boundaries to eradicate duplicate processes, ineffective hand-offs and disconnects between and among enterprises.

Virtual corporations are being created that have shared business goals, common planning, and performance management tools. *Industry Process Reengineering (IPR) also known as commerce process reengineering (CPR)* is the competitive weapon for designing and implementing hyper-efficient business processes that are integrated in real-time and jointly owned by suppliers and customers. Cheaper, better, and faster takes on a whole new meaning in these 21st century corporations.

As companies embrace the Internet to redesign business processes that cross company boundaries, they enter Phase 1 of industry process reengineering. Figure 4 illustrates a small sampling of inter-company business processes being integrated electronically across corporate boundaries (indicated by the lines that span companies).

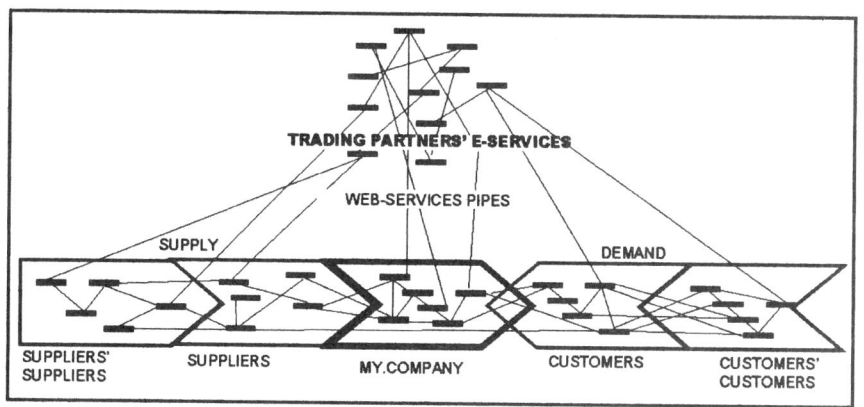

Chapter 3 - The New Way of Competing: Value Chain Optimization 59

Figure 4. Industry Process Reengineering (IPR) Phase 1: Reengineering and Innovation Across Industries Using Internet Technologies

In addition to the primary activities of the value chain, these companies reach out electronically to their trading partners for support activities delivered in the form of electronic business services (e-services). These e-services may include both primary and support activities provided by individual companies (e.g., FedEx for shipping) or through emerging digital marketplaces, hubs and exchanges that broker business services (e.g., the Covisint[5] exchange consortium conceived by GM, Ford, and DaimlerChrysler for auto makers and their suppliers).

The Value Web: Structure of the New Economy

Companies that pioneered inter-company process innovation did not take long to learn that the value chain no longer had to be linear. For example, the Covisint business model no longer lines up the players. Instead a hub of activities is made available to all participants as shown in Figure 5. Covisint intends to harness the power of Internet technology to create visibility within a company's supply chain — transforming the linear chain into a far more productive and efficient network model.

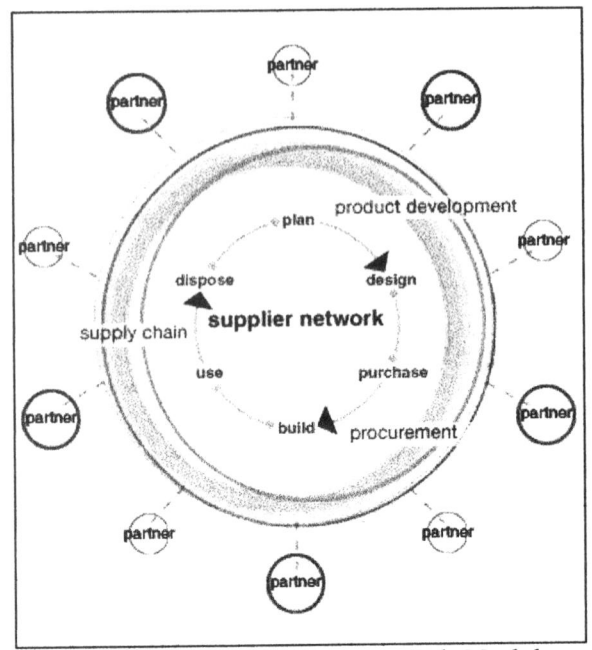

Figure 5. The Covisint Network Model
(Source: Covisint)

But that's not all. The next step beyond the network model is the totally decentralized value web. As shown in Figure 6, IPR Phase 2, formerly rigid, linear supply chains are blown to bits by the Internet. Reassembling the business process bits into a coherent infrastructure is the centerpiece of the 21st century economy, as depicted in Figure 7. The result is a web of any-to-any connections that can drive supply chains, demand chains, and even the business processes that represent the core competencies of an enterprise.

Chapter 3 - The New Way of Competing: Value Chain Optimization 61

Figure 6: IPR Phase 2:
Linear Supply Chains are Blown to Bits by the Internet

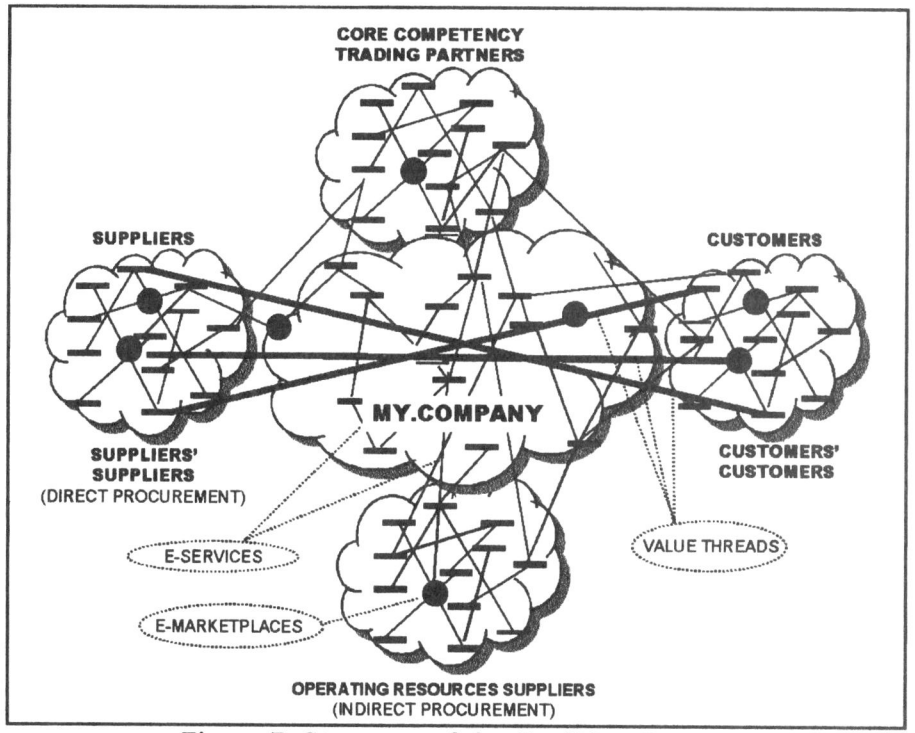

Figure 7. Structure of the *Real* New Economy

The digital corporation of the 21st century will thrive in a business world where the traditional linear supply chain will give way to dynamic, customer-driven value webs. This brave new world can be understood by examining how the business processes and activities of Porter's value chain are reassembled into the dynamic business ecosystem portrayed in the figure.

Business activities and processes are realigned with real-time connections between and among a company's customers, suppliers and trading partners. As shown, Porter's primary and support business processes of a company are realigned around four realms of interwoven activities involving:
- suppliers and suppliers' suppliers (direct procurement)
- operating resources suppliers (indirect procurement)
- core competency trading partners (value added activities) and
- customers and customers' customers (selling through private and public electronic marketplaces).

Three elements apply to all facets of a digital business participating in the new business ecosystem: e-marketplaces, e-services and value threads. The first two elements are discussed at length in the next chapter. For now, let's focus on the critical importance of managing multiple, simultaneous value threads —the hallmark of success in 21st century competition.

From Value Chains to Value Threads

Traditional supply chains are linear. They involve tightly linked suppliers and trading partners and are made up of large sets of complex business processes. In large companies such as Wal-Mart, supply chains are tied together with complex and expensive EDI systems that are out of the reach of smaller companies. As the monoliths that they are, such systems are difficult to build and maintain, and they cannot adapt to the dynamics of markets being made possible by the Internet.

In the digital economy, once rigid supply chains must become light weight, fine grained and agile. In the era of mass customization and personalization, a unique value chain may be needed for just a single customer and a single transaction. Others may serve multiple customers over long periods of time. A typical company will need to manage both kinds of value chains.

As coarse grained value chains are reengineered to be lightweight, fine grained and adaptive, they become *value threads*.

Value threads are woven through the tapestry of the any-to-any connections of the Internet enabled business ecosystem. They can be bundled, unbundled and rebundled in response to changing market realities. They allow a company to participate in multiple marketplaces or reach out directly to individual customers. The successful company will manage and optimize multiple simultaneous value threads.

Optimizing Value Chains

As the lines between B2C and B2B electronic commerce blur into seamless business ecosystems, a new form of competition emerges. The new competition is no longer company versus company, it is value chain versus value chain. Future battles for customers, however, will be won with "value chains of information," not traditional supply chains of supplier-squeezed, lowest-cost inventory.

Early entrants in B2B and B2C Internet markets gained their customer base through first-mover strategies and initiatives as witnessed by Amazon.com's surprise attack on the book industry in the mid-Nineties. But as the novelty of electronic commerce begins to fade, it's the power of a company's value chain – not just its initial customer base – that will rise up as the deciding factor for future success.

Companies that "get it" realize that competing in the future is about turning a company, and its entire value-chain, over to the command and control of the customer. For example, when a customer goes to Dell for a build-to-order computer, Dell's suppliers and the suppliers' suppliers are linked into the transaction in real-time to trigger fulfillment and inventory replenishment. The customer is in the driver's seat initiating activities that ripple throughout the value chain.

Customers, who can use the Internet to compare prices and search for competing suppliers without leaving their browsers, hold absolute power —they are but one eighth of a second from going to a company's competitor. Instead of owning the product and pushing it to market segments, successful companies are turning over control to empowered customers, making it easier for them to pull products and services from a multitude of suppliers to meet their individual needs.

GE's Trading Process Network (TPN) pioneered this business concept in the B2B market space, bringing together multiple buyers and suppliers with aggregated catalogs and sophisticated bid-ask trading. In the B2C space, when a consumer buys through *volumebuy.com*, purchasing power is no longer limited to an individual but instead increases with the buying power of everyone trying to buy the same products.

Joelle Tessler of the San Jose Mercury News explains, "Much like online auction sites, which bring together buyers and sellers who might never find each other offline, group buying sites enable something that could probably never happen on the same scale in the brick and mortar world. They let shoppers who could not join forces offline band together on the Web to build up buying power and negotiate discounts from suppliers. The concept, called 'demand aggregation,' is simple: The more people who sign up for a group purchase, the more buying power they have — and the more the price goes down."[6]

Powered by demand aggregation software from companies like the *mobshop.com, SHOP2gether.com* and *etrana.com,* such instant buyer cooperatives were not possible before the advent of the Internet. Unlike reverse auctions alone, demand aggregation is a dynamic commerce model that promotes what has been dubbed "viral marketing" (because it's so contagious) or word-of-mouth activity among buyers who understand that prices will fall as more people order. Auctions actually discourage this type of activity. While auctions are good for low-volume sales and one-of-a-kind items, demand aggregation encourages larger trading volumes.

Demand aggregation software can embody several dynamic pricing models, enabling virtual buyer groups to obtain lower prices through pre-negotiated volume discounts and group bids, group reverse auction and spot group exchanges. Demand aggregation can bring together smaller business buyers who otherwise do not have the purchasing strength of a GE to participate in large transactions. Suppliers who do not embrace such radical new business models will not appear on the buyer's radar.

As the Internet calls to us to reengineer complete value chains, competition between companies like Sears and J.C. Penney or Home Depot and Lowes will become less about brand and more about the strength and efficiency of each company's value chains. Value chains are business assets that must be invested in, carefully managed, protected and continually enhanced. How does a company protect its position in its value-chain?

The struggle is to own the primary relationship with the ultimate customer served by the value-chain. In a bold move of "antidisintermediation," Home Depot sent a letter to 1,000 suppliers including Black & Decker, Scotts, and General Electric, stating that it will hesitate to do business with suppliers that also market their products online. Home Depot said it would be happy to partner with them on selling via the Internet, but maintaining the primary relationship with the ultimate customer is Home Depot's obvious rule of engagement.

Managing a Company's Value Threads

The lesson is simple: companies with dynamic value chains that can own the primary customer relationship, and rapidly respond to – and even anticipate – customer demands will be the winners. But putting the concepts into practice is the hard part. So, what are companies to do?

Foremost, companies must recognize that the challenge of continuous value chain optimization goes beyond their companies' walls to their trading partners — companies cannot go it alone. Nor will they gain sustainable advantage if they use the B2B exchanges and other Internet-based procurement mechanisms simply to put the price squeeze on suppliers. The entire value chain must be optimized with win-win relationships forged from end-to-end.

This has three implications. First, senior management and line of business managers must be intimately involved as they are the ones with the deepest relationships with a company's trading partners.

Second, IT managers must participate in the appropriate inter-company alliances and consortia that are defining cross-company business vocabularies and standards, centered primarily around XML technologies. Interoperability initiatives are underway in most industries and a quick visit to www.xml.org will reveal activities in many industries. Today's IT managers must provide leadership not just within their companies, but also must become directly involved in the multi-company organizations defining the value chain rules of engagement of the economy.

Third, the reality is value chains, not value chain. As companies progressively aggregate total solutions for their customers and reach out to new markets using the Internet, they must manage multiple simultaneous value chains. Large corporations such as GE must manage thousands of value threads as it competes for both consumer and business markets.

A given value thread may exist for only one sale as in the case of building a skyscraper, or may endure over decades as in the case of a commodity market. As cross-selling is realized to a far greater extent and new market opportunities are discovered, a company will need to reach out to its web of suppliers to source the best mix of resources to meet a specific need. As a result traditional value chains must be more tightly focused and customized to meet the needs of customers on a one-to-one basis —they must become value threads.

Collaboration makes it possible to create customer-driven value threads by harmonizing demand and supply channels. Significant leverage can be achieved. Companies can radically reduce the cost of doing business across company boundaries, speed time-to-market, achieve flexibility and tap dynamic markets by making decisions based on who can deliver the required products or services at the right price, quality and place.

Figure 8 shows the technologies involved in managing value threads. The enterprise network or intranet ties together the connections within the enterprise, traditional supply chain management is enabled with extranets, private networks and EDI. Extended supply chain management uses the Internet for the breakthrough. In the figure, customers and their customers, suppliers and their suppliers are joined into a complete business ecosystem. The need for rapidly connecting these participants in a secure environment for collaboration has led to the demand for *peer-to-peer* technologies (discussed in Chapters 6 and 8) to enhance the basic protocols and functionality of the native Internet.

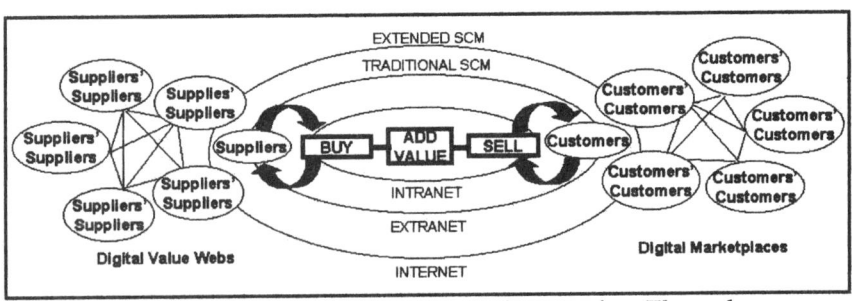

Figure 8. A Customer-Driven Value Thread

Chapter 3 - The New Way of Competing: Value Chain Optimization

A central core competency of a company becomes its ability to manage and optimize multiple simultaneous value threads. That means reaching out to digital value webs on the supply side and delivering personalized goods and services through private and public marketplaces. An organization must build the capability to codify and share its knowledge base, its know-how and business intelligence. Collaborative planning, forecasting and replenishment (CPFR), vendor managed inventories (VMI) and dramatic cycle time reductions provide the foundation for value thread management.

How do companies and whole industries revamp their supply chains? The approach to reinvention is not new, it is the application of business process reengineering to whole value chains: IPR. To many business people reengineering had become passé. But with the challenge of value chain optimization, no longer. Déjà vu – IPR is reengineering all over again, only this time it's on steroids.

BPR is a tool for analyzing a company's internal business model, disassembling the actors and roles contained in the departmental stovepipes of traditional companies and reassembling them around end-to-end business processes that are seen by and add value to customers. In their classic BPR book, *Improving Performance,* Rummler and Brache use "managing the white space on the organization chart" as the book's subtitle and metaphor for this process.

Just as the BPR movement eradicated duplicate processes, ineffective hand-offs and disconnects between departments within a company, the new, real-time interconnections enabled by e-commerce allows a business to tear down process barriers between its customers, suppliers and trading partners. *While BPR crosses departmental boundaries, IPR crosses enterprise boundaries and is about "managing the white space in the value chain."*

BPR didn't happen overnight, companies required several years of hard work, missteps, retrenchments and failures before transitioning from functional to process management. Because BPR deeply affects what people do, organization challenges were major roadblocks. There is no doubt, BPR was a very painful process in many organizations, not a silver bullet to streamlining businesses.

By extrapolating the difficulties of BPR to IPR, it becomes clear that building the digital corporation and restructuring industries will be a difficult road ahead. If people challenges were the primary challenge of BPR, it is easy to see the level of difficulty in affecting the politics, organizations and processes of entire industries. People issues will overshadow technology issues during the transitions ahead. Governance and control will be the determining factor in building B2B marketplaces and exchanges such as the Covisint exchange. While Internet technology is the enabler of an electronic economy, leadership will be the ultimate determinant of success.

Leaders must master the art of digital business. Companies must gain the skills needed to participate in and operate digital marketplaces, capture and extend know-how digitally, and build holistic customer relationship systems that integrate all customer and supplier touch points. The success of these endeavors will determine the winners and losers in the 21st century economy.

References

[1] President William J. Clinton and Vice President Albert Gore, Jr., *A Framework For Global Electronic Commerce,* July 1, 1997.

[2] Porter, Michael E. *Competitive Strategy: techniques for analyzing industries and competitors,* Free Press, 1980; *Competitive Advantage: creating and sustaining superior performance,* Free Press, 1985. 1998. ISBN: 0684841460, and *On Competition.* Harvard Business School Press. 1998.

[3] Michael Hammer and James Champy, *Reengineering the Corporation,* HarperBusiness, 1993.

[4] Smith, Adam. *An Inquiry Into the Nature and Causes of the Wealth of Nations.* London: W. Strahan and T. Cadell in the Strand. 1776.

[5] Named after "cooperation," "collaboration" and "communication; "vision" and "visibility;" and "international" and "integrated, '

[6] Tessler, Joelle, "Buying Sites Are Branching Out To Bigger Clients," San Jose Mercury News Group, October 24, 2000. http://www.mobshopbusiness.com/company/ar/102400.html

Chapter 4

The Art of Digital Business

"It's not hyperbole to say that the 'network' is quickly emerging as the largest, most dynamic, restless, sleepless marketplace of goods, services and ideas the world has ever seen."[1]
—Lou Gerstner, CEO, IBM.

The Art of Digital Business

Competing for the future with digital commerce is not just about technology. It is not just about business. It is inseparably about both, and fusing the two must be a top management priority of the 21st century.

Just as Barnes and Noble.com created a digital mirror world of its brick and mortar bookstore, minus the coffee shop, the Internet will drive a mirror world of the real economy. Digital incarnations will transform markets from places to spaces and redefine customer relationships by making knowledge and business services pervasive. These digital simulations of a given company or entire value chain will look and act much like today's physical marketplaces.

To build digital mirror worlds of a company and entire value chains, businesses will need to master the art of
- building digital marketplaces,
- rendering their services electronically (e-services),
- managing knowledge digitally, and
- building holistic customer relationship management systems.

Each of these facets of the 21st century business activities merits detailed study and mastery. Because businesses are moving into uncharted territory, there are no preset rules or predefined solutions. The effort is more one of art, of business architecture, rather than a specific management technique. It's an art of managing discontinuous change.

Digital Marketplaces

Whether it's the ancient storyteller square at the Khyber Pass in Asia, the corner grocery store or the stock exchanges on Wall Street, a marketplace is simply where buyers and sellers congregate to buy and sell goods and services. The difference the Internet makes is that markets move from *places* to *spaces*.

EDS' former CEO, Les Alberthal, describes the impact of this shift, "By now we know the revolution will never abate. In the next 10 years we will witness one of history's greatest technological transformations, in which the world's geographic markets morph into one dynamic, complex organism."[2]

In the past companies were often protected by geographic boundaries where customers did not have full information about buying options outside those bounds. No longer. In the Internet age, marketplaces must serve *communities of customers* that, because they can collaborate, have the power to demand the best possible value. Anything less will not be tolerated. "Click." That's the sound of a customer moving on to a company's competitor who may be anyone, anywhere.

Derek Leebaert writes in *The Future of the Electronic Marketplace*, "Anyone with access to electricity can make a market at will. The marketplace is the place of exchange between buyer and seller. Once one rode a mule to get there; now one rides the Internet. An electronic marketplace can span two rooms in the same building or two continents. How individuals, firms and organizations will approach and define the electronic marketplace depends on people's ability to ask the right questions now and to take advantage of the opportunities that will arise over the next few years."[3]

How big are those opportunities? Forrester Research estimates that online trade between businesses will reach $2.7 trillion by 2004. The company also predicts that roughly $1.4 trillion of that will be conducted through digital marketplaces.[4]

To be successful, a marketplace must attract customers with compelling value, handle customer transactions and retain customers through excellent customer care. The entire framework must be carefully managed to bring about reliability, cost reductions and continuing process improvement – all judged from the customer's perspective.

Based on the nature of a given industry and the fragmentation of buyers and sellers, three major digital marketplace structures have emerged to capitalize on the capabilities of the Internet, as shown in Figure 1.

A *seller's market* is typical of business-to-consumer marketplaces where a single seller does business with many buyers. The business model is one-to-many. Seller's markets are generally *private*, enterprise marketplaces. Private marketplaces restrict participation of either buyers or sellers. In the private seller's market, the marketplace is open to any and all buyers, but multiple sellers are not invited. For example, all customers are welcome at borders.com, but Barnes and Noble is not invited to participate as a seller.

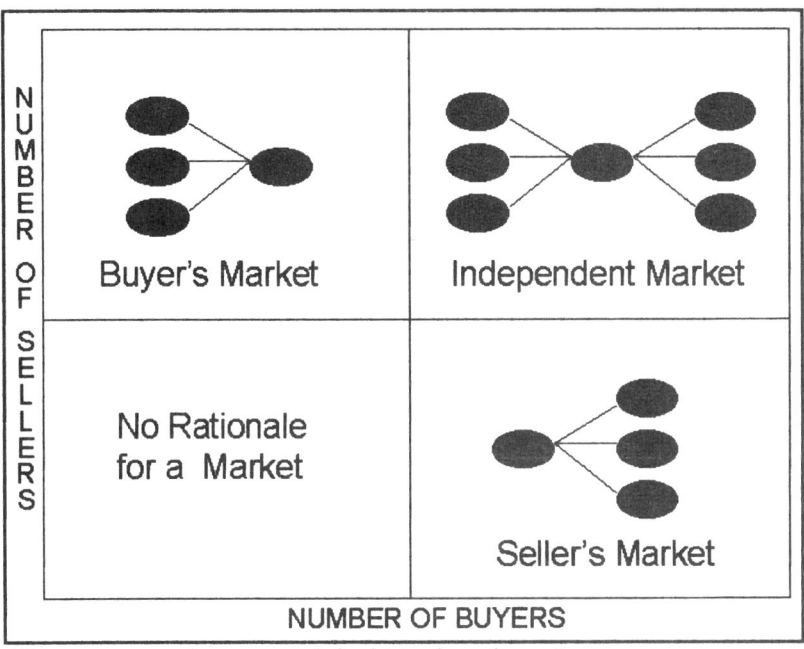

	Buyer's Market	Independent Market
NUMBER OF SELLERS	No Rationale for a Market	Seller's Market

NUMBER OF BUYERS

Figure 1. Digital Marketplace Structures

A *buyer's market* is typical of the B2B exchange where one large company or a tightly controlled consortium of companies in a given industry procures goods and services from many suppliers. The business model is many-to-one (or few). Buyer's markets are either *private* as is the case with GE providing procurement services for its many subsidiary companies, or semi-private, involving large companies banding together form buying consortia, pooling their buying power. Examples include the Sears & Roebuck, Carrefour and Oracle joint venture (GlobalNetXchange), and the Ford, DaimlerChrysler, GM buying consortium (Covisint Internet Exchange). These consortium business models assume preexisting business relationships with suppliers and trading partners, and the value proposition is one of gaining efficiencies by eliminating the friction involved in most transactions — all the faxes, emails, phone calls, letters and so on.

Regardless of the compelling arguments to reduce friction and streamline relationships in supplier trading, the B2B trading exchange has absolutely no guarantee of success. First generation exchanges and buying consortiums have mostly been a disappointment for buyers and sellers. One supplier expressed this view, "Let's see, you want me to put all my products and prices online so my customers can beat me about the head and shoulders. Then I can commoditize myself even more to take my razor-thin margins down to microscopic level. Finally, I get to pay transaction fees for this privilege. What am I missing?"[5] Trading exchanges must provide win-win relationships between buyers and suppliers. They can do so, not by strangling suppliers, but by offering automated trading services that cut the costs of doing business for both parties.

Where there are many, fragmented buyers and sellers, an *independent market* can aggregate goods and services of many sellers. They serve as a one-stop buying site by consolidating multiple product catalogs for buyers. The business model is many-to-many and is sometimes referred to as a "butterfly market." The independent market-maker is the central node, and buyers and sellers represent the wings. Independent markets usually are open, *public* marketplaces, and it is the market-maker's challenge to gain enough traction to connect fragmented buyers and sellers and to provide sufficient value to get the wings flapping— hence "butterfly."

For an independent butterfly marketplace to make sense and succeed, the market must be large and geographically dispersed with significant fragmentation among buyers and sellers. Price volatility, high search costs and perishable products make up other rationales for operating these open marketplaces. The marketplace aggregates supplier offerings, simplifying matching and searching for the buyer. Conversely, the marketplace brings an aggregation of potential buyers to the seller whose tasks of getting buyer attention are reduced. The independent marketplace model requires the functionality of both buy-side and sell-side forms of commerce plus sophisticated market processes for discovery and mediation between buyers and sellers.

Early public marketplaces did little more than aggregate catalogs and facilitate transactions between buyers and sellers. Unless they reached incredible volumes, transaction fees and advertising were not sufficient to make the venture profitable. Considering existing relationships with their suppliers and the availability of Internet search engines, many companies have shied away as they have not seen a clear value proposition. Many public marketplaces already have come and gone.

Some independent electronic markets have succeeded by specializing in conducting *auctions*. The interactivity of the Internet has led to the growing use of auctions in both business-to-consumer and business-to-business markets. Whether it is selling antiques to consumers or putting surplus inventory on sale, auctions are becoming commonplace in the digital economy. Auctions can be the preferred mechanism for liquidating surplus at the best possible price while offering a wide range of buyers the opportunity of bidding for lower than market prices. Sellers also use the auction format to help set prices on first-run goods.

Auctions go beyond negotiated fixed pricing and utilize a number of dynamic pricing mechanisms. Generally, auctions are segmented into four major one-sided formats: the ascending-price English auction, descending-price Dutch auction, first-price sealed-bid, and uniform second-price (Vickrey). In one-sided auctions, only bids are permitted, but not "asks." Double auctions allow bids and asks to take place at the same time.

According to a report released by Forrester Research, online business-to-business auctions are expected to approach $52.6 billion by 2002. The computer and semiconductor industries have been early adopters of Internet auctions because their fast-moving product cycles often cause inventory management problems. The auction market is also touching commodity industries like oil and gas.

As shown in Figure 2, two broad types of digital marketplaces have appeared on the business scene. *Horizontal marketplaces* connect buyers and sellers across many industries, primarily providing indirect procurement resources. Horizontal MRO (maintenance, repair, and operations) marketplaces for office supplies, travel, shipping and financial services are now commonplace. To participate in these marketplaces, companies typically need automated requisitioning and procurements systems capable of interacting with the marketplace.

Vertical marketplaces provide products that are specific to trading partners in a given industry (e.g., textile, oil and gas, and retail industries). They also can serve as hubs for integrating business processes between companies. To be successful, they must provide much more than the simple aggregation of goods and services into an electronic catalog. They must add value chain services and collaborations well beyond the basic catalog-transact business model typical of horizontal MRO marketplaces.

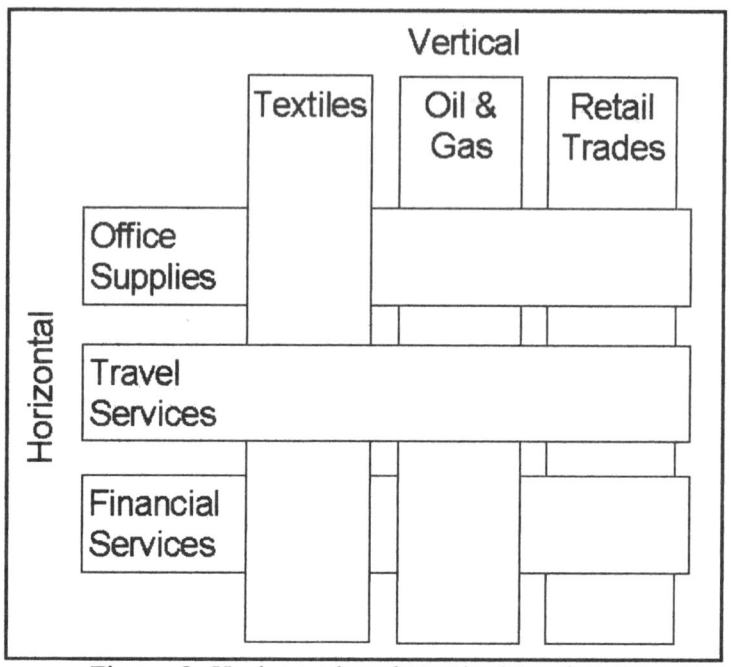

Figure 2. Horizontal and Vertical Marketplaces

One of the fastest growing vertical marketplaces is the B2B trading exchange. One or more have sprung up in most industries. These marketplaces go beyond procurement activities for operating resources and focus on the supply chain. According to the Aberdeen Group, "Electronic marketplaces have accelerated the shift to e-Business, providing a single Web-based hub for brokering buyer-seller interactions for select vertical industries, business processes, or groups. E-Markets can efficiently match buyers and sellers, reduce transaction costs, and ease trading-relationship management."[6]

Romesh Wadhwani, Vice Chairman of i2, revealed how the B2B e-commerce landscape is shifting, "Putting in e-procurement systems for the management of indirect materials and office supplies is what we call the 'tinkering around' approach. The market is changing from an emphasis on public e-markets to private e-markets and the real transformation of companies into digital businesses. Since the supply chain is a closed loop —as opposed to the freewheeling nature of a public e-market— private e-markets make fertile ground for custom supply-chain management software."[7] With this trend, the primary role of the public marketplace will be handling low-margin, commodity operations.

A blurb at Ariba's Web site states that, "Ultimately, all businesses will buy on a marketplace, sell on a marketplace, host a marketplace or be marginalized by a marketplace."[8] Taking these notions one step further, companies will likely do all three. Companies will ultimately maintain connections to multiple public and private marketplaces. Least-common-denominator functionality such as auctions, spot buys and open sourcing will be handled at public marketplaces. Business process integration and unique knowledge that creates competitive advantage will be handled within the private vertical marketplace. The knowledge base will be shared with only the most intimate of trading partners, and it represents the vital ingredient missing from most first generation digital marketplaces, *collaboration*.

Collaborative marketplaces go far beyond the first generation B2B exchanges to add all the business conversations and interactions that surround the transaction component of commerce. Collaboration, not the transaction, is what B2B digital commerce —and the real world of business-to-business commerce— is about.

Business encounters are not simple *see-buy-get* transactions typical of consumer markets. They are long-lived collaborations involving such dimensions as multi-party discovery, negotiation, supply and demand planning, joint product design, shared documents and workflows, change management and the many other facets of real world commerce. Often, multi-company interactions must occur in real-time and cross the political, cultural and legal frameworks of trading partners scattered across the globe. Trading services applications must provide facilities for maintaining negotiation-collaboration boards, creating resources within the boards, defining user privileges and managing resource sharing among users. With these facilities, companies can develop buy-side RFQ applications, sell-side auctioning platforms, and partner collaboration environments with the facilitates of the marketplace.

And they must be able to tap third party business services such as logistics, shipping, insurance, bill presentment and payments —they must be connected to any number of additional industry marketplaces. Forrester Research explains, "eMarketplaces will create point-to-point connections with specialty service providers ...satisfying customers' needs for more extensive commerce help than simply matching bids and offers. ...eMarketplaces will actively create Net-based service offerings that participants can't access offline. These novel services... help sites build stickiness with all user groups. ... eMarketplaces will fulfill customers' visions of one-stop shops by connecting the process of product research information all the way through to trade settlement and clearing —as part of one connected transaction process."[9] Networked digital marketplaces are the essence of the digital economy.

Forrester Research elaborates, "Demanding participants will look for marketplaces to play dual roles: acting as one-stop shops for a variety of products as well as offering highly specialized industry-specific services. To accomplish this near-Herculean task, sites will be forced to leverage the capabilities of other marketplaces. Those marketplaces that try to fly solo will find that they're beaten out by others that aggressively create alliances."[10]

To gain collaborative commerce facilities, marketplace software vendors are rushing to expand their offerings. Ariba acquired Agile Software Corporation, a leading provider of collaborative commerce solutions; Freemarkets hopes to extend its sourcing offering into supply-chain collaboration and optimization with its acquisition of Adexa, a collaborative supply-chain commerce company; and i2 Technologies' $9.2 billion buyout of Aspect Development Corporation was aimed at beefing up i2's component supply-management technology.

Collaboration does not mean revealing all of a company's competitive secrets to everyone who may look on. Instead, a Web of potential connections —public and private— capable of deep collaboration down to the business process level is needed. Collaboration proceeds to deeper levels as relationships are formed and naturally deepen.

Relationships can be casual and short-term, or highly selective and deeply rooted as is often the case with long-standing trading partners. Collaborations can range from very open information sharing in public marketplaces, to very privileged information and resources shared only in private marketplaces with invitation-only "collaboration rooms."

Relationships may range from simple information presentment to real-time business services (e-services) whereby companies come together to form virtual corporations. Relationships may last for a single project consummated in seconds or minutes or endure for many projects over many years.

The digital marketplace must support *encounter models* and facilities so that individual participants can control the depth of their relationships, information sharing, business process integration, knowledge sharing and collaboration with others. In this way, companies can protect their proprietary information and unique business processes.

When companies master e-marketplaces, each seller and each buyer will build its own private marketplace and also belong to one or more public marketplaces. In each model, the seller or the buyer transforms its non-proprietary information into e-services to exchange with public marketplaces. At the same time, the seller or the buyer keeps to itself and its most intimate partners proprietary information, such as customer purchasing histories, that gives the company a competitive edge. Mastering collaborative digital marketplaces is not an option, it's an imperative — from every company's customers.

E-Services: The Cathedral and the Bazaar

According to Hewlett Packard's crisp definition, "E-services are modular, nimble, electronic services that perform work, achieve tasks, or complete transactions. Almost any asset can be turned into an e-service and offered via the Internet to drive new revenue streams and create new efficiencies. E-services are business activities versus computer 'applications.'"

E-services are digital versions of real-world business services — they transform services that are required to conduct business in the physical world into a form necessary for the digital economy. Examples include scheduling, credit and financial services, logistics, shipping and supply chain functions.

United Parcel Service of America (UPS) launched a project in 1997 that distributed vital customer service functions. UPS is integrating its package-tracking capabilities directly with corporate customers' sites. Puzzled by the initiative, Computerworld's Sharon Machlis asked, "Why, when conventional Web strategy is to create more links to your site and increase public traffic, is UPS moving the other way?" [11]

Ross McCullough, electronic-commerce group manager explained, "We want to enable the merchants to speak directly to their customers." By helping retailers offer more services to consumers, he said, those retailers might generate more repeat sales – and thus more shipping business for UPS. By linking the confirmation number with a shipping number when an order is first entered, customers get the information they need to track the package immediately – there is no need to check in another time for the shipping number. And the tracking information is integrated with the retailer's site, so a user would get status information from the site where the order was placed, not from the separate UPS page where 4.7 million tracking requests were logged in December 1997. UPS's strategy cements its place in the value chain by way of making its e-services pervasive.

Today's business world is dominated with large corporations using monolithic information systems —massive cathedrals where people must conform to the worldview in business processes represented by the ornate structures of the business and its technology. By contrast, the Internet is a bazaar filled with dynamic business structures and processes. The architects and builders of 21st century businesses must answer a most fundamental question, should they build a cathedral or a bazaar? The short answer is the bazaar.

The Internet is a virtually limitless, ever-changing and constantly adaptive marketplace of business service offerings. To accomplish a particular goal, the savvy business can enter the bazaar with the mindset of exploring, choosing, testing, rejecting —in effect, assembling a unique combination of software-based business services in a rapid and efficient manner, creating a set of services that may never be recreated by any other user.

The first generation of buy-side and sell side applications were cathedrals, monolithic point solutions, automating a single aspect of a business with little or no facilities for integrating other digital commerce applications. On the other hand, large companies such as Home Depot have identified over 70 Internet commerce initiatives. If these initiatives were addressed as 70 stand alone efforts, integrating them with existing legacy systems and each other would be a nightmare. Maintaining them could be even worse.

Instead, what's needed is a commerce resource platform capable of integrating dynamic e-services from both within and outside the enterprise —a platform capable of rapidly and in many cases automatically, bundling, unbundling and rebundling e-services with a limitless number of online participants in digital marketplaces.

Everything that each participant brings to a marketplace —be that the service the company provides —the unique information or knowledge the company holds, or the relationships the company has with its own customers, partners and suppliers —has the potential to be accessible as an online business service. These e-services can be accessed by any user, including external marketplaces or other businesses, to deliver total solutions to customers.

In the Internet bazaar, marketplace participants can pick and choose only those business services that they require at the moment and find new services as necessary. Each will supply a complete set of functionality independent of all other e-services. This enables the plug-and-play ease that participants require to join and move between digital marketplaces without difficulty.

Industry analyst Patricia Seybold explains, "We're about to embark on a new era in which most companies will begin to focus on a few very strategic business processes. Innovative companies will package up their strategic processes as services that can be provided and launched via the Internet. Soon, many business-to-business activities will be handled by a series of e-services locating one another, negotiating with one another, and handling each other's requests."[12]

The level of automation is low among the Small and Medium Enterprises (SMEs) yet they represent a major part of the economy, making up as much as 80% of some manufacturing industries. To include first time business users in value chain networks they must be provided facilities allowing them to start out with very simple, yet highly effective, business activities rendered digitally as e-services.

To make it possible for SMEs to participate in value chains, e-services hubs or business service providers (BSPs) are a natural as they can eliminate hassles and computer system conversions. Private and public e-service hubs can serve as the foundation of extending the supply chain to even the smallest of suppliers and their suppliers —all they may need is a Web browser. The key is simple "task" automation, not complex, monolithic "application" automation.

Knowledge Management

In the same way that the computer itself heralded the start of an information age, new developments in network-centric computing herald a new age of knowledge rather than of information. Not only can future technology distribute information, it can distribute an enterprise's knowledge base by interconnecting people and digitally codifying their expertise.

Such knowledge management requires that a company go well beyond providing data and information contained in spread sheets, databases, and documents. It must include the tacit information and digitally capture an experts' know-how.

Dr. David Skyrme explains, "Knowledge management is the explicit and systematic management of vital knowledge and its associated processes of creating, gathering, organizing, diffusion, use and exploitation. It requires turning personal knowledge into corporate knowledge that can be widely shared throughout an organization and appropriately applied."[13]

We are not speaking of artificial intelligence technology as we know it today. We are speaking of amplifying the knowledge contained in individuals' heads and in business rules stored in computer systems, and of *selectively* making it available to anyone or any system anywhere, at any time. Knowledge management involves capturing, classifying, evaluating, retrieving and sharing all of a company's information assets in a way that provides context for effective decisions and actions. These are daunting tasks within a single enterprise, but become even more challenging when all the participants in a value chain are included.

As corporations become more extended and externally integrated, then the community memory and organizational knowledge must reside in the information systems. Consequently, not only are new types of systems necessary, but also new ways of human interaction with information systems are needed. With current systems approaches, the onus is on humans to try to make sense of information from disjointed presentations of data. New types of information systems are needed that place the onus on the computer system to correctly convey information in a context that both humans and the automated computer systems of a company's suppliers, customers and trading partners can process naturally.

The information must reflect reality as perceived and understood by humans, not the artificial constructs of computer files characteristic of today's systems. Where it once stood on the sidelines, cognitive science plays a central role in new era information systems. Systems rooted in human cognition can enable instant use (no training required), correct assimilation, confirmation of user intentions and error-free communication between man and machine and machine and machine. Such systems are essential to the extended enterprise.

Thomas Davenport clarifies that it is not the rise of a new form of artificial intelligence software, but that "the workhorses of knowledge management will be contained in object-oriented modules for easy maintainability."[14] The object approach organizes data and processes into understandable entities such as people, places, things and events. Ontologists and library scientists will one day be called on to help corporations to categorize and classify their knowledge base so it is as intuitive and expandable as possible. The goal is to classify and provide information with context, not create information overload.

In *The Digital Economy,* Don Tapscott explores the promise and peril of the phenomena of networked intelligence.[15] This capability truly empowers individuals and computer applications (whether on the shop floor or in a customer's office or two enterprise's computer applications interacting with one another) to make optimal business decisions on-the-spot, wherever and whenever required. It is this magnitude of empowerment that is required for true business innovation.

What happens when an enterprise codifies, digitizes and makes available its rules, policies, techniques, workflows, business processes, and decision-making to its entire workforce as well as its customers and suppliers? By making customers, suppliers and trading partners as smart as the enterprise itself, a whole new work force evolves. People inside and outside the business become not just connected together, they work with one and the same knowledge base as illustrated in Figure 3.

In his classic book, *Things That Make Us Smart,* Donald Norman reveals that it's the information we surround ourselves with as we do a task, that makes us smart. But mountains of data and disjointed tidbits of know-how are of little use unless they are distilled and made available to the people or computer programs that need meaningful information at the right place at the right time —they need information context. It is information context that provides the cornerstone of digital commerce, customer relationship management.

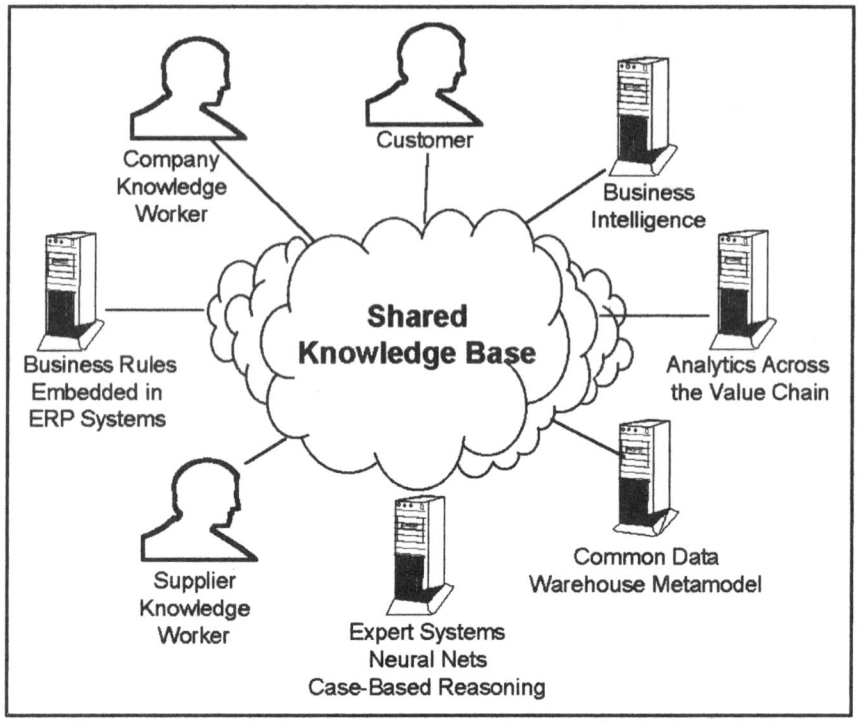

Figure 3. Knowledge Management Across the Value Chain

Customer Relationship Management: The Soul of Digital Commerce

Successful digital commerce requires much more than just selling. That something more is excellent customer service and support. Customer relationship management has grabbed the attention of business executives who are charting their course for conducting business on the Internet —and for good reason. Customer relationship management —from customer acquisition to building loyalty— is the heart and soul of a customer-driven company.

The goal is to maximize the life time value of a company's most profitable customers. The strategic results can include improving the quality of customer service while reducing costs, and putting the customer in control by providing self-service and solution-centered support. The ultimate business goal is to earn customer loyalty and gain a lifetime of business.

Chapter 4 - The Art of Digital Business

To sustain life-long relationships, customers and companies must have access to a common pool of "know-how," provided not just by the enterprise but also by customer communities. When customers are recognized as equals, not some static target at the end of a value chain, strong relationships can be developed.

Customer interactions become conversations, interactive dialogs with shared know-how, not just business transactions. While the Internet cannot totally replace the phone and face-to-face communication with customers, it can strengthen these and all customer touch points. Web-based customer care can become the focal point of customer relationship management and provide breakthrough benefits for both the enterprise and its customers — substantially reducing costs while improving service.

That impact is summed up by Kevin Kelly, "The central economic imperative of the Industrial Age was to increase productivity. The central economic imperative of the network economy is to amplify relationships. Since a relationship involves two members investing in it, its value increases twice as fast as one's investment. Outsiders act as employees, employees as outsiders. New relationships blur the role of employees and customers to the point of unity. They reveal the customer and the company as one. In the network economy, producing and consuming fuse into a single verb: prosuming. And whoever has the smartest customers wins. The world's best experts on your product or service don't work for your company. They are your customers, or a hobby tribe. The network economy is founded on technology, but can only be built on relationships. It starts with chips and ends with trust."[16]

By extending Kelly's notions to suppliers and trading partners as well, companies can weave a tapestry of knowledge sharing throughout the entire value web. The scope of relationship management changes drastically and becomes multidimensional, not just the traditional company-customer relationship. Companies can blend the knowledge of their suppliers' experts with their own and that of their customer communities to transform the process of relationship management.

When customers conduct their business on the Internet, they see —and they steer— entire value-chains. The Internet "Looking Glass" is a two-way mirror world, and its field of vision is the entire value-chain as illustrated in Figure 4. Customer communities-of-interest can see the entire value chain, including other well informed customers.

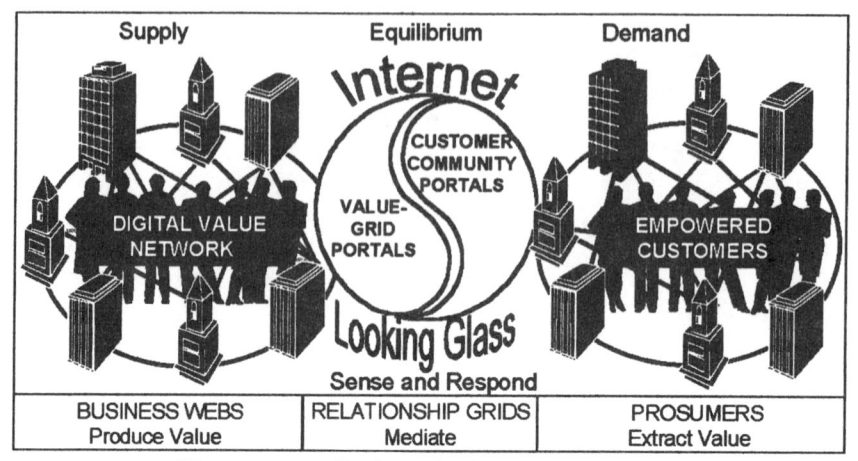

Figure 4. Holistic Relationship Management

To exploit the ability to connect the entire value chain into a unified whole, traditional customer relationship management must be taken to new levels: Value Chain Relationship Management (VCRM) and Customer Community Relationship Management (CCRM). Companies must manage their relationships not just with customers. They must reach out to entire customer communities, and with supplier and trading partner communities as well.

The transformation is from customer service "atomism" to integrated business ecosystems. Customers are the experts and have the most experience when it comes to the *use* of a product or service. Suppliers are the experts on each of the components that go into a complete product. Thus a company is surrounded by experts whose knowledge can be of immense business value if only it can be tapped. As shown in the figure, healthy business ecosystems feature relationship portals for both the demand channel and the supply channel. Through these channels flows the information and knowledge needed to optimize entire value chains, producing unrivaled value for customers.

The definition of "the customer" is sometimes blurred within a single commerce transaction. In many business-to-business scenarios, customer versus supplier is a function of *role,* not entity. In some transactions the same entity plays multiple, simultaneous roles of producer and consumer —prosumer.

When looking at the value chain as a whole, the question of where the customer will get help in repairing that Black and Decker drill remains an open question: from Home Depot, a third party service company, Black and Decker, or one of its component suppliers? This question, along with issues of protecting each participants' proprietary information and know-how, must be answered. Answers, furthermore, will change as a business ecosystem evolves. Clearly, digital relationship management systems must be capable of rapid bundling, unbundling and rebundling. Relationships are about connections, dynamic and adaptable connections.

Relationship management strategies and systems that tap the power of the Internet can yield innovation and promise great competitive advantage. These same strategies and systems pose a great challenge in their conception, design and implementation. The very best business and technical minds will be needed to build the relationship management systems needed in the digital economy.

Content, Community, Commerce and Context

The art of digital business involves content, community, commerce and context as companies build digital marketplaces, render their business services electronically, codify their know-how and manage holistic customer relationships. The fit, balance and compromise of these dimensions must be managed diligently to optimize relationships in the overall interest of the business and its purposes. Putting the pieces together is the challenge of every company that wants to succeed in digital commerce. Getting there requires mastery of new enabling technologies and incorporating digital strategy into overall business strategy.

References

[1] "IBM's Gerstner Speaks On E-Commerce," Newsbytes News Network, March 19, 1998.
[2] Les Alberthal, "The Once and Future Craftsman Culture," in *The Future of the Electronic Marketplace*, MIT Press, 1998.
[3] Derek Leebaert (Editor), *The Future of the Electronic Marketplace*, MIT Press, 1998.
[4] Kafka, Steven J., Bruce D. Temkin, Matthew R. Sanders, Jeremy Sharrard and Tobias O. Brown, "eMarketplaces Boost B2B Trade," Forrester Research, February 2000.
[5] Phillips, Charles and Mary Meeker, "The B2B Internet Report: Collaborative Commerce," Morgan Stanley Dean Witter, April 2000.
[6] Aberdeen Group, April 2000.
[7] http://www.line56.com/articles/default.asp?NewsID=2024
[8] http://www.ariba.com/com_plat/b2b_marketplace.cfm
[9] Lief, Varda, Bruce D. Temkin, Kathryn McCarthy, Jeremy Sharrard and Tobias O. Brown, "Net Marketplaces Grow-Up," Forrester Research, December 1999.
[10] Lief, Varda, "Net Marketplaces Grow Up," Forrester Research, December 1999.
[11] Sharon Machlis, "Integrated tracking," *Computerworld*, 11/24/97. http://www.computerworld.com/home/print9497.nsf/all/SL47UPS16F5E
[12] Patricia B. Seybold, "Preparing for the E-services Revolution: Designing your next Generation E-Business," April 30, 1999, http://www.hp.com/e-ervices/article_sey_1.html
[13] Skyrme, D., "Knowledge management: making sense of an oxymoron," *Management Insight*, 1997. http://www.skyrme.com/insights/22km.htm
[14] Davenport, Thomas H., "The Future of Knowledge Management," *CIO Magazine*, January 1, 1996, pp 30-32.
[15] Tappscott, Don, "The Digital Economy: Promise and Peril in the Age of Networked Intelligence," McGraw-Hill, 1996.
[16] Kevin Kelly, *New Rules for the New Economy: 10 Radical Strategies for a Connected World*, Viking Press, November, 1998.

Chapter 5

The Commerce Resource Platform

The goal is to manage the white space in the value chain and streamline inter-enterprise business processes to increase their value to customers.

From ERP to CRP:
Agile Software Powering the Agile Corporation

Most commercial IS shops simply did not have the knowledge and skills needed to build enterprise-class systems. As a result several software vendors emerged with complete Enterprise Resource Planning (ERP) systems. Today most large companies have installed ERP systems from software companies like Peoplesoft, Baan, J. D. Edwards and SAP. The trend continues to the small to medium enterprise (SME). To capitalize on the growing adoption of ERP systems by SME's, on December 21, 2000 Microsoft announced plans to acquire Great Plains Software, a leader in this field.

An ERP system is *not* a specific application or point solution to a business problem. Instead it is a conglomerate of many applications that are integrated with one another —ERP systems are platforms for building information systems with an enterprise-wide reach. Companies do not "program" their ERP systems. Instead they "configure" them to derive the desired functionality. But even this process is complex, and the services of systems integrators can cost more than the software itself.

Although ERP systems are complex, when their domain is extended from a single intra-company scope to multi-company value chains, the complexity can be daunting. Digital commerce is about consolidating and harmonizing the many islands of disparate information and systems scattered throughout a value chain, creating a unified whole. *The goal is to manage the white space in the value chain and streamline inter-enterprise business processes to increase their value to customers.* It's about making intranets, extranets and the Internet work together to deliver business concept innovation. It's about business reengineering on a grand scale.

To manage the complexity of the inter-enterprise systems needed for digital commerce, companies will again turn, not to point solutions, but to a comprehensive software platform, a Commerce Resource Platform (CRP).

The choice in commerce platforms has serious implications. CRP systems must be more eloquent than their predecessor ERP systems. They must be capable of easy and rapid integration with any number of other companies' systems and marketplaces. The CRP must make it easy to join existing marketplaces, create marketplaces, add new suppliers to a value thread and add new customers to shared spaces for customer service and support. Companies require a comprehensive platform so they can implement multiple simultaneous market models: seller, buyer, market maker and community builder. Digital business demands great agility without which a company will be severely constrained.

To reach this end, flexible CRP systems incorporate component-based architectures and intelligent technologies which are discussed in greater detail in the following chapter. With such a modular and adaptive platform, business solution developers can assemble and tailor prebuilt business components into complete solutions. Figure 1 shows the architecture and functionality needed in a CRP.

The architecture is layered. The top of the framework shows that a given company will need to participate in several marketplaces (financial, procurement, distribution and industrial), playing multiple simultaneous roles (seller, buyer, market maker, and community builder). The top layer represents the external renderings of the services provided by the platform. The business services that a company delivers to these marketplaces may be rendered to people through a browser, a network appliance, or wireless WAP-enabled devices such as cell phones. They may also be rendered as application to application interactions, no humans involved.

Community and Marketplace Management. The community and marketplace management layer of the architecture handles information boundaries among the participants. As needed in any online system, user management authenticates members and authorizes them to enter the marketplace. At the business process level, what is needed is authentication so that no one else can pretend that he or she is an authorized user, and access control so that a particular user can gain access to only those portions of the business for which he or she is authorized. On the stateless and session-less World Wide Web, the user needs to know he is communicating with the right server, called server authentication, and the server needs to know it is communicating with the right user, client authentication.

Chapter 5 - The Commerce Resource Platform

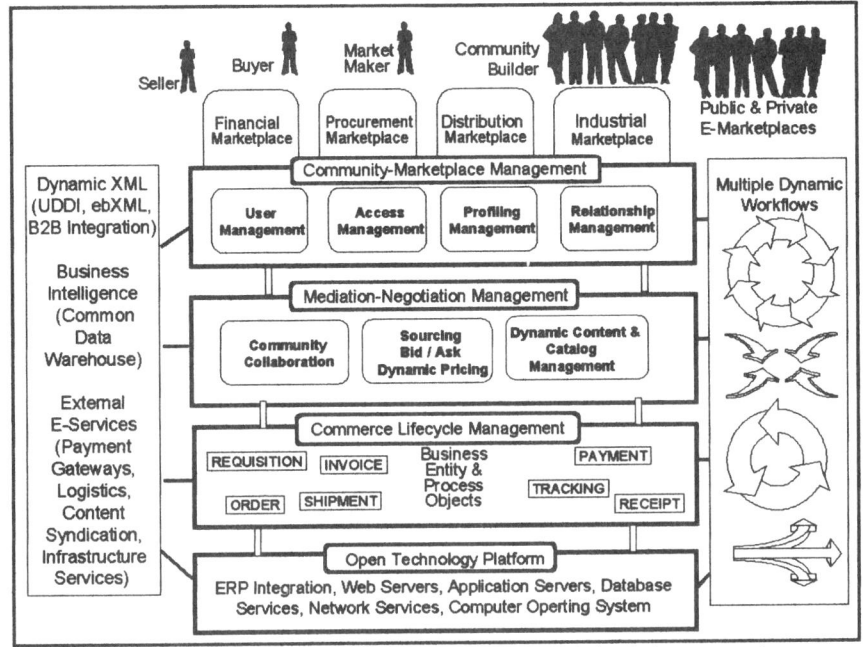

Figure 1. From ERP to CRP: The Digital Corporation

Authentication procedures must provide convenience as well as security. For example, in a business-to-business context, authentication should provide a single, universal user logon to multiple applications running on multiple servers while controlling access to resources on the system: files, directories and server universal resource locators (URLs). In fact, a single sign-on is a requirement in most business-to-business digital commerce environments. Parties to transactions must feel comfortable in their asumption that they are in fact doing business with who they believe they are. Doubt as to the identity of other parties must be eliminated by a security system that authenticates by verifying information that the user provides against what the system already knows about the user.

Access management involves the control of access to a particular information space once the user has been authenticated. Access controls delineate the user's privileges or permissions such as 1) creating and destroying information, 2) reading, writing and executing files and programs, 3) adding, deleting and modifying content, and 4) exporting and importing abilities.

Business rules and authorization limits may be unique to different divisions, operating units, individual employees and *roles* (e.g. buyer, administrator and manager). Authorizations can be assigned to individuals, groups or roles and the administration of these vital business controls can be delegated to the appropriate managers and organizational units, inside or outside the enterprise. Human resource systems are a key point of integration needed for managing user profiles and roles. Role-based task allocation is essential to accommodate organizational change and the multiple roles employees play.

Profiling and relationship management are essential to personalization. For example, the profiling component will capture and store information that can be used to personalize content delivery such as access to specific account and billing information. Such profiles may be role-based, eliminating the need to assign access privileges on an individual basis. For example, a purchasing agent may have access to all company purchase orders, whereas individual employees can see only those they have initiated.

The profiles of the users of the system must be dynamic as well as able to provide more static access controls. For example, users typically want the system to start where they left off as they suspend and reinitiate work sessions. Because purchasing agents are time constrained, they want the system to bring to bear all the resources for the task at hand in a convenient manner that allows them to do their work efficiently. Often a task cannot be completed in one work session, and users will want to continue where they left off with these successive, work-in-progress, sessions. Dynamic profiles also can be used to individualize content by tracking and analyzing individual usage of the system.

Dynamic profiling is a key to a complete customer relationship management system which, in turn, is a central component of the community-marketspace management layer. As we noted in Chapter 4, CRM is the soul of digital commerce, bringing together dynamic information from all customer touch points. The profiling component captures customer interaction information from people and customer application systems, then the CRM system analyzes the information to enable 1-to-1 customer relationships.

Mediation and Negotiation Management. Once inside the market space, discovery, mediation and matching, collaboration, negotiation and content delivery become the critical components of the commerce resource platform. Users may enter a marketplace just for these purposes without actually buying or selling —at this level of the framework the basic task is providing information and collaboration facilities. Is a particular product available? What's the price? What are the terms? What's the status of an order? Has an engineering change order been processed? In sourcing applications, the mediation-negotiation management layer of the platform must provide for requests for information, availability to commit, requests for quotations and auctioning capabilities such as bid/ask facilities.

Dynamic content and catalog management components of the platform must be robust in most industries. Up-to-the-second catalog information must be synchronized with the information contained within a given company or aggregated from multiple suppliers. Catalog management systems come in a variety of flavors and catalog interoperability requirements are not unusual. Advanced catalog search techniques such as parametric search engines are needed in most industrial marketplace applications.

Commerce Lifecycle Management. When users of a marketplace want to conduct the business of buying or selling, the commerce lifecycle comes into play. At this level of the framework, business entity objects (e.g., requisition, order and invoice) and process objects (e.g., shipping, paying and receiving) are used to initiate transactions and carry through all the way to satisfaction and settlement. The business objects in the commerce lifecycle are not lined up in a serial flow from requisition to receipt. The reason is that the real world of commerce is essentially not linear. If it was, every participant's activities would have to be synchronized before business was conducted. Instead the activities of the digital commerce life cycle are asynchronous, as in the real world of commerce. They are governed and coordinated by dynamic workflows.

Open Technology Platform. The foundation layer of the CRP is an open technology platform that provides essential computing services such as transaction processing, permanent storage of information, event handling services and integration with existing ERP systems. The technology platform includes application servers, web servers, database services, network services and computer operating systems. Well known component-based technology platforms include Sun Microsystems Enterprise Java Beans, OMG's Corba Component Model and Microsoft's COM+. The technology platform is an infrastructure that supports "plug-and-play" business application components which, in turn, are used to build the commerce framework.

Multiple Dynamic Workflows. An extremely important requirement of a commerce resource platform is the capability to manage multiple dynamic workflows. To conduct digital commerce and integrate value chains, workflow systems must provide end to end business process control, from the initial request for a price quotation, all the way through to the delivery of goods to a customer.

Workflows control the movement of work through a business process. Work tasks can be performed in series or in parallel and usually involve automated computer applications and people.

Workflows in early e-commerce application packages were hard coded into the commerce lifecycle such as the procurement process. Changes in workflows required recoding of the workflow steps and processes, an increasingly complex and time consuming task as more and more participants join a value chain or marketplace. In a robust commerce resource platform, on the other hand, workflow management is separated out from the commerce lifecycle —they are orthogonal to the commerce lifecycle management component as shown on the right of Figure 1.

Companies have installed workflow systems to automate their internal workflows. But when multiple companies are involved in the various stages of a business process, each potentially using different workflow systems, two problems become apparent. First, external workflows must be jointly owned by participants in a value chain. Companies may have their own internal workflow systems, but inter-company workflows are the key to digital commerce. The second problem is that there must be a mechanism for external workflows to trigger tasks within each company's internal workflow systems. Because workflow systems embed a company's unique business rules and policies, these systems must be leveraged, not discarded.

To solve these problems, interoperation standards are increasingly vital as new, shared workflows are jointly designed and owned. An emerging standard, Wf-XML of the Workflow Management Coalition (WfMC) is especially important to watch. Wf-XML complements work being done by other XML groups.

External Resources. As shown on the left of Figure 1, a commerce resource platform provides the ability to plug in external resources as integral parts of the commerce resource platform. Unlike systems of the past, digital commerce systems now rely on the services and activities of external entities. These services are the digital equivalent of the resources needed in the real world of commerce. Key among these external resources are dynamic XML frameworks, business intelligence that spans an entire value chain or marketplace and e-services.

The eXtensible Markup Language (XML) is a standard that is used to define data and to send structured messages between trading partners. It is used by various industry standards organizations to create consistent data definitions and pre-defined business conversations in the form of structured documents such as purchase orders and invoices. We cover XML in greater depth in the next chapter. For now we introduce one of the core XML initiatives to indicate its role in a commerce resource platform.

Universal Description, Discovery, and Integration (UDDI) is an XML-based registry for businesses worldwide to list themselves on the Internet. Its ultimate goal is to streamline online transactions by enabling companies to find one another on the Web and make their systems interoperable for digital commerce. UDDI is often compared to a telephone book's white, yellow and unique "green" pages that describe how to do business with a company. UDDI allows businesses to list themselves by name, business category, product, location, and the Web services they offer.

Business intelligence applications are used by companies for gathering, storing, analyzing and providing access to data to help make better business decisions and enable customer relationship management. Business intelligence systems bring together decision support applications, query and reporting, online analytical processing, statistical analysis, forecasting and data mining. Business intelligence is vital to optimizing value chains and delivering customized goods and services to customers.

For years companies have used data warehouses and data mining techniques to drive decision support systems. Now the challenge is to bring these techniques to provide business intelligence to the entire value chain. Standards such as the Object Management Group's Common Warehouse Metamodel Interchange (CWMI) provide the mechanism for integrating the data warehouses of individual companies to broaden the scope of business intelligence from a micro to a macro perspective. With CWMI data can be taken from one type of data repository and worked with in another data warehouse.

E-services round out the sampling of external resources that can be incorporated into the commerce resource platform. Each service a trading partner provides, for example, the unique information or knowledge a supplier holds, has the potential to be accessible as an online e-service. As we discussed in Chapter 4, typical e-services include credit verification, payment gateways, logistics and content syndication which can play a vital role when building on-line communities.

Software components throughout the commerce resource platform may be changed without affecting the others. The component model is ideally suited to e-services as it is a services-based architecture. With a component-based CRP, multiple digital commerce applications can be assembled, disassembled, and reassembled. In this way, the platform can allow a company to play multiple simultaneous roles of buyer, seller, market maker and community builder. The platform becomes a software greenhouse where a company can grow its digital commerce solutions as business models evolve.

Building the Commerce Resource Platform

When a company recognizes the need for a comprehensive commerce resource platform it faces a very challenging array of options for building its CRP. When ERP systems were introduced, selection was limited to picking one of several vendors like SAP, J. D. Edwards, Baan or Peoplesoft. CRP systems, on the other hand, automate so many dimensions of a business that no one company has emerged as a clear leader, as SAP did in the ERP world, with a total solution. Even if such a company with a "total solution" were to appear on the scene, its solution would still have to be integrated with the systems of a given business' suppliers, customers and trading partners — a tedious and expensive process at best.

To overcome the integration problems, a new generation of application architectures is needed that is independent of operating systems, existing application programming interfaces, programming languages or object models (such as CORBA and DCOM). With such an architecture, business services can be developed in any language or underlying object model. By using services-based architectures native to the Internet, companies can expose their business processes (embedded in their existing and new commerce applications) as e-services to interact and collaborate with trading partners without concern for the technologies they deploy. Using the e-services technologies and standards described in the next chapter, companies can "compose" their commerce applications from e-services, embed them in their CRP platforms and deploy them in secure virtual private networks in a fully distributed environment.

Enabling services-based application architectures is the current focus throughout the computer industry (e.g., Sun Microsystems' Sun One and Microsoft's .net, Hewlett-Packard's Netaction, IBM's Application Framework for E-business, Novell's Net Services, and Oracle's Dynamic Services Framework). The industry will need time before services-based architectures reach maturity, but the demands of dynamic commerce will ensure the rapid transition.

As companies face commerce resource platform decisions today, they should make sure that their software suppliers have a road map to the fully distributed world of e-services. Companies threw away their first generation e-commerce point solutions for selling or procurement in favor of the more integrated platforms of today. To avoid the "throw away" problem in the future, alliances should be formed with software companies committed to a clear migration path to the e-services paradigm. Because the CRP will be the bedrock of digital commerce, businesses must carefully select, deploy and manage this most fundamental business asset.

Chapter 6

The New Way of Competing Demands New Technology

"Things are getting more complicated, so we needed these assistants [intelligent software agents]. And since we have them, we can afford to let things get more complex."[1] —Milind Tambe

21st Century Business Software: A Change in Kind

First generation e-commerce solutions are already out of date as they automate only the simplest catalog-transaction commerce activities. They do not contain the intelligent software needed for collaboration, knowledge management, intelligent task management or intelligent support, which is the key to customer relationship management. Their technologies are based on outdated client-server architectures. Their workflows are synchronous, not the dynamic asynchronous workflows of real commerce. They rely on central servers for content management rather the up-to-the-instant updates at the source. They only handle 10% of business interactions, the transaction. First generation digital commerce applications seem as though they were aimed at pleasing Wall Street, rather than solving the deeper business problems needed for digital commerce.

By now it has become obvious that we need a new kind of software capable of handling all facets of conducting real commerce. Real commerce is fraught with complexity and tacit information that to date has only been held in the heads of humans. We simply need new kinds of software to drive the commerce resource platform, value webs and customer-dominated business ecosystems. In short, when it comes to software the new competition needs a change in kind.

The Requirements of a Commerce Resource Platform

Current software development methods, tools, and architectures have hit technical and information walls when it comes to meeting the requirements of a commerce resource platform. The CRP must embrace open standards to reduce the friction of integrating new customers, suppliers' and trading partners' information systems. The CRP must be engineered for rapid assembly of new commerce applications to provide the agility needed to embrace change as market realities change. They must speak a business language that can be understood by trading partners and marketplaces. They must be intelligent enough to manage overwhelming complexity.

The ingredients to build and maintain a commerce resource platform include both new technologies and new approaches to software development. For software development companies building a CRP, these ingredients form the basis of their work. For companies selecting a CRP, these ingredients form the requirements definitions and selection criteria. They include component-based, peer-to-peer and model driven architectures; business vocabularies derived from the extensible markup language (XML); e-services and software agents.

The Importance of Component-based Architectures

The complexity of the inter-enterprise computing systems needed is overwhelming. Component-based architecture provides a blueprint for mapping complex technology onto the requirements of a business. It produces the mental representations that are intelligible to all the information system participants, business managers, designers and builders. While the complexity does not go away, the complexity can be managed. Furthermore, if component-based systems from one company are to be compatible with those of their trading partners and customers, they must be based on open standards.

The Electronic Commerce Reference Model of the Object Management Group is an example of a standards-based component architecture for the design of a commerce resource platform. As shown in Figure 1, the architectural model includes logical components such as catalog management, trust management, registry and directory services, encounter models, community management and collaboration. These and other components are arranged and interconnected to bring about fit and balance in the overall interest of the system.

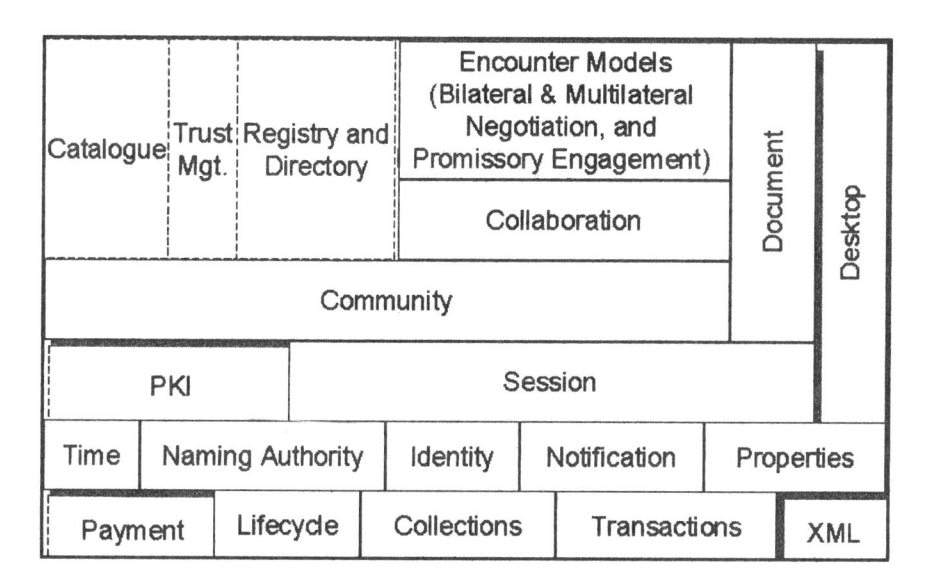

Chapter 6 - The New Way of Competing Demands New Technology 105

Catalogue	Trust Mgt.	Registry and Directory	Encounter Models (Bilateral & Multilateral Negotiation, and Promissory Engagement)	Document	Desktop
			Collaboration		
Community					
PKI		Session			
Time	Naming Authority	Identity	Notification	Properties	
Payment	Lifecycle	Collections	Transactions	XML	

Figure 1. OMG's Electronic Commerce
Reference Model Architecture

Components do not act alone, they plug into *component frameworks* that connect participating components and enforce rules of component interaction. Commerce resource platform components will not be delivered to corporations as a big pile of parts and pieces. Instead the components will be preassembled into industry specific component frameworks. These component-based frameworks represent digital commerce applications that are somewhere between 60% - 80%, complete.

Component architectures are s*ervice-based:* end-user services, business process services and data services. Application components rely on distributed computing infrastructure services, freeing solution developers from the complexity and intricacies of the underlying technologies. This separation of concerns is the key to agile software capable of rapid bundling, unbundling and rebundling in response to changing market requirements.

Component architectures divide software into construction and consumption. Once built in compliance with standards, newly constructed software components can register the services they provide, while other components can subscribe to and consume these services —*this is key to the e-services model of fully distributed computing.* Component builders are technologists who use component-based software engineering disciplines to *produce* components of extreme quality. Solution developers *consume* these prefabricated components during business process modeling and application assembly.

The task of solution developers is to customize and extend the framework to incorporate the unique business rules and processes of a given company. Because they are insulated from the technology plumbing, solution developers can concentrate on the unique character and knowledge of the company that provides competitive advantage.

Much of the extension and tailoring of components focuses on the user interfaces and involves both graphical and task-centered customization. Integrating the e-services of suppliers and trading partners is the other key activity in tailoring the framework.

With the component framework approach, corporations no longer design and code their applications. Instead they buy component-based platforms and plug in and configure just the functionality needed for the moment. Component-based commerce resources platforms, however, cannot be the complex, hard to understand and configure packages seen in today's ERP world. They should be frameworks based on distributed computing architectures that allow individual components to be mixed and matched even though they are built by a variety of software vendors.

The XML Factor and the Tower of Babel Challenge

The ultimate purpose of standards is the development of *consistent business semantics* that can be used by all participants in a value chain or marketplace —a common language of digital commerce. These semantics provide commonality to names and relationships of processes, workflows and data across value and supply chains.

A new standard for defining and naming data on a Web page, a potential lingua franca for business, was adopted by the World Wide Web Consortium (W3C) in 1997. The eXtensible Markup Language (XML) will likely revolutionize the Web by allowing structured data — with standard names and consistent semantics — to be moved around the Web in a simple, straight-forward manner as easily as HTML. XML is a native Web approach that enables extensible data-exchange formats, and gives industries the flexibility to create their *own* data tags to develop a shared Internet file system. A number of XML industry vocabularies are being developed by individual companies, vertical industry consortia and software industry groups.

XML is a document-centered technology ideally suited for message passing between trading partners in a digital commerce ecosystem. Document messaging is a way for commerce applications to interoperate in a loosely-coupled, request-for-service, communication process. The document type definition (DTD) alone can identify a given document type in a business-to-business transaction. This is similar to the various document types defined for the EDI community. For example, an ANSI X12 EDI 850 is a Purchase Order transaction set. By sending such a document to an EDI enabled system, the receiving organization knows what processing services to perform on the data. Such data hand-offs trigger business processes in the receiving organization based simply on knowing the document type contained in the message sent to it.

XML, as a potential replacement for EDI-like systems, is, however, no "silver bullet." In some ways XML is little more than the reintroduction of the "unit record concept" introduced with the punched card in the 1950's where chunks of data (fields) were tagged with names giving us attribute/value pairs bound together as a stand-alone document (record). After all, XML is simply text (ASCII) data and must have links to a powerful, underlying object infrastructure to handle the adaptive business processes and workflows needed for digital commerce. Thus XML is simply an enabler, not a guarantor, of the consistent business semantics needed for digital commerce. The truly hard part is to gain global agreement on the semantics —an effort that has eluded information systems designers since the introduction of centralized corporate data bases in the 1960s. Ask any experienced Data Administrator and they will tell you they cannot even get departments within the same company to agree on data names, much less their meaning.

The capability to create industry vocabularies is both a blessing and a curse. It basically gives the world of business an alphabet that lets them create their own languages and dialects from the alphabet. But already there are so many industry "vocabularies" and predefined "business conversations" that the result is alphabet soup. A quick Web visit to The XML Cover Page reveals over 400 "XML: Proposed Applications and Industry Initiatives."[2] In its early life, XML has already demonstrated its capability to build a Tower of Babel.

The tasks of integrating, or in any way unifying the rapidly growing list of XML vocabularies will be monumental. The Tower of Babel problem will need to be solved to create interconnected marketplaces: Commerce One uses Common Business Library (CBL), Ariba uses cXML, and Oracle uses OAG XML (OAGIS). Many corporations need to support these three dialects as well as maintain those of their traditional EDI systems. Covisint, for example, is built using technology from Commerce One and Oracle, so it must contend with the CBL and OAG XML formats. In addition, the Big Three auto makers and most of their first tier suppliers also use electronic data interchange (EDI) systems for processing invoices and communications, adding yet another layer of confusion. The good news is that several initiatives are underway that may result in universal XML specifications that can be understood and deployed by all, paving the way for a service-based Internet and "service oriented programming".

XML Technologies Power E-Services

The need for a service-based Internet goes beyond just sharing data in an understandable format. As the Internet evolves from simply serving up Web pages, dynamic e-services (a.k.a. Web services) are needed to perform tasks involving multiple steps executed on a user's behalf. These tasks usually require one e-service to call on other e-services, at the level of program-to-program or application-to-application interoperation. To solve these problems two ambitious *core* XML specifications are being developed for business-to-business interoperation: electronic business XML (ebXML) and the Universal Description, Discovery and Integration (UDDI) business registry.

UDDI somewhat overlaps ebXML and was motivated in part by its creators who wanted to move faster than the ebXML initiative. Both are similar to previous initiatives that did not reach critical mass including CommerceNet's *eCo Framework* and Hewlett-Packard's *e-speak* which is now being integrated with UDDI. It is also encouraging to note that the UDDI and ebXML organizations are beginning to collaborate, realizing the duplicate standards specifications do not serve the larger needs of business.

Chapter 6 - The New Way of Competing Demands New Technology 109

In September 1999, the United Nations (UN/CEFACT) and OASIS joined forces to develop ebXML, a set of specifications that together enable a modular electronic business framework. The vision of ebXML is to enable a global electronic marketplace where enterprises of any size and in any geographical location can meet and conduct business with each other through the exchange of XML based messages.

UN/CEFACT is the United Nations body whose mandate covers worldwide policy and technical development in the area of trade facilitation and electronic business. OASIS is the international, not-for-profit, consortium that advances electronic business by promoting open, collaborative development of interoperability specifications. In the future the ebXML standard could open up business-to-business data exchange or "Web-based EDI" to millions of companies and individuals who would have never considered expensive EDI systems. One factor that may contribute to the success of the ebXML initiative is that its developers are dealing with an established body of inter-enterprise business semantics derived from the traditional EDI world.

The other core XML initiative, UDDI, would be little more than a search engine type of directory service without its green pages that define how electronic exchanges are performed. The Web Services Description Language (WSDL) is the cornerstone of UDDI. WSDL is based on the Simple Object Access Protocol (SOAP) and IBM's Network Accessible Service Specification Language (NASSL). WSDL is an XML format for describing network services as a set of endpoints operating on messages containing either document-oriented or procedure-oriented information.

While under the roof of a single enterprise or between close trading partners who can agree on protocols, the solution for creating rich application-to-application communication has been to employ an object model such as Microsoft's DCOM or the Object Management Group's Internet Inter-ORB Protocol (IIOP) or Common Object Request Broker Architecture (CORBA). But as systems developer Pete Loshin explains, "these technologies have some limitations when it comes to creating Web services. In particular, DCOM and IIOP/CORBA are rich environments, which means that implementations and applications that use them tend to be complex and symmetrical. In other words, to build a distributed application using them, you typically need the same distributed object model running at both ends of the connection. But, the Internet doesn't guarantee what specific kind of client or server software is running at the other end of your connection, just that it speaks HTTP. Also, it is often politically or technically impractical to get everyone to run either IIOP or DCOM.

"SOAP is simple. SOAP doesn't care what operating system, programming language, or object model is being used on either the server side or the client side: it is utterly agnostic, except that it needs HTTP as a transport. SOAP works with the existing Internet infrastructure. You don't need to make any special accommodations on any of your routers, firewalls, or proxy servers for SOAP to work."[3]

SOAP does not, however, replace the rich distributed object models. Because SOAP is XML-based it consists of verbose sets of ASCII text and cannot compete with the performance of binary middleware like CORBA or DCOM. In addition, CORBA and Microsoft's COM+ include other facilities and services unavailable in SOAP, including robust and proven transaction capabilities. As a result, SOAP will play a vital role *between* companies while traditional distributed computing middleware will continue to tie together the systems within companies and tightly coupled trading partners.

UDDI and ebXML are a part of a larger movement that will place e-services at the heart of the computing paradigm. Programming will never be the same. By extending service-based component software to the native Internet, a whole new world emerges. Solution developers will be able to assemble services needed to *compose* computer applications. They will be able to focus on business requirements and logic, shielded from the complex technical plumbing, transaction processing and file system.

Microsoft's .net, Sun Microsystems' Sun One (Open Network Environment), Hewlett-Packard's Netaction, IBM's Application Framework for E-business, Novell's Net Services and Oracle's Dynamic Services Framework are examples of the Internet native service-based architectures for creating, assembling and deploying e-services. Such infrastructures must support streams of innovation coming from many fronts including wireless devices (e.g., cell phones, Palm Pilots, pagers, PDAs, and GPS in fleet trucks) that are driving mobile commerce. Other innovations will be of the soft kind such as intelligent support, knowledge management and predictive customer relationship management.

Peer-to-Peer:
Commerce on the Edge of the Internet

The use of the Internet for digital commerce has, to date, focused on a client-server computing model, where the client is either a browser or another computer application. Client-server computing architectures are a holdover from the enterprise-wide network model. In the client-server model, functionality is broken into layers or tiers with the server handling business logic, database access and business rules. The client layer renders a user interface: a graphical user interface in the case of human users as clients and some form of application program interface (API) in the case of computer applications calling on each other for services.

In many ways, the real world of commerce is not broken into such convenient tiers: real commerce is a tierless world where clients can be servers and servers can be clients. Peer-to-peer architectures overcome many of the limitations of the client-server model, and by eliminating central servers, allows information to be shared directly with producers and consumers of information.

Although peer-to-peer computing architectures have been around for years, their use in collaborative commerce is compelling and a number of companies are pushing the approach to the forefront. Peer-to-peer and collaboration are two sides of the same coin. Its importance can be measured on the scale of what Netscape meant to the Internet, a whole new experience, a whole new Internet.

Userland's Dave Winer elaborates, "Version 1 was the pre-Web Internet, the playground of techies and geeks and professors and programmers. Gopher, FTP, email, newsgroups."

"Version 2 was the Web, instant messaging and email. Broad adoption. You can buy movie tickets on the Web. Internet kiosks and cafes are everywhere. URLs on all business cards. Who needs the Yellow Pages when we have Yahoo?"

"Internet 3.0 will realize the groupware vision of the late 80s which was really Doug Engelbart's vision of the 60s and 70s. Shared writing spaces with good boundaries. Structures that link to each other but are capable of managing greater complexity than the page-oriented metaphor of the Web."[4]

Peer-to-peer computing allows users to collaborate in a shared information space where any information artifact can be utilized, added to or commented on. Such "groupware" facilities can be used to build public and private collaborative commerce communities. For example, it is in highly secure shared spaces that the deep collaboration of tight business partners will take place. Peer-to-peer shared spaces provide an alternative to virtual private networks (VPNs), one of the most secure network technologies in use today. Not only does the technology obviate the need for centralized servers, it avoids delays and security issues inherent in today's e-mail and Internet messaging systems like chat.

Rapid integration is another key requirement of collaborative commerce. Because trading partners can come together for a single transaction or form long lasting operational relationships, the ability to integrate new trading partners in near real-time is highly desired. Peer-to-peer computing enables immediate *direct* interaction among people and computer systems and the business processes they embody for:

- ☑ trading,
- ☑ conversing,
- ☑ chatting,
- ☑ designing,
- ☑ conducting research,
- ☑ planning,
- ☑ negotiating,
- ☑ clarifying,
- ☑ reporting,
- ☑ messaging,
- ☑ correcting errors,
- ☑ handling exceptions,
- ☑ sharing knowledge,
- ☑ mining shared marketplace data,
- ☑ auctioning,
- ☑ distributing and maintaining content (e.g., software, catalogs, marketing product data, and data warehouses)
- ☑ harnessing idle computing cycles (power),
- ☑ integrating ERP systems, and
- ☑ managing projects

All these business activities can take place in shared spaces, dynamic virtual private networks that are highly secure, invitation-only and real-time. Peer-to-peer collaboration is about connecting people-to-people, people-to-information systems, information systems-to-people and information systems-to-information systems. Importantly, those connections happen naturally in peer-to-peer ecosystems, the way they do in the real world.

A First Albany report elaborates, "We think P2P's spontaneity, and its ability to offer multi-channel, synchronous and asynchronous connections that can harness vast amounts of storage and computing power will have a profound impact on expanding the scope of work done by computing devices. We see P2P driving applications design to a new level of ease of use. We believe that, over the next several years, software will increasingly have to mold itself to the user rather than the other way around. The 'peer-to-peer experience' will demand a high degree of spontaneity, give users multiple channels and modes of communications, and become ubiquitous. As such it will represent another step function improvement reducing the "hassle factor" in using software."[5]

John Gantz, a senior vice president at International Data Corporation noted, "Napster, the brainchild of a 19-year-old college student, Shawn Fanning, has 58 million users. Often, more than a million users are trading MP3 files at a given time. It takes only nine people to manage the Napster server."[6] Such self-organizing systems have to be the envy of corporations attempting to integrate their customers, suppliers and trading partners.

In peer-to-peer computing environments, clients can be servers and servers can be clients. The well known Napster music sharing system uses central servers for mediation and making the connections between peers. Other systems such as Gnutella are server-less, they distribute the search engines to each peer system. Gnutella is a fully-distributed information-sharing technology.

According to a Web site that serves as a hub for the technology, "Gnutella is an open, decentralized, peer-to-peer search system that is mainly used to find files. *Gnutella is neither a company nor a particular application.* It is also not a Web site; in particular, it is not this one, which is merely a hub for Gnutella information. It is a name for a technology, like the terms 'e-mail' and 'web'. Gnutella client software is basically a mini search engine and file serving system in one. When you search for something on the Gnutella Network, that search is transmitted to everyone in your Gnutella Network 'horizon.' If anyone had anything matching your search, he'll tell you. So, time to give a brief explanation of the 'horizon'."

"When you log onto the Gnutella network, you are sort of wading into a sea of people. People as far as the eye can see. And further, but they disappear over the horizon. So that's the analogy. When you log on, you see the host counter start going crazy. That's because everyone in your horizon is saying 'Hello' to you. After a while, it stops counting so rapidly, because you've counted most everyone in your horizon. Over time the people in the horizon change, so you'll see the counter move slowly. If you log in another day, you should see a whole bunch of fresh faces, and maybe you'll have waded into a different part of the network. A different part of the crowd. Different information."

"There is all kinds of stuff on the GnutellaNet, and when you get a search hit, it's virtually guaranteed to be there. No stale links. No irrelevant hits."[7]

This description of peer-to-peer technology sounds very much like what's needed to enable the dynamic connections of private digital marketplaces. Of course, encounter management systems will be needed for determining the kind and depth of information and knowledge sharing in these dynamic commerce spaces.

Collaborative commerce logically embraces a combination of server-centric and peer technologies. As shown in Figure 2, a server-centric universal discovery, description and integration (UDDI) registry can enable the mediation requirement of commerce, while peer-to-peer technologies bring the actual conduct of business into private, collaborative shared spaces.

Although peer-to-peer computing is still in its infancy as an Internet technology, developments are occurring at a rapid pace. For example, Sun Microsystems has already developed Jxta, a technology that can "juxtapose" the core elements of peer-to-peer and allow multiple peer-to-peer networks to work in concert. Jxta will include ways that computing tasks can be linked together in "pipelines" that span a peer-to-peer network. In addition, Jxta will offer a mechanism by which tasks can be monitored and controlled.

Peer-to-peer computing is sure to become a cornerstone of digital commerce. As Bob Anderson of Groove Networks explains in his in-depth chapter in Part II of this book, "Peer-to-peer is ideally suited to the types of just-in-time, decentralized, cross-organizational business activities that characterize 21st century commerce."

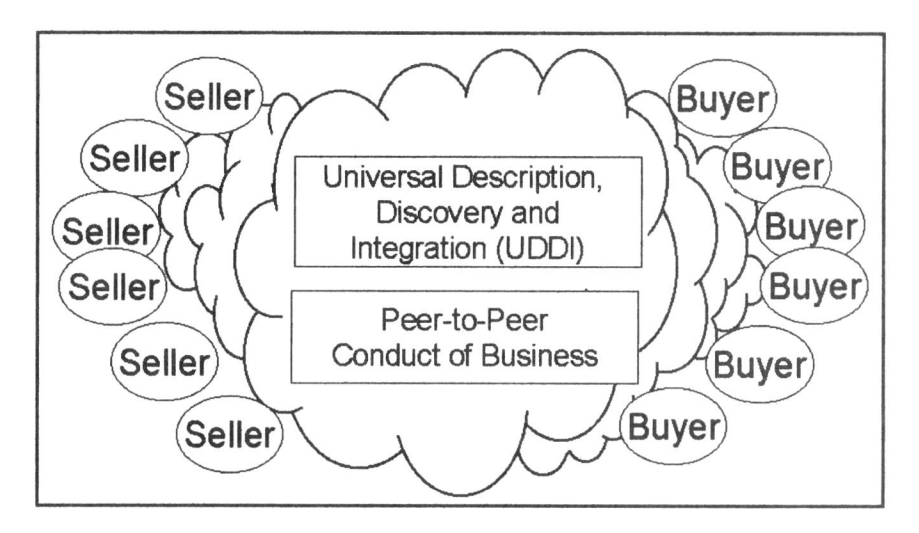

Figure 2. Peer-to-Peer Collaboration Technology

Model Driven Architecture

Although peer-to-peer technologies can provide the collaborative environments needed for digital commerce, the challenges of fusing business and technology do not go away. Businesses need the capability of aligning technology with the dynamic business models of digital commerce.

To gain the agility that is needed in digital commerce requires a *model driven architecture*, where business models can be changed and then automatically implemented in software as illustrated in Figure 3. In essence, a model driven architecture can fuse together business engineering with software development, aligning technology with business goals, strategies and dynamic business processes. Technologist David Taylor explains, "Instead of managers posing problems for technologists to solve by creating new applications, the two groups must work together to create working software models of the organization."[8]

Philip Colbert, Vice President Enterprise Systems, of USAA further elaborates, "Achieving our strategic business objectives is heavily dependent upon establishing a rich information base that closely models the business environment in which we anticipate having to function."⁹ Model-based business systems hold great promise for managing complexity and mapping the complex real world of business to the complex machine model of technology —component-based software development provides the paradigm for model driven development.

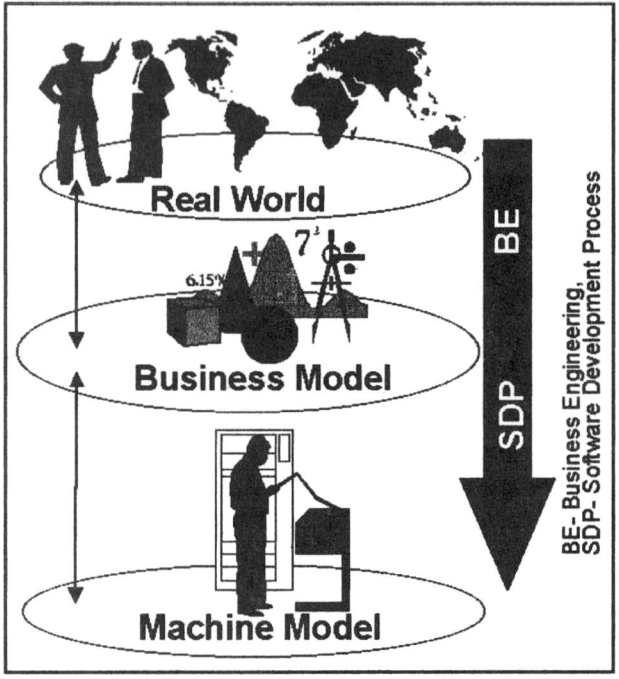

Figure 3. Model Driven Architectures

As a means of addressing complexity, the model driven architecture approach adds useful "levels of abstraction" for problem-solving. Problems are partitioned into major layers, beginning with business engineering (BE) and proceeding through work breakdowns to the software development process (SDP). At each layer, the prevalent vocabulary and concepts are used to describe that part of the domain.

At the highest level, concepts center on the real world business. At the lowest level vocabulary and concepts center on the technology, the machine model. The business model fuses the real world and machine models by representing the real world in such a way that business concepts can be reified into software — from concept to code.

Chapter 6 - The New Way of Competing Demands New Technology 117

Business concept innovations can be proposed and reflected in the processes and workflows of the business model. With model driven architectures, technology based details can be suppressed, allowing more focus on the problem to be solved and on the business process to be reengineered.

The notion of business-centric modeling to drive the software development process is formalized in Peter Herzum's and Oliver Sims' business component architecture, a hierarchy of software components that are isomorphic with business concepts —the software is architected with tight mappings to the ways business people speak and define their world of business organizations, policies and processes.[10] From elementary "distributed components" to "federations" of business component systems, each higher-level construct encapsulates the lower-level components and business objects.

A distributed component (DC) is a design pattern for an autonomous software artifact that can be deployed as a binary component in a run-time environment with a network accessible interface, always passed by reference. Moving up the hierarchy, a business component (BC) represents and implements an autonomous business concept such as *customer* by encapsulating all its software artifacts. In effect, it provides an interface to a whole collection of DC's necessary to realize a single business concept. Next, a Business Component System (BCS) combines multiple BCs and provides a common interface that renders complete business processes such as *invoice management*, while Federated Component Systems (FCS) provide the interfaces for BCS's to interconnect with other BCS's across the Internet and perhaps belonging to different organizations —the essence of digital commerce applications.

An interesting problem is inherent in designing the intercompany processes that cross complete value chains. How can companies share and integrate their business models? This is the problem that has captured the focus of the Object Management Group's Model Driven Architecture (MDA) initiative. It blends together several critical standards including UML, XMI and CWMI.

The Unified Modeling Language (UML) is a standard notation for the modeling of real-world objects, as a first step in developing a software design methodology. It has been endorsed by almost every maker of software development products, including IBM and Microsoft for its Visual Basic environment.

Although UML is the standard for component modeling, differing analysis and design methods and tools are used by different corporations. XMI (XML Metadata Interchange) makes it possible for separate enterprises to share UML models and is essential to inter-enterprise development of digital commerce applications. In addition, XMI can also be used to exchange information about data warehouses.

The Common Warehouse Metamodel Interchange (CWMI) is a specification that describes metadata interchange among data warehousing, business intelligence, knowledge management and portal technologies. CWMI incorporates the best features of a once competing standard, the Open Information Model (OIM) of the Meta Data Coalition. Metadata interchange is essential to the continued growth of e-business, as data from increasingly diverse sources and applications needs to be exchanged both within the enterprise, and more importantly, outside the enterprise across the value chain.

The whole idea of the Model Driven Architecture development is summed up by OMG's CEO, Dr. Richard Soley, "the focus is on making sure that you can integrate what you've built, with what you're building, with what you're going to build."[11] By staying above the technology platform with a model driven approach, component models can be distributed and incorporated to gain maximum benefit from technology now and in the future, both at the business modeling and systems deployment phases. MDA provides the foundation for the widespread deployment of e-services in digital marketplaces.

Managing the Complexity with Software Agents

The real world of commerce is not only complex, it is laden with a multitude of *tasks*. And most tasks are not just straight forward "do this, do that" lists. Successful computer systems underlying digital commerce require judgment and the knowledge of experts such as buyers, contract negotiators and marketing specialists.

Agent technology authority Jeffrey M. Bradshaw explains, "Recent trends have made it clear that software complexity will continue to increase dramatically in the coming decades. The dynamic and distributed nature of both data and applications require that software not merely respond to requests for information but intelligently anticipate, adapt, and actively seek ways to support users. Not only must these systems assist in coordinating tasks among humans, they must also help manage cooperation among distributed programs."[12]

A digital marketplace is a complex and non-deterministic system, often producing results that are ambiguous and incomplete. Auctions and contract negotiations are obvious examples. Knowing when to sell in an auction requires judgment based on estimates of demand and price elasticity — the kind of judgment traders use in traditional financial and commodity markets. In addition, configuring and reconfiguring software to participate in different, often simultaneous roles in digital markets could not be accomplished using the old fashioned way of manually configuring software. Further when a price change occurs in a product or product component, real and virtual catalogs, in each trading place where they can be found, must be updated accordingly.

Adding to this the need to profile customer preferences and create communities of like interest, humans would be simply overwhelmed by the zillion knowledge-based tasks inherent in digital commerce. What is needed is software that can take on these tasks. Such software needs to be "smart" enough for the tasks at hand, simple stimulus-response for handling simple tasks or highly deliberative for mining databases of customer information. Such software must be able to "play the game" of the markets in which they compete. It must be goal seeking just as a salesman is goal seeking in the game of competitive selling. The essence of such software is taking task knowledge now contained in the heads of the traditional commerce workforce and codifying it into software systems.

IBM's Deep Blue playing world class chess, case-based reasoning determining credit approvals at American Express, and expert systems of all sorts are well known and used today. They deploy various techniques and knowledge from the field of artificial intelligence (AI), a field that was overhyped decades ago and fell from grace in the commercial computing press. Quietly, however, AI has continued to play a significant role in many leading information systems. Its use has been limited due to its complexity, monolithic designs and lack of knowledgeable systems developers. On the other hand AI is making a very strong comeback, as it is now crucial in nondeterministic systems such as workflow, data mining, production scheduling and supply chain logistics. Its new form is not the monolithic AI systems of the past, but distributed artificial intelligence (DAI), popularly known as intelligent agent technology.

Computing literature is replete with discussions of software agents. Like other Internet buzzwords, however, the term is overused and misused. Various names have been used — knowbots, softbots, personal assistants, shopping bots and smart computer programs.

Cutting through the hype, the importance of agent technology, varying in "intelligence" from simple stimulus-response sensors to highly deliberative agents capable of learning, is the central feature of software agents: *the ability to independently carry out tasks delegated to them by people or other software*. Robust marketplaces being built today simply could not function without being able to delegate to software the multitude of tasks that would otherwise be left to armies of people to handle.

Backing away from technology for a moment, the everyday term, agent, provides a starting definition: "one who acts for, or in the place of, another." A software agent is a software package that carries out tasks for others, autonomously without direct intervention by its master once the tasks have been delegated.

The "others" may be human users, business processes, workflows or applications. A basic software agent has three essential properties: autonomy, reactivity, and communication ability. The notion of autonomy means that an agent exercises exclusive control over its own actions and state without being under the control of some external software entity. Reactivity means sensing or perceiving change in its environment and responding through effectors. And, even the most basic software agent has the ability to communicate with other entities (human users, other software agents or objects) giving them various forms of social ability.

"Agenthood" can be measured along two axes: agency and intelligence. Agency is the degree of authority and autonomy given to the agent as it interacts with its user and other agents in an environment. Intelligence is the degree of reasoning and independent learning abilities of the agent.

Even "dumb" software agents incorporate simple Boolean logic: "If the stock price drops to $50, notify the user." If only the world of commerce was so absolute, our discussion would be complete. But what we need are knowledge-based agents that can reason under uncertainty, goal-driven agents that can plan and agents that learn. To pursue these characteristics we turn to the artificial intelligence technologies of fuzzy systems, artificial neu-

Chapter 6 - The New Way of Competing Demands New Technology

ral networks, and evolutionary processes such as genetic algorithms.

If an agent needs to reason with imprecise or incomplete information or linguistic variables, it will need to incorporate fuzzy logic. *Fuzzy systems* extend Boolean logic to handle degrees of truth that fall in between being completely true or completely false, for example the variable 'Age' whose linguistic values are young, old or middle-aged. Such unsharp boundaries are commonplace in the domain of commerce - after all, cheaper, better and faster are not absolute values. Fuzzy systems enable the building of intelligent agents that can be used for business process monitoring, scheduling, planning, forecasting and natural language processing.

Artificial neural networks are composed of groups or layers of interconnected processing elements analogous to the neurons of the brain. Each neuron has one or more inputs and one output, and uses the weighted sum of the inputs to produce a value for output or not — determining if the neuron "fires." What is important is not a single neuron, but groups of them whose initial weights are set to initial values. Inputs are applied, and comparing the output to some goal results in measurable errors. Then the weights are reset and the process repeated until the goal is reached. The resetting of the weights is done according to a set of rules, and the backward propagation of errors through the net provides feedback that can "train" the net. In this way the net organizes itself, it learns. Using noisy or incomplete historical or real-time market data, a neural net can train itself to learn patterns that lead to critical market conditions, predict trends, and enable agents to improve their performance of tasks over time.

Evolutionary computing techniques can give agents the ability to evolve their reasoning and behavior in environments where conditions are dynamic, such as multi-buyer, multi-seller market places. Techniques such as genetic algorithms "evolve" software processes through simulations constrained by the laws of reproduction, natural selection, and mutation. Individual processors that prove unfit are eliminated or "die out" through a process of natural selection. Parent solutions to a problem produce offspring that change or "mutate" the parent's behavior. Then the offspring are subject to their fitness as a solution. Evolutionary computing techniques are suited to optimization problems such as resource and job scheduling and production control needed in most supply chain environments. These techniques are relevant in situations where there are many interacting variables that can result in many possible solutions to a given problem. The intelligent agent using such techniques can produce optimal solutions from among all possible solutions. Physical distribution of finished goods, task scheduling in workflows, cash flow optimization, concurrent design and engineering, and dynamic network configuration are typical applications.

To sum up these "soft" computing approaches in digital commerce we turn to the notion of taking a vacation. Today several resources are available on the Web to reserve and book flights, local transportation and lodging (Travelocity, Expedia, theTrip). Price and availability are the two criteria used to match a user's needs. But what if we wanted to design an intelligent travel agent that could optimize our vacation? For example the lowest airline fare may have us taking an all night red-eye with multiple connections instead of what could have been a 1 hour nonstop flight for a few dollars more. Using price alone and arriving exhausted may not be the optimal start to the vacation we had in mind. Our intelligent travel agent will have to look at many variables including subjective fuzzy variables to become a really good travel agent.

In their book, *Developing Intelligent Agents,* Knapik and Johnson paint the scenario, "Where a nonintelligent agent may compare airfares to find the lowest fare to a specific destination, an agent that provides successive generations of better and better vacation solutions would be much more adept at pleasing the user. You could use a genetic algorithm tool to encapsulate the process, which lets a vacation-planning agent not only formulate a vacation plan, but find the best one for its user's interest, available funds, time, and so on. This would involve dynamically modeling many possible vacations and ranking them based on current criteria. The agent may find that there is snow at a user's favorite ski resort, but that lift-ticket prices just went up. It may also detect additional funds in the user's vacation account, so a little fancier vacation might be possible. As a wide range of vacations are thus modeled and judged for maximum expected utility, a short list of winners eventually emerges, and can be evaluated by the user. If none on the short list is satisfactory, the user can kick the whole process off again, whereby the parameters would be combined or mutated by the genetic algorithm to arrive at a new set of vacation solutions." [13]

Chapter 6 - The New Way of Competing Demands New Technology

This illustration of soft computing with appropriate and multiple intelligences woven throughout software is the future of digital commerce. All possible intelligence, however, is not simply thrown into all possible agents, and there is no single, all-knowing intelligent agent. It is the building in of the right kind of intelligence for the right purpose that is the key to successful design.

"Intelligent agents" build on the three pillars of a basic software agent. They add the ability to plan and set goals, to reason about the effects of actions, and to improve their knowledge and performance through learning. The architecture of contemporary intelligent agents is object-oriented and is essentially an extension of an object. Objects encapsulate data (attributes) and procedures (methods). Add to this the intelligences of fuzzy systems, artificial neural nets and evolutionary computing techniques, and an object becomes an intelligent agent.

Intelligent agents can act autonomously, in the background of mainstream applications, to perceive their environment through sensors and act on the environment to perform and optimize their tasks: information retrieval, monitoring and notifying, information filtering, data mining, coaching, negotiating, configuring and so on —all the multitude of tasks needed in a robust digital commerce environment. The following table highlights the diverse requirements and uses of intelligent agent technology in digital commerce.

Data filtering and analysis	Information brokering
Condition monitoring and notification	Workflow management
Personal assistance & task delegation	Collaborative application integration
Collaborative systems integration	Simulation and gaming
Risk management	Data mining
Document management	Knowledge sharing
Real-time software configuration	Distributed systems management
Task automation	Customization
Learning / performance improvement	Tutoring
Negotiation	Product configuration
Resource scheduling	Optimization
Bandwidth management	Collaborative filtering
Communications	Arbitration
Production control	Profiling

An intelligent agent usually operates as a part of a community of cooperative problem solvers, including human users. Each agent has its own roles and responsibilities. Such multi-agent systems are essential to digital marketplaces, especially considering the multiple dynamic and simultaneous roles a single company may need to play in given market sessions (a manufacturer may need to be a broker, provider and merchant, simultaneously). Behavior of intelligent agents (the tasks that they perform and how the tasks are performed) can be modified dynamically, due to learning or influence of other agents —a selling agent that just lost several rounds of a bid-ask negotiation would certainly modify its behavior in the next round by calling on other agents to help out. As illustrated in Figure 4, the selling agent could collaborate with a price forecasting agent, a data mining agent, a trading rules agent and a risk management agent, all with their market data feeds and historical task knowledge.

Figure 4. A Multi-agent System

In summary, business objects make a major contribution to modeling information in the enterprise; intelligent business agents extend this capability to provide the breakthrough in modeling knowledge in the enterprise —task knowledge that was once confined in the heads of specialized human workers. Intelligent agents can facilitate the incorporation of reasoning capabilities. They can learn and improve their performance. Intelligent, task centered user interfaces can provide intelligent assistance to end-users and be a boon to productivity in the world of commerce.

Chapter 6 - The New Way of Competing Demands New Technology 125

While most of the literature about software agents describes the use of agents to assist end users (Web bots that search other search engines, bargain finders that search for the best buy) this is only the tip of the iceberg in the use of agents. They are needed to handle multitudes of tasks attendant to operating digital marketplaces. As shown in Figure 5, they are needed throughout the information architecture of digital commerce systems.

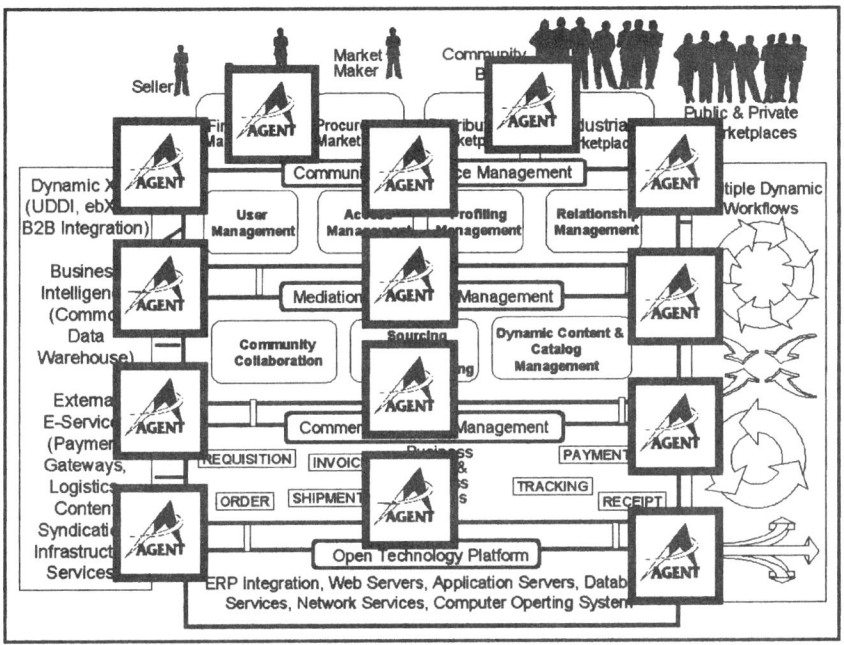

Figure 5. An Agent-Mediated Commerce Resource Platform

This discussion of digital commerce using intergalactic object-oriented intelligent agents is neither science fiction nor should it be off-putting. Many of the topics we have discussed are actual commercial offerings of software vendors, but no one vendor or industry consortium can claim to have the total solution for the digital economy. This examination does, however, provide a framework for the future as shown in Figure 6.

The architecture's form, like building architecture, follows function. The functions are those inherent in the real world of commerce as we already know it. They are complex, non-deterministic, and often fuzzy. Yet, they are the way of real commerce and must be the way of digital commerce. The components of the architecture include commerce places, business objects and an object Web that glues together the e-services essential to building commerce resource platforms for the digital economy.

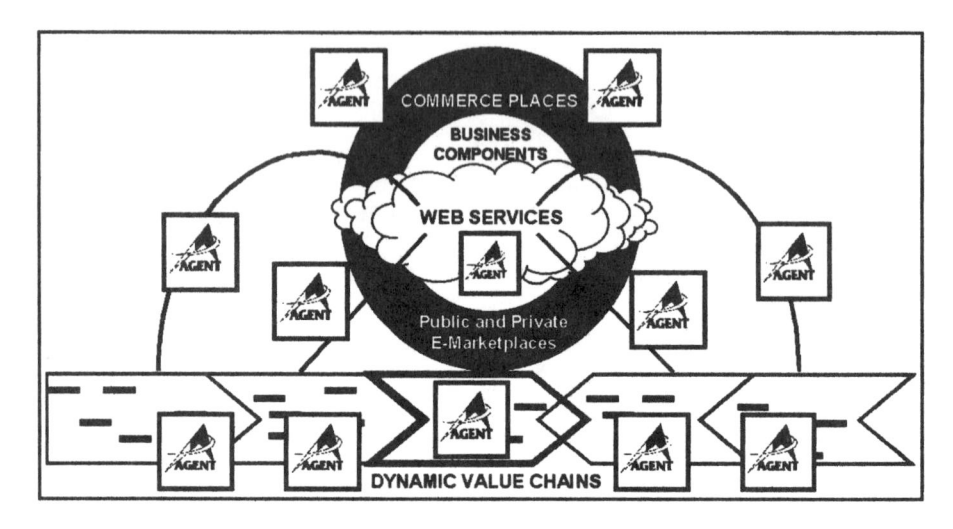

Figure 6. Digital Commerce Using Intergalactic Object-Oriented Intelligent Agent Architecture

Putting It All Together

Because the domain of automation is radically expanded as companies take on digital commerce, the new way of competing demands a change in kind in software. As this chapter has explained, a whole new set of software technologies, some seemingly very exotic, are needed to power digital marketplaces and create shared spaces for collaboration. Building and maintaining such software are monumental tasks beyond the capabilities of individual companies. As a result, companies and independent market makers must develop and manage strong technology alliances. Technology capital is now a first class business asset. Just as companies establish relationships with financial and investment partners, they will build tight relationships with technology partners to acquire and evolve their commerce resource platforms.

Is there a single, comprehensive package a company can go out and buy? Not today. Furthermore, some of the technologies described in these pages are immature. Others, such as intelligent agent technology, have been around in research labs for some time, but not in commercial environments. Regardless of their maturity, business demands will drive the advancement of these software technologies, step by step.

Competitive pressure and market realities will demand that each step taken toward the fully open digital market economy will place increasing competitive pressure to take yet the next step. Since the ultimate digital economy is not a single end-state, corporations are in for a long journey. Those that succeed will do so not with the systems they have in-place today, but with solid, well managed systems developed through technology alliances. This stuff is simply too complex for a company to go it alone.

However, just as a well managed company does not turn over control to its financial partners, it will not turn over control to its technology partners. Managing technology alliances is moving from the IT department to the executive suite as technology capital gains the strategic status of land, human and financial capital in the digital economy. Model driven business and technology architectures provide the foundation for managing this first-class business asset.

References

[1] Bots-CNN.html
[2] http://xml.coverpages.org/siteIndex.html#toc-applications
[3] Pete Loshin, "Web Services and the Simple Object Access Protocol," December 10, 1999. http://msdn.microsoft.com/xml/general/soap_webserv.asp
[4] Winer, Dave, "Internet 3,0," February, 2001. http://davenet.userland.com/2001/02/19/internet30
[5] First Albany Corporation, "Peer to Peer - More Than Architecture," Financial Research Report, February 5, 2001.
[6] John Gantz, "Jump on the P2P Bandwagon," *Computerworld*, November 20, 2000.
[7] "What is Gnutella?" http://gnutella.wego.com
[8] Taylor, David A., *Business Engineering with Object Technology*, John Wiley & Sons, 1995.
[9] Fingar, Peter, et al, *Next Generation Computing: Distributed Objects for Business*, SIGs Books, 1996.
[10] Herzum, Peter and Oliver Sims. *Business Component Factory: A Comprehensive Overview of Component-Based Development for the Enterprise.* Wiley (2000).
[11] Soley, Richard, Model Driven Architecture, OMG White Paper Draft 3.2, November 2000.
[12] Bradshaw, Jeffrey M. (Editor)., *Software Agents*, MIT Press, 1997.
[13] Knapik, Michael and Jay Johnson, *Developing Intelligent Agents for Distributed Systems: Exploring Architecture, Technologies, and Applications*, McGraw-Hill, 1998.

Chapter 7

Digital Strategy

"Both architects and business managers live in ill-structured, unbounded worlds where analytic rationality is insufficient and optimum solutions are rare. Both have perspectives that are strategic and top-down. Top managers, like chief architects, must architect strategies that will handle the unforeseeable, avoid disaster and produce results satisfactory to multiple clients –to boards of directors, customers, employees and the general public. Their common modus operandi is one of fit, balance and compromise in the overall interest of the system and its purposes."[1] – Eberhardt Rechtin, Systems Architecting.

Business Strategy: People, Process and Technology

With the death of "e," the first rule of digital strategy is not to have one. Digital strategy should just be a part of business strategy. This would seem obvious, but too often strategy is vaguely defined by executive management and left to the information systems to implement. Who should be in charge of digital strategy? At GE, it's CEO Jack Welch, not just the IS department.

The elements of business strategy --product, pricing, promotion and place -- pose the same problems for business analysis whether or not the Internet is involved in the equation. The Internet does, however, affect these elements. To gain the Internet perspective on strategy development, the paramount question to be asked, "What is it that the company can do now that was not possible before it could connect any with any, anytime and anywhere that will significantly add value for customers?" This question should be on the minds of strategists at all times during the business strategy process.

Business strategy is not a single plan, it is an ongoing process. For the process to be repeatable, a framework is needed. Figure 1 shows the elements of a business strategy framework centered on people, process and technology. The blending of these elements into a cohesive whole to achieve a business purpose results in a business "architecture." Today's business architecture must build on the current legacy foundation of systems and business practices and create a framework for digital commerce.

Architectural thinking allows for change. *In today's business world, the ability to change is more important than the ability to create, and the velocity of change is only going to increase.* Change may result from new business requirements or the adoption of new Internet technologies. Neither should impede the other. Accommodating change requires deliberate planning, one of the key goals of business architecture.

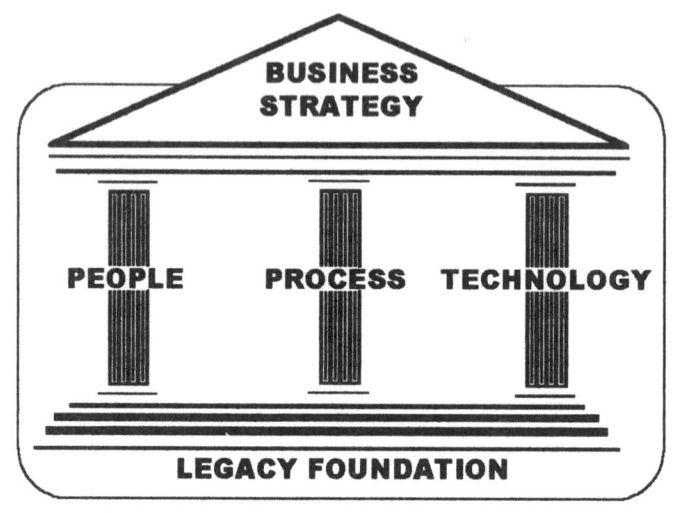

Figure 1. Business Strategy Framework

The reality is that all businesses have an architecture. The real questions are how visible is the architecture and does it provide for business and technological evolution? Including architectural planning in the business strategy process helps ensure the longevity of business models and information systems. Commerce resource platforms created under a well defined architecture exhibit conceptual integrity. This quality helps organize development projects and lays the foundation for business and technology evolution.

During planning, tasks that will be executed in the near term are defined in detail. Long-term tasks are more generally scoped, abstractly defined and roughly estimated at this stage of planning. A mechanism must be provided to replace general or abstract tasks with more detailed versions as initiatives progress and more is learned. The situation is similar to planning a cross country drive from New York to Los Angeles. Before setting out on the journey, a general direction is set and major highways selected, but navigating the maze of streets in each city along the way is left until the details are needed. Although the entire trip could be planned in detail from the outset, it would require a tremendous amount of work that would have to be redone as roadblocks and detours are encountered en route. General direction and main highways are enough to get started on the long journey. In business, an architecture sets the general direction and accommodates the details as they are needed.

Two major sources of change are the business itself and the marketplace. The detailed initial plans are based on current business goals and objectives. On the other hand, adopting digital commerce is a long-term commitment, and it is reasonable to assume that business conditions will change during the journey ahead.

While the elements of business strategy are universal, their scope and complexity increase dramatically when applied to entire value chains. Business processes become inter-company commerce processes. People no longer work in one standalone organization, their work spans organizations throughout the value chain, starting with the customer. Technology can no longer be controlled by one company's IS department, disparate systems are scattered across the value chain participants. Together, these facts result in the need for new leadership, new inter-company business processes and integration of technologies. Simply put, companies can no longer go it alone in developing successful business strategies and need inter-enterprise business architectures that span entire value chains.

In Switzerland, the famous Matterhorn casts a shadow over the cemetery at its feet in the town of Zermatt. The cemetery is a warning to those who would proceed up the steep slopes. Early pioneers who had neither maps nor guides are buried there, along with the primitive tools they thought were up to the task. Today, Swiss law prohibits the inexperienced from climbing the steep slopes without a guide.

Today's business and technology professionals tasked with adopting Internet generation computing, new knowledge management systems, customer relationship management and digital marketplaces should heed the message sent down from the Matterhorn, "Don't go it alone." Because the trek is through territory unfamiliar to the inexperienced, even years of knowledge and skill in somewhat related domains do not directly apply. Too much is at stake to go it alone without an experienced guide to point out opportunities as well as pitfalls. The guide's map shows many alternative paths, and the guide charts the paths based on current circumstances and the goals of the climber.

Planning and formal approaches to business strategy are not new to large corporations. Successful businesses already know how to formulate strategy, plan, and execute otherwise they would not be in business today. To presume that a whole new approach is needed for digital strategy is nonsense, although many consulting firms behave as though they bring enlightenment to a business world of dullards. Entire books written by self-anointed digital gurus and big six consulting firms are pumped full of digital strategy checklists and detailed formulas for success. Such static checklists and cookie-cutter approaches should be a red flag for companies seeking outside assistance.

This is not to say that outside help is not appropriate. On the contrary, success requires using people that are experienced with the emerging technologies, standards and trends. The path to incorporating the Internet into mainline business is an obstacle course littered with methods, tools, techniques, complex technologies and hype. Today's down-sized business workers already have their plates full with day to day operations of the current business and find it increasingly difficult to keep up with the onslaught of new technologies and Internet business models.

While outside help can be appropriate, consultants must be properly managed, not handed control. In addition, they should be used as mentors in an apprenticeship model of technology transfer. Training classes alone are not enough. People learn by doing, and there is no substitute for hands-on experience, guided by a master practitioner who has "been there, done that."

Business and technology alliances, partnerships and joint ventures are becoming commonplace as companies simply cannot go it alone when jointly operating and managing entire value chains. Multi-disciplinary, multi-company teams are needed for each pillar of business: people, process and technology.

People. The key to ensuring successful adoption of Internet technologies and new business models is to successfully transition the knowledge and skills of all participants in shared value chains. Current staffs embody significant value and intellectual capital. They understand the current systems and infrastructure. They also possess extensive domain knowledge that takes years to accumulate and that may not exist in written form. Successful business and technology transitions build on the current intellectual capital and, through careful inter-organization design, bring together all the people inside and out of the organization needed for the endeavors at hand. Specialized consultants with relevant experience can be used to fill the gaps, but their role should also include knowledge transfer as a centerpiece of the services they offer.

When business processes change, that change has a direct impact on organization. People can be disintermediated inside and outside a company as the functions they performed are migrated to digital commerce systems. This process can undermine long standing internal relationships and those with people and organizations of trading partners. As internal and business process change, leadership is needed to build the individual tolerance, flexibility and new team skills of the people affected. Overcoming resistance and building a shared vision become the challenges of leadership. Organizational change is a tough cultural issue and must be addressed as such.

Process. Inter-company business processes must be jointly owned and designed. Recognizing this need for multi-company process design, many industries have formed consortia to foster business process design. For example, RosettaNet is a consortium of major information technology, electronic components and semiconductor manufacturing companies working to create and implement industry-wide, open e-business process standards. Most industry standards groups center their efforts on expressing their business processes as XML vocabularies and business process conversations. Companies wanting to maintain leadership in their industry will also maintain their leadership in their industry standards organization.

Business process engineering tools based on methods such as Rummler and Brache are suitable for inter-enterprise business modeling; along with use case methods and Unified Modeling Language (UML) tools for requirements gathering and analysis. Simulation tools and methods will grow in importance as a means of conducting the "what if" analyses needed to optimize entire value chains. Such model-driven business process design techniques go hand in hand with the model driven architecture discussed in Chapter 4. Together they provide a means for going from "concept to code" that can be implemented in the commerce resource platform. They provide the means to align technology with business in a way that yields speed and agility.

Technology. Technology alliances are critical for companies transitioning to digital forms of business and wanting to implement comprehensive commerce resource platforms. Adopting new technologies places extensive demands on systems developers and their managers. Both are expected to change the way they think and work, as individuals and in groups, as automation is extended to new and unfamiliar domains.

With the advent of e-services, the selection of a commerce resource platform, technology alliances and partnerships become strategic issues. Companies need partners, not vendors. Selection should be heavily biased toward those platform providers that embrace component-based technologies that incorporate open standards, both business and technology. The resulting architecture will create a framework for plug-and-play e-services, mixed and matched from multiple sources as needs change. The ability to not just accommodate, but to embrace, change is an essential characteristic companies must demand in their commerce resource platform.

The Planning and Implementation Process

The effective blending of people, process and technology is the challenge of formulating business strategy. It is within this framework that planning and implementation of digital business models proceeds. Figure 2 presents the process for strategy and execution. The major steps in the ongoing process include customer value analysis, business strategy formulation, value chain engineering, implementation and, closing the loop, feedback.

Customer Value Analysis. Until now, the Industrial Age meant producers making products and pushing them to consumers. In the Internet Age, the equation is reversed. Thus the engineering of customer-driven value chains must begin with the customer -- this is reverse value chain engineering. Emphasis at this point is placed on the buying processes and patterns of current customers and predicted patterns of future customers.

Traditional market research and industry analysis provide the context for a thorough analysis of customer buying processes and behavior. From this assessment, initial gaps and disconnects are uncovered that represent opportunities for business innovation. Customers' problems become a company's opportunities. With knowledge of customers' requirements and the competitive landscape, the strategy team can then explore scenarios for answer-

Chapter 7 - Digital Strategy 137

ing the question, "What can the Internet let us do to offer new value to our customers?"

```
┌─────────────────────────────────────────────┐
│  ┌───────────────────────────────────────┐  │
│  │        CUSTOMER VALUE ANALYSIS        │◄─┤
│  │            Buying Process             │  │
│  │  Market Research      Industry Analysis│  │
│  └───────────────┬───────────────────────┘  │
│            Goals,│                          │
│       Requirements,                         │
│         Constraints                         │
│                  ▼                          │
│  ┌───────────────────────────────────────┐  │
│  │     BUSINESS STRATEGY FORMULATION     │◄─┤
│  │   Strengts, Weaknesses, Opportunies, Threats │
│  │            SWOT Analysis    Commerce  │  │
│  │      Organizations          Platform  │  │
│  └───────────────┬───────────────────────┘  │
│            Goals,│                          │
│       Requirements,                         │
│         Constraints                         │
│                  ▼                          │
│  ┌───────────────────────────────────────┐  │
│  │        VALUE CHAIN ENGINEERING        │◄─┤
│  │              Business                 │  │
│  │   Suppliers  Processes    Customers   │  │
│  └───────────────┬───────────────────────┘  │
│            Goals,│                          │
│       Requirements,                         │
│         Constraints                         │
│                  ▼                          │
│  ┌───────────────────────────────────────┐  │
│  │           IMPLEMENTATION              │  │
│  │              Program                  │  │
│  │   Proof-of-Concept  Management   Incremental │
│  │                                  Releases │
│  └───────────────────────────────────────┘  │
│              Feedback of Results            │
└─────────────────────────────────────────────┘
```

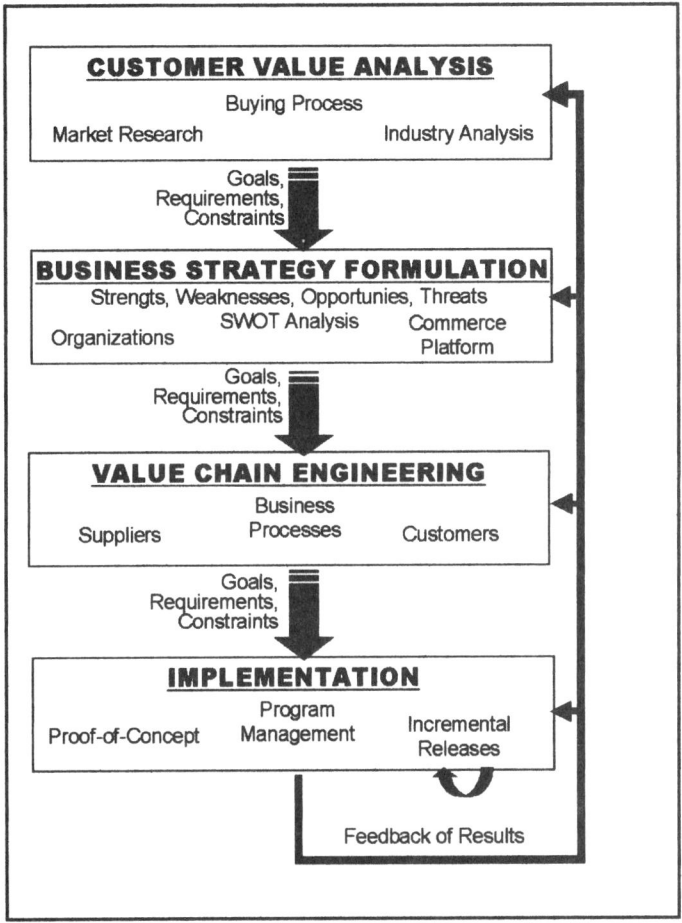

Figure 2. Business Strategy and Execution Process

Breaking this question down into its parts, a decision framework can be established:
- What are the current customer buying channels?
- Are customers using automated buying processes?
- What channel conflicts would be created by digital marketplaces?
- Does the industry already contain digital marketplaces?

- If so, are they pure play Internet companies or brick and mortar incumbents?
- What kind of traction have current marketplaces gained?
- What are the revenue models for the market maker?
- What e-services can our company bring to existing marketplaces?
- Will our company's current market advantages be diluted by joining an existing marketplace?
- If the industry does not currently support digital marketplaces, can our company establish one?
- If so, what is the business case? The revenue model? The results of market research?
- Should our company host a public marketplace?
- What competitive advantage could be gained?
- Which market model will most likely succeed? Butterfly? Seller's?
- What kinds of partnerships will be needed?
- Which trading model will work best? Catalog-based, fixed pricing? Forward or reverse auctions? A combination?
- Can efficiencies be gained from creating an industry buying consortium?
- Who in the value chain would be disintermediated and what will be the impact?
- Is the market emerging, mature or declining?

The results from customer value analysis, market research and industry analysis will result in initial, first-cut goals, requirements and constraints to be fed into the next step, business strategy formulation. The results are vital to evaluating a company's core competencies, identifying competitive advantages, mapping the competitive landscape and developing a portfolio of digital commerce initiatives.

Business Strategy Formulation. Business strategy involves domain experts who define the initiatives to be pursued based on an analysis of a company's strengths, weaknesses, opportunities and threats (SWOT). Because a company is dealing with an entire value chain, suppliers' and customers' input must be included in the SWOT analysis.
- What are our customers' Internet expectations?
- How does the Internet allow us to change our value proposition for our customers?

- How does the Internet as a communication medium affect our value chain?
- Should we cannibalize our value chain?
- If we do not, who will?
- If we do, what will happen to our existing value chain relationships?
- Which business model do we use to reintermediate: aggregator, open marketplace or value chain integrator?
- At a high level, how can our internal business processes be remapped and integrated with our business partners, customers and suppliers?
- What is their readiness for process integration?
- How does the Internet blur the boundaries of our existing industry?
- What new goods and services can we aggregate to more fully serve our customers?
- If we do cross industry boundaries, what is the competitive landscape and how will we differentiate our offerings?
- If we use the Internet to reach global markets, how do we internationalize our logistics, language and legal frameworks?
- What is the business case for each potential digital initiative?
- What compelling value can we offer customers that will gain the most traction?
- The revenue and cost projections?
- The ROI?
- Where is the low hanging fruit that offers the greatest initial return?
- Which initiatives will be most difficult for fast followers to replicate?

Strategy formulation creates the vision, frames market opportunity, sets the major goals, defines the metrics needed to measure achievement of the goals, *prioritizes* the initiatives needed to reach the selected goals, and defines the first-cut organizational infrastructure. Clearly, participation from all the stakeholders in the value chain must be included in the process.

Business strategy formulation will serve as a basis for developing the business and technology architectures needed to support the initial digital commerce initiatives selected for implementation. The focus must be on architecture because initial projects and commerce applications will mark only the beginning of many to follow.

Business architecture will greatly impact organizational design, within the company and within customer and supplier organizations. All participants must be fully involved as the lack of willingness to change organizations by any one party can be an insurmountable obstacle.

One important aspect of the architectural approach is the selection of the commerce resource platform that is capable of supporting initial commerce applications and extensible to naturally accommodate those to follow. For example, if initial digital commerce initiatives involve creating a private marketplace for selling direct to customers, the platform must be capable of being extended to support the role of seller in a public marketplace, and later a buyer in a trading exchange. Without such an overall architectural model, cohesion will be lost as a company takes on more and more digital initiatives.

The scenario is similar to a college campus master plan. The entire campus is laid out providing a total vision of what is to come, but only those buildings that are to initially go up are designed in detail. The master plan incorporates both. So should it be with business architecture if a hodgepodge is to be avoided.

Value Chain Engineering. The business strategy phase identifies "what" to do. The value chain engineering phase addresses the "how."

The task at hand is the mapping and engineering of the inter-enterprise business processes. The entire process is driven first and foremost by customer business processes.

Work activities, steps and hand-offs are redesigned using the methods and tools of business process reengineering, only this time the mappings are inter-enterprise. Inter-enterprise processes may be loosely coupled as in the case of open markets where pass-throughs are made from the digital marketplaces to individual organizations. Or they may be tightly coupled as in the case of a supply chain partners where applications are integrated in real-time with binary machine code.

As mentioned earlier, best practice BPR methods, such as Rummler and Brache[2], are suitable for extending process definitions across organizational boundaries. There is no need for a company to change the process modeling methods and tools it already uses, as long as the customer is at the center of everything. What is different, however, are the external actors and resources that will result from modeling inter-enterprise business processes. Also new is the incorporation of emerging standards such as Wf-XML to facilitate the interoperation of workflow systems rather than the migration of process definitions from one system to another.

Process and workflow engineering should use a model-based approach to problem-solving. As functional requirements are passed through to the process engineering phase, a repository of previously developed models can be searched for processes that match the requirements. A growing repository of the artifacts produced by business and systems modeling becomes a major corporate asset.

Implementation. The business modeling artifacts produced during value chain engineering should contain a standard representation of requirements, *use cases*. Use cases not only serve as a way of capturing the requirements of a system, they also trigger later development steps from analysis through design, implementation and testing. Each step provides further elaboration of previous steps. The use cases bind the steps together providing traceability and thus permit the management of inevitable change. Use cases are a part of the Unified Modeling Language (UML) which has become the standard for modeling business systems. UML is designed to model components and guide in their construction, assembly and reuse. It is a central part of a model driven architecture that can speed implementation and maintain quality.

Building the digital corporation is not a single project nor can it be accomplished all at once. Program management is needed to coordinate and integrate multiple digital commerce projects. Any one initiative will require a project team and project management techniques. By implementing a program management organization, parallel projects can be undertaken, sharing a common architecture and management organization.

Web-based e-business projects introduce change in virtually all facets of development: a new development paradigm, new infrastructure and developer skills, new roles, responsibilities and organizations. This much change all at once is a sure formula for high risk. Fortunately, risk management can be achieved through proof-of-concept projects that introduce these new facets in a controlled environment.

A proof-of-concept project is planned in the same way as any other project. The differences lie in goal selection, project scope and duration and development pace. The development pace for a proof-of-concept project is generally slowed to allow developers time to learn. Tasks are structured to provide early opportunities for success. It is important that developers build confidence in themselves, the architecture and system design before moving on to more aggressive schedules. New concepts require hands-on experience and time to be assimilated. The goal of a proof-of-concept project is to balance risk and rapidly validate design assumptions. The project must demonstrate value to the organization without introducing unnecessary risk and allow time for individual and team learning.

With the proof-of-concept project successfully concluded, initial commerce applications can be developed and put into production. Incremental delivery can set a sustainable pace. To constrain the scope, initial implementations will not contain all the functionality that will be included over time. Using the 80-20 rule, the 20% of the functionality that handles 80% of the requirements is implemented first. The goal is to "release early, release often." Over a three year period, GE's TPN project teams implemented over 40 releases.

Incremental releases are the key to risk management, sustainable growth and reduced cycle times needed to respond to market realities. Frequent deliveries allow the organization to change priorities and direction when appropriate. This arrangement also enhances credibility with customers and builds morale among developers. From a quality perspective, each delivery provides useful feedback for continuous process improvement.

Feedback and Measurement. Throughout the strategy and execution process, metrics must be established to enable measurement of success. Feedback of results is essential to continuous improvement and uncovering fresh opportunities for innovation.

Because digital commerce changes the way a company operates, it calls for new measures of business performance. It follows that if companies are reengineering to do new things, they need new, consummate, measures of business-critical performance. How else could they measure their progress in translating vision and strategy into day-to-day business reality? A modern jet airliner requires many more instruments to measure flight-critical performance than an automobile needs for its simpler operating environment. Business-critical performance in the digital commerce environment requires measuring the right things, those things that create competitive advantage in digital age competition.

Robert S. Kaplan and David P. Norton, developers of the Balanced Scorecard method, write, "The emergence of the information era in the last decades of the twentieth century made obsolete many of the fundamental assumptions of Industrial Age competition. The balanced scorecard retains traditional financial measures. But financial measures tell the story of past events, an adequate story for industrial age companies for which investments in long-term capabilities and customer relationships were not critical for success. These financial measures are inadequate, however, for guiding and evaluating the journey that Information Age companies must make to create future value through investment in customers, suppliers, employees, processes, technology and innovation."[3] More than a financial measurement system, the Balanced Scorecard, is a strategic management system for achieving long-term goals. Kaplan and Norton show how to use measures in four categories –*financial performance, customer knowledge, internal business processes*, and *learning and growth*– to align individual, organizational and cross-company initiatives and to identify entirely new processes for meeting customer and shareholder objectives.

The Balanced Scorecard serves as a learning system for testing, gaining feedback and updating an organization's strategy. The four perspectives provide a balance between short-term and long-term performance and include subjective as well as objective measures. When applied to digital commerce initiatives, measures may include process cycle-time, transaction per employee ratios, cost per transaction, volume of transactions, percent of customers supported with digital customer care systems, time to fulfill service requests and inventory costs. Kaplan's recent research initiatives have extended activity-based analysis to technology and product development; and interorganizational measurement systems between manufacturers and retailers that capture supplier and customer profitability.

Putting It All Together

In summary, a model driven approach to developing digital commerce systems fuses business architecture with technology architecture. Business strategy involves domain experts who define the initiatives to be pursued based on an analysis of customer requirements, industry structure and the company's strengths, weaknesses, opportunities and threats.

Business strategy determines what problems are to be solved, generating requirements, goals and constraints. Value chain engineering defines how the requirements are to be satisfied through new or modified organizations, processes and data shared among a company's partners, suppliers and customers. Component-based commerce resource platforms implement the newly designed business processes, leveraging best of breed e-services from a variety of sources. The entire process is guided by an architectural approach that enables rapid development of business solutions through reuse of all elements in a growing repository of models and software components.

According to Yankee Group analyst, Chris Selland, "there's no reason to lag behind –the time has come to develop your company's e-commerce strategies. But getting your corporation to jump onboard can be difficult at best. The trick is to plan well and start small. You need to take many things into consideration in connecting the dots:

- What kinds of tools and technology do we need?
- What do we outsource, and what do we insource?
- How do we compete online?
- What marketing efforts are needed to establish our presence quickly?
- How do you increase that presence?
- Do we have to restructure the business to support the Web business?
- What back-office support issues will arise?
- How will this impact our billing and payment systems and our distribution channels?
- How can we use the Web to enhance relationships with customers and vendors?"[4]

Over and above answering these specific questions, companies will need to team with their trading partners to develop an inter-enterprise business architecture. With this architectural approach, they must rationalize, arrange and connect business and technology components to produce the desired results, now and in the future. They must build high performance, inter-organizational work teams with shared vision and goals. To master their new environment, they will need to use the first principles of general systems thinking to transform their companies into customer-driven value webs.

Meaningful communication that keeps all participants fully informed and organizational learning are the key to mastery. Over a decade ago, Arie DeGeus of Royal Dutch/Shell wrote words in the Harvard Business Review that today describe the ultimate critical success factor for digital commerce, "The ability to learn faster than your competitors may be the only sustainable competitive advantage."[5]

References

[1] Rechtin, Eberhardt, Systems Architecting: Creating and Building Complex Systems, Prentice-Hall. 1991.

[2] Rummler, Geary A. and Alan P. Brache, *Improving Performance: How to Manage the White Space on the Organizational Chart,* Jossey-Bass Publishers, 1995.

[3] Kaplan, Robert S. and David P. Norton, *The Balanced Scorecard : Translating Strategy into Action,* Harvard Business School Press, 1996.

[4] http://www.erpsupersite.com/newsletter/e-commerce-strategy.htm

[5] DeGeus, Arie, "Planning as Learning," Harvard Business Review, p. 74 (March-April 1988).

Part II: Thoughts From The Thought Leaders

Chapter 8

Peer-to-Peer Commerce

With Bob Anderson

The Connection Age

We are now at the threshold of a new era, driven not by the technologies of production and transportation as previously, but by the technologies of information, communication, and coordination. These technologies hold the potential to completely transform the nature of relationships throughout the world – directly and indirectly - for individuals as well as the conduct of business.

However, phrases such as *Information Age* or the *Computer Age* – without an implicit emphasis on communication – somehow fail to capture the full scope of the time we have entered. For it is not the ability to perform more computations per second or to get access to useful and timely information that seems so fundamental to this new age. Instead, it appears that the transformational dynamic of this era is our newfound *ability to make a connection with each other*, at the same time or at different times, in the same place or different places, and to have a meaningful and purposeful interaction as a result of that connection. In short we find ourselves at the advent of the *Connection Age*.

How will this ability to connect people impact how business and commerce are conducted? As this Connected Age is dawning, what forces are also driving (and accelerating) the need for such connection? And, what form will solutions take? One emerging set of capabilities lies with peer computing technologies.

Complex Adaptive Systems

Certainly business has always been shaped by management's ability to deploy and strategically use technology to benefit the organization whether internally or as organizations focus in on collaborative commerce, with an ever more dynamic portfolio of trading partners. Conventional thinking for decades has assumed that the best way to deal with a complex, competitive business environment was through structure, control, and predictability. To this end, businesses have recently assumed that deploying complex ERP technology yielded significant strategic advantage to the few large enterprises that could afford it.

Gradually however, in the past decade, business leaders worldwide realized that they must now radically rethink the structure and operations of their enterprises to operate and thrive in an unpredictable and continuously changing business environment. For organizations, the key challenge in the coming years will be to design and produce products and processes that rapidly respond to unpredictable changes in their environment. This endeavor, inherently complex and non-deterministic, belies traditional notions of control.

We should distrust any elaborately planned, centrally developed, and carefully deployed business system or process. Successful systems and processes will be agile and dynamically adaptive: they'll grow and evolve as needed over time in support of multi-dimensional collaboration in the Connection Age. And, this collaboration will not be just system-to-system, rather it will involve people stepping out of business processes in real time to collaborate on design issues, negotiate conditions, respond to exceptions or emergencies, or conduct other value-adding activities that have typically stalled processes and extended efficient completion of processes.

Thus where business processes are inherently imbedded in center-based systems, business practices, or how people get work done, are typically 'at the edge'. Should we therefore empower at the center (leveraging ERP systems, CRM systems, KM repositories, trading partner relationship portals, ...) or at the edge (leveraging human capital, interaction and agility)? The answer is resoundingly, both: sometimes it's best to centrally locate storage services and applications (that is, with browser appliances), and sometimes it's best to fully distribute or peer them (that is, in mobile-disconnected use, or when issues of trust or reliability exist).

As companies have evolved the wholesale restructuring of business from vertically integrated hierarchical monoliths into complex multi-company value networks, this has presaged something deeper than just a move toward efficiency: it is largely about the customer-perceived effectiveness of the products and services offered. It is about the richness and meaning of our interpersonal relationships: what we share, and how we interact.

Nobel Prize economist Ronald Coase wrote in 1937 that the firm existed as an enterprise in large part as an entity that minimized transaction costs. That is, it was much more cost efficient for a company to assume directly the full set of tasks – production, sales, marketing, distribution, ... – that comprised its business. By bringing these functions in house, the services of each function were available "at cost."

In the Connection Age, there is a momentum towards the so-called "frictionless economy," in which transaction costs are rapidly dropping. Many business analysts see the essential dissolution of traditional firms as a result. Of course, Coase himself recognized that while avoidance of transaction costs is the primary *raison d'être* of the firm, it is not the only one, and that we are not about to witness today the complete disappearance of the firm as we have known it for centuries.

Nonetheless, the last decade has seen an obvious trend towards outsourcing and strategic alliances as a new model for conducting business on any scale. 'Virtual companies,' 'supply chains,' and 'value networks' have become essential terms of the connected economy.

More and more, work in the connected economy is conducted by teams of employees. The days of the individual contributor working in blissful (or bored) isolation may be numbered. Inside the firewall in every organization, teams of employees are working together on projects of all types: ad hoc and regularly planned, crisis-driven and seasonal, customer-facings and internal in nature. Connected technologies have made these teams relatively easy to form across time and geography, and are increasingly relied upon to improve the performance of those teams.

This does not mean that every worker in the connected workplace will necessarily be a high performing team member. Nevertheless, each person's function within the organization is rapidly becoming inextricably tied to the functions of altogether new and far-flung coworkers. The connections among them are making this a reality, for better or worse.

Outside the firewall, a similar dynamic is evident. Teams increasingly include outside members: specialty firms, independent contractors, temporary employees, etc. This has become practical in large part because these team members are now more and more able to enjoy the appropriate level of access to information and to other team members as if they were actual employees. They are connected.

Outdated Notions of Corporate Boundaries

Given this, the competitive nature of e-business and e-commerce has led businesses of all sizes to seek solutions for economically and securely interconnecting their mobile workers and telecommuters to company information sources, and to their strategic partners, suppliers and customers.

Many businesses are evaluating, considering and implementing Virtual Private Networks (VPN) as the preferred method of secure external network connectivity. Surveys indicate, however that the focus of these efforts is primarily on internal company use - telecommuting employees and remote office connectivity – rather than on extending their network to their value chain partners, suppliers and customers. In essence, companies are using VPNs to securely extend the "inside" of their firewall-protected corporate networks to employees working remotely.

But VPN technology isn't being use broadly to connect partners, suppliers, and customers because it generally exposes too much to them. And so these parties – important as they may be to the core business—continue to be treated as "outsiders" from a networking perspective. As a result, the quaint notion of "corporate boundaries" no longer matches the actual structure of workgroups that now naturally span the firewall—freelancers, colleagues on different continents, contractors, and whoever else is able to get the job done quickly and efficiently. If this is the case, how do we reconcile the existing notion of firewalls and in today's business environment, how do we distinguish between "inside" and "outside"?

As with all other boundaries, tunnels have been dug to subvert the firewall. These take the form of laptops, Palm Pilots, portable memory cards, unencrypted mail, and public file-sharing Web sites. We've all gotten used to working this way in the interest of "just getting something done". Of course all of this activity defeats the original purpose of the firewall — to protect a company's assets from unwanted intruders.

Perhaps it's time for information technology professionals to revisit the notion of security as something done at the lower levels of the ISO stack. Perhaps it's time to augment these existing network-level security solutions with secure applications that allow workgroups to form quickly, work securely, and integrate intelligently with existing business systems.

Perhaps it's even time to introduce yet another acronym into our lexicon — VPNAP, or virtual private network application platform: a platform that enables applications to be extended securely yet transparently to people inside, outside, and across firewall boundaries.

Systems must match the way we actually work (business practices), with whom we need to work, and they must be end-to-end secure. We must focus on securely connecting groups of people, not just computers. What are the characteristics of such an application platform and how might they come together? How will peer computing help make such application platforms operational consistent with business needs?

Peer Computing Comes to the Internet

A new sense of excitement is running through the Internet. Peer-to-peer computing, in a new instantiation that leverages client devices (earlier incarnations have leveraged the connectivity of large computers, such as at globally distributed universities) has captured the imagination of consumer, developers, businesspeople, entrepreneurs, copyright holders, and technology companies.

Typical uses include new twists on Internet search, file swapping, resource sharing, micropayments, personal communications and other applications. So far, these peer computing innovations can be categorized in three different areas:

- **Direct access to information.** Peer-to-peer search and file transfer tools, such as Napster and Gnutella, have burst onto the Internet, disrupting not only the business models of copyright holders, but reorienting user notions of what content is available and desirable. While the Web is full of interesting and useful content, often times the most urgent and personally relevant content – music, photos, work files, drafts and works-in-progress, calendars and schedules – are found on the desktops of individuals, beyond the reach of any centralized or Web-based search engine. In this light, there is no mystery to the popularity among end users of tools that easily discover and retrieve content at the "grass roots" or "edge" of the network.

- **Direct access to computing power.** There is a class of computations involving such massive amounts of data that they require supercomputer to perform them. Examples of these include pattern detection algorithms to help discover trends for weather forecasting, credit card fraud detection, stock market tracking, economic analysis, and corporate data mining. Peer-to-peer computing can greatly economize these computations, distributing the number crunching to peer computers found across a network. SETI@Home, which distributes the computations that listen for clues to the existence of extraterrestrial intelligence, is an example of such a peer computing application deployed over the Internet.

☑ **Direct access to people.** When one looks at the most popular uses of the Internet in general, it is readily apparent that email far outdistances Web browsing and electronic commerce. In survey after survey, email remains the primary driver of Internet use and adoption. It is no wonder then, that the most widespread use of Internet peer computing is not music- or file-sharing, but rather instant messaging. Interestingly, like Napster and SETI@Home, this communications application is actually a blend of computing architectures: centralized, server-based "awareness" capabilities combined with direct, text-driven, peer-to-peer interaction.

As with peer-to-peer file sharing, the adoption of instant messaging has been driven by *individuals*. In the absence of a single organization imposing a technology, this peer technology has naturally lent itself to ad hoc conversations within relatively small circles of "buddies" in business and non-business settings alike.

Clearly, peer computing has a bottom-up, grassroots appeal to it. This appeal is mirrored by a business-driven dimension that attracts innovative developers, systems integrators and business managers. So, what is it about peer computing that has immediate appeal to end users and technologists and business people alike?

Peer Computing in the Enterprise: Tools, Platform, and Infrastructure

The pattern of peer-to-peer adoption is reminiscent of other significant shifts or inflection points in the history of computing. This pattern has distinctive phases: early adoption of innovative tools by consumers and by 'change agents' in businesses; the broad adoption of a more complete platform for general purpose business use; and the full-fledged integration of a robust platform as part of a strategic business technology infrastructure.

We can expect the next phase of this trend to unveil a general-purpose platform — like the desktop operating system or the Web server — upon which a wide variety of applications can be built and deployed. And, beyond that stage, we can expect IT management and systems integrators to begin to tie this new breed of peer-to-peer applications together with existing systems.

Nevertheless, the appearance of a promising technology on its own is not enough to bring about a major inflection point in computing. Some technologies, such as push, have appeared and faded. Other technologies, such as email, have seen broad adoption as infrastructure, but have failed to drive the business value and usage of technology to a new order of productivity and magnitude. Indeed, file sharing has already had a less than dramatic impact on computing since it first appeared on corporate networks over a decade ago. For peer computing to be adopted like the Web and personal computing before it, it needs to generate demand for commercial business solutions.

Only when there is a financial stake in its success on the part of those who deploy it (and not just on the part of suppliers of peer technologies), will peer computing impel a true inflection point. Demand for business solutions will drive innovation among tool and platform vendors, solution developers and systems integrators.

A Peer-to-Peer Platform for Business Solutions

From the perspective of an e-business or a solution developer, peer-to-peer can represent more than a tool — as introduced earlier, it can be a platform upon which a wide variety of business solutions can be developed and securely deployed and support the following communications capabilities.

- ☑ **Transparency.** It can be used by many business people to make direct connections with customers, partners, suppliers and others – some who may sit on the other side of a corporate or personal firewall. This requires that the platform provide peer connection services automatically and transparently cross firewalls and network address translators, so that users never need to go through special steps to set up a shared space.

- ☑ **Awareness.** The platform will need an awareness capability that keeps track of other devices and users who are online at any given moment, and what they are doing. For example, if there are three active members in a project planning space, all members can see that one member is in the shared document library, that another is browsing a competitive site on the public Web, and that the third is updating the project timeline. They should also see that there are two members who are online at the moment, but not active in the space, and that the other three members are not online at this time.

- ☑ **Adaptability.** To truly embrace collaborative commerce and multi-dimensional communication with a diverse set of trading partners, the platform must enable use over a variety of networks (LANs, intranet, Internet) and connections (T1, cable modem, dial up modem, wireless). The platform must also provide an architecture that enables checking users' online status, their position inside or outside a firewall or behind a network address translator, and how to most efficiently move content across the network.

- ☑ **Mobility.** Members of a shared business space will frequently be disconnected from the local network or the Internet. The platform should enable disconnected members to continue to work in a shared space, propagating all changes made by all members when he or she reconnects. This keeps all members up to date even when they are not online at the same time, a key difficulty of Web-centric solutions.

Beyond these communications capabilities, the platform must be designed for solutions at the intersection of peer-to-peer interaction and back-end business systems to truly leverage both the center and the edge. As such it must support such hybrid "peer-to-Web" solutions by encapsulating content and function from server-based systems, so that business process and business practice can be interwoven in a single shared space. In doing so, it must provide security that can flexibly manage who has access to back-end resources, both within and outside corporate firewalls, lending itself to reliable business-to-customer and business-to-business interaction.

An approach to achieving such integration is by using system "bots," or agents, that act as virtual members of a shared space.

Chapter 8 - Peer-to-Peer Commerce   157

In this way, systems have a direct connection with the content and activities of a shared space, and can pull from or push information back into centralized systems, such as knowledge management systems, so that content, lessons learned, skills identification and other knowledge assets created or discovered, can subsequently be shared across an enterprise.

Benefits of Peer-to-Peer Communications

Peer computing may make possible a wide array of new capabilities and applications: dynamic, distributed search; distributed content storage and management; massively parallel and distributed processing. Another important peer computing function is personal communications. In fact, peer-to-peer communications has the potential to more fully transform the personal computer into a personal communications device with which employees communicate easily, intuitively, and purposefully with coworkers, customers and partners.

To that end, most organizations have deployed messaging systems, and have begun to investigate or deploy Web-based group communications capabilities. In this light, why should a business consider developing and deploying peer-to-peer group communications applications? Why can't the Web serve as a person-to-person communications platform as well as an information distribution platform? After all, there exist already Web tools and expertise to support things like private spaces where families or co-workers can meet, interact, share content, even talk live. The answer is not that the Web *cannot* adequately serve as a communications platform, but rather that peer computing simply may be more *cost-effective,* more *personally efficient and* more *flexible and adaptable* to person-to-person communication.

Cost effectiveness. There are several specific ways that widespread use of peer-to-peer communications among many small groups can be more cost effective than a center-based approach: reduced centralized management resources, reduced server storage resources, and optimized computing resources.

☑ **Reduced centralized management resources.** Let's say a team of a dozen coworkers and contractors needs to meet regularly, investigate options, make decisions, and share documents, updates and ideas. They could use a shared space on a Web site or create a shared space on a peer network. For one team, the difference in cost between center-based and edge-based approaches may not be great. However, if the Web site needed to accommodate hundreds of such teams, any number of which may be actively online at any given time, the Web site would need to expand in capacity. Because of the resources consumed, administrators would have to police who can and who cannot create spaces; they would have to do backups of these spaces; and, since most of the time no single member of a team assumes the responsibility of declaring the collaboration to be "over," administrators would have to prod people to delete their shared spaces.

In an edge-based peer environment, each member of a team makes use of his or her own local computing resources, without any worst-case capacity planning necessary. There is no need to have bandwidth, processing and storage enough to support the entire universe of users, only enough to support his or her own usage. And, when an individual user finds that stored assets no longer merit storage on a local machine, he or she can delete them without having to ask permission of the rest of the team. This eliminates the administrative burden of managing access to services, backing up resources that may be obsolete, and tracking down abusers of the system.

☑ **Reduced storage resources.** Consider an even simpler person-to-person interaction: e-mail file attachments. Everyone is aware of the network inefficiency of sending a single email with a file attachment to ten recipients, only to have some recipients reply to all with the file still attached. Not only does this unnecessarily tax the network, but also most client/server messaging systems will store a replica of the message and its attachments on both the client and the server. Peer-to-peer file transfer can minimize network traffic while eliminating redundant storage. This is not to say that peer file transfer will displace email, but rather that the appropriate and judicious use of peer computing will naturally lead to a reduction in server-based storage requirements.

Personal efficiency. Regardless of the cost effectiveness of peer computing at large, such savings are unlikely to be appreciated or even noticed by individual end users. Peer computing will have to have some other attraction than IT cost savings before it becomes a popular means of communication by individuals. The appeal of free music notwithstanding, the visceral attraction of peer computing for many people is sense of personal empowerment it engenders. In a peer-computing environment, all a user needs to do is make a connection to someone else, and a shared session has begun. Like making a simple person-to-person phone call, there is no up-front setup required. This sense of personal control and the intuitiveness of initiating contact with someone have an innate appeal to end-users. Everything that is needed to make a connection is in place. What's more, with most peer communications, it is a nearly effortless task to bring additional members into the interaction as needed.

Flexibility and Adaptability. This sense of personal empowerment only grows as innovation continues to occur at the edge of the network. For example, in a Web computing setting, when coworkers need to increase functionality of their project spaces, they must turn to a centralized development or deployment team to enhance the shared application service. This necessarily means a lag between requirement and fulfillment. In a peer-computing environment, functionality can be added directly (and more quickly) at the edge of the network. It is up to the end user to add the function, with no need to convince a centralized development team to make changes at the server.

What's more, in the case where a collaborative application needs "active content" (e.g. automated agents and background processes involving custom code), there arises a potential danger to other shared information on the centralized server, or even to the stability of the shared service. The relationship between "customers" and centralized administrators sometimes turns adversarial. Administrators naturally try to "protect" the service and its other customers, while the consumer of the service simply wants the requisite functionality to do their job. Peer computing has the potential to diminish the natural tension between administrators and end users.

Is There a Future for Peer Computing?

The pattern of adoption of peer computing bears some of the earmarks of other significant shifts in the history of computing technology. This pattern is comprised of distinctive phases: early adoption of innovative tools by consumers and by 'change agents' in businesses; the broad adoption of a more complete platform for general purpose business use; and the full-fledged integration of a robust platform as part of a strategic business technology infrastructure.

Innovative, standalone peer computing tools such as Napster and Gnutella may indeed represent the 'thin edge of the wedge' that will open up into an entirely new dimension of computing. If so, we can expect the next phase of this trend to unveil a general-purpose platform – like the PC or the Web server – upon which a wide variety of applications can be built and deployed. And, beyond that stage, we can expect IT management and systems integrators to begin to tie this new breed of peer-to-peer applications together with existing systems. If the market does *not* witness these dynamics, then perhaps peer-to-peer computing will likely suffer the same fate of other technologies; such as push technology, which never managed to evolve beyond the 'interesting tool' stage.

There are several characteristics of a peer-computing platform that are fairly straightforward requirements:

- ☑ **System Level Services.** Interesting and innovative peer-to-peer tools – search, directory, file transfer, instant messaging – have value in and of themselves, but so far they have not proved extensible. They have not been widely leveraged to build other applications or solutions. A general purpose platform will provide a consistent set of system level services, such as an application development model, user identity and awareness, information security, information transfer and synchronization, task coordination (e.g., for workflow scenarios) that can be applied consistently across a spectrum of peer tools and applications. In the past, this type of platform has emerged sometimes as a single offering, sometimes as the result of a set of independent standards, and others as some combination of each.

- ☑ **Seamless System Integration.** No matter how a peer-computing platform might emerge, history and common sense dictate that it fully embrace existing systems. No one expects to read headlines extolling the death of the Web, just as the Web did not replace the client/server and transaction processing systems that preceded it. For example, a conversation among co-workers, among business partners or between a customer and relationship manager will have greater context, meaning and purpose if the content of that conversation includes information that is pulled from company data or customer records. Clearly, the value of peer computing increases when applications leverage the strength of centralized computing assets.

- ☑ **An Ecosystem.** Any legitimate "wave" of computing can only be successful if and when an ecosystem emerges to support, sustain and propel it. Such an ecosystem is made up of a diverse community that will supply the full range of products and services to make peer computing thrive: development talent, skills transfer, training, consulting, subsequent tool innovation, and eventually integration with existing systems. Today, peer computing tools and skills are scarce in comparison to the technology and talent available for Web applications.

An Example: Peer Computing at the Edges of Net Markets

Net Markets: Current Conventional Wisdom. Not long ago, trading exchanges (also known as "net markets") were the rage of the marketplace. With the promises of billions of dollars in annual transactions, the business plans of these exchanges, often generated by industry outsiders and focused on disintermediation of non-value adding participants, were rife with the notion of charging single-digit percentages of each transaction, and making tens of millions of dollars in the process. These exchanges would further drive down the cost of goods and in the grandest sense, streamline supply chain management processes by delivering on the promise of supply chain collaboration. The use of the word "collaboration" in this segment is in the domain of system-to-system connectivity rather than human-based collaboration. It was the idea, for instance, that a consumer product goods company's SAP Materials Management module would "speak" directly to the exchange, which would speak directly to a chemical company's SAP system, and affect just-in-time replenishment.

Over the last two quarters, we have seen how this centralized exchange model has failed in a number of key vertical industries. While these exchanges have failed, we are seeing phone-based spot markets in these verticals, serviced through intermediaries (e.g., brokers, trading companies, and distributors), flourishing. The irony here is that these are the same constituencies that were to be disintermediated. Net market makers are now trying to determine how to best reposition themselves given this phenomenon.

Many theories abound, but a common theme is centered on the importance (and misconception) of the exchange resembling what many call, "the fat butterfly" (www.nmm.com). It's the notion that an exchange needs a critical mass of at least 10 participants: five on each side (wing of the butterfly) which needs to remain fairly balanced: having a single dominant member defeats the intended value. But this approach typically has ended up focusing only on commodity goods and thus accounts for about 20% of what is actually being sold: relatively standard product, excess inventory, and indirect goods and services. The remaining 80% is concluded in much more complex human interactions and transactions that can often involve intermediaries and other net markets.

Another theory is rooted in something akin to the exchange acting as the "dating service". Buyers and sellers are indeed connected initially through the exchange, but as the collaborators become more comfortable with one another, they move away from the exchange and do things directly with one another. One could argue that something deeply anthropological is occurring here: humans like to trade person-to-person and use person-to-person communications models to do so.

Jupiter Research released research last summer that showed that only 50% of all exchange transactions went to the lowest bidder, hence trust and relationship may continue to be playing into the equation. One could also argue, though, that as the goods trading between supplier and buyer move farther away from indirect goods (commodity, non-customized) and towards direct goods (essential for product manufacturing), the need for specificity of materials as well as direct human interaction increases.

But even when buying commodity goods, procurement departments are often constrained by requirements to solicit bids from multiple vendors or require negotiation for contract of delivery considerations: people are involved. The real value of net markets or the killer business plan, will be for a market that provides significant value to the participants beyond merely posting goods and services and making introductions. It will be to provide additional tools, configurators, or industry and process expertise that would otherwise not be readily available to its members and it will provide visibility across the network of trading and collaboration partners rather than just one partner removed along the supply chain. Hence, discussions to date with net market makers suggests that the actual value propositions of the net market may actually be these people-focused value-added services that surround the center-based activity of transaction handling.

The Human Communications Aspect of Net Markets

Net markets are, indeed, the quintessential example of what we call a "center-based system": a system that embeds repeatable business process into a large-scale, managed, and centralized service. The movement towards mass human interaction around these processes is indicative of "edge-based" practices, the market segment where a peer-to-peer application platform is directly applicable. As discussed, such a platform would enable the creation of self-organizing, highly adaptive, secure, shared virtual spaces: not just a temporary instance, but a persistent repository for capturing content as well as capturing and evolving best practices.

Discussions with the net market makers have revealed that a great deal of activity is occurring at the edges of their communities. This edge-based communication is happening using tools like the telephone, fax, email, and instant messaging, each of which is peer-to-peer in nature, but each has been able to only provide limited functionality or context.

A peer-to-peer application platform is of interest to these net market makers because of the ability to create contextualized spaces that enable richer forms of human interaction, well beyond the capabilities of the fax and phone, around the exchange process.

In our discussions, we have identified a number of potential drivers for secure, edge-based collaboration in an exchange environment: human activities, activity constituencies and semantic webs. We believe that the functionality enabled will most likely make the next generation of net markets more successful. Net market makers are interested in leveraging the secure shared spaces offered by a peer-to-peer application platform as key facilitators of:

Human activities. These are the larger classes of collaboration that occur around a transaction. They are ad-hoc in nature, limited in scope and duration, and are influenced (they don't happen without some level of interaction by one or more humans), and typically, they are not well documented or leverage and transformed as best practices. Recent business experience indicates the need for human-focused collaborative capabilities addressing activities such as:

- **Negotiation.** Buyers and sellers will break out of center-based process to create and respond to offers, identify terms and conditions, agree to financial terms, specify customization criteria, and establish delivery terms (timing, quantities, locations, 3PL, 4PL, returns).
- **Logistics.** Buyers and sellers will work together to identify how the goods will get to the buyer. They will also likely need to work together to identify scenarios where goods must be sent back because of defects or end of life cycle and reuse considerations.
- **Exceptions.** Perhaps the largest area of interest, exception handling covers anything that derails the transaction (slows or stalls the center process) and must be mediated to salvage a potential deal. This is an area where peer-to-peer based solutions have the potential to enable significant cycle time reductions.

Activity constituencies. There is often a need to reach across the organization, but more importantly, outside of the organization, in facilitating the collaboration necessary to the activity. Fundamental to the concept of a peer-to-peer application platform is the speed of traversing organizational barriers, either physical, or logical while ensuring preservation of content in a highly secure environment.

- **Intra-Enterprise.** While transactions often require the organization's procurement entities, they are also likely to embrace legal and accounting as well, on as as-needed or specific basis.
- **Extended Enterprise.** Transactions could also require collaboration with external entities such as a leasing company,

financial services, regulatory agencies, or outside contractors. To the earlier discussion, a peer-to-peer-enabled VPNAP is especially adept at securely crossing firewalls and creating secure, application-layer VPNs.

Semantic Webs. Edge-based collaboration is nearly always influenced: decisions are made by people, with other people based upon a number of factors, not all of which are predictable, but rather are based on the unique circumstances and set of collaborators. Key constituencies involved are connected to others in the organization through task, interest or hierarchy. These linkages are almost always leveraged in an edge-based business practice. With these linkages comes domain knowledge (expertise, artifacts) as well as conventional wisdom (personal bias, cultural bias) that affect the decision-making process. Peer computing has the potential to be the tool to rapidly bring the right people together and the information they need to achieve consensus.

The Future

The interest in peer computing application platforms by net market makers suggests that a shift is indeed occurring in the net market space. Transactions will still occur, but the value proposition for these net markets may be in value-added services that have a dramatic impact on communications, human connectivity and interactivity. The future may be subscription-based collaborative B2B hubs where value-added-services like UDDI yellow pages, contextualized collaborative spaces, custom edge-based tools, and discrete toolsets for negotiation and exception handling are the hooks.

It is likely that there will be further consolidation among hubs, as well as among point solution capabilities where net market makers will try to enable the broader functionality described above. The common link may well be peer computing solutions that continue to offer the people (practice)-focused communications platform that can complement these center-based, domain-specific solutions with capability that enhances their inherent value.

Peer-to-Peer Collaborative Commerce

In conclusion, while peer computing is coming to market in multiple forms, leading organizations are beginning to embrace the important role a secure peer computing platform can play both within their enterprises and in the conduct of collaborative commerce: with their trading partners as well as their customers.

Solutions enabled by this emerging technology will be most effective when used to enhance the value inherent in the business systems of one or more company by facilitating rapid instantiation of self-organizing, secure, shared spaces in which the right people can collaborate with the meaningful tools. In so doing, they will be able to leverage the content within their center-based systems to reach resolution, and use and capture evolving best practices to complete business activities more efficiently. Given the dynamic, complex nature of business, there is reason to believe that peer computing will effect the emergence of a robust, survivable computing ecosystem that parallels complex adaptive systems in nature, and will be the core methodology enabling agile, fit businesses to move forward.

Chapter 9

Collaborative Commerce

With Manoj Saxena, Dr. S.P. Rana and Tim Harmon

BEYOND THE TRANSACTIONAL EXCHANGE: THE COMING ERA OF COLLABORATIVE COMMERCE

Imagine you are building a new home. To ensure this home reflects your personal preferences and tastes, you decide to customize the design and layout. What lies ahead is an extremely complex set of cooperative and collaborative activities. Indeed, success in the world of home building is attained through a web of interactions among buyers, developers, builders, construction firms, real estate agents, banks and many other service providers.

Unfortunately, this array of complicated trading arrangements is something that cannot be replicated by a transaction-oriented exchange on the Internet. You cannot simply buy your customized house on the Web. It doesn't exist until you participate in its creation.

But this isn't the only element of the home design and building process that doesn't lend itself to today's Web-based exchanges. Builders, for instance, look for trustworthy contractors who have a track record for meeting their obligations on time. They also want to cultivate partners for future jobs. In order to determine the value of a deal, ideas and information must be shared. Mutual opportunities must be explored. Commitment levels must be gauged. Negotiations must take place. Success is tied not merely to the exchange of products and services but also to the development of a business relationship.

This raises important questions about the future of electronic exchanges – questions we must examine and take seriously as the hype surrounding such exchanges continues to rise. Gartner Group predicts the number of business-to-business (BtoB) Internet exchanges will climb to 10,000 within the next three years. Forrester predicts that BtoB commerce will reach $1.3 trillion by 2003. And yet, many companies are beginning to recognize the severe limitations of transaction-based exchanges. It will become increasingly clear in the coming years that the alternative is collaborative commerce, a model of trade based on perpetual interaction, dynamic processes and powerful relationships.

The Limitations of Transactional Exchanges

At this point, most BtoB exchanges tend to revolve around "commodities" such as steel, chemicals and auto parts. Some of the more notable sites include Chemdex, MetalSite and PlasticsNet. At such sites, goods may be offered at pre-negotiated prices or made available for competitive bidding. However, the key factor behind most current exchanges is price. There doesn't tend to be an opportunity to negotiate enhancements to products in order to have them match unique customer needs and requirements.

This is certainly a key limitation. The question is why price is the only variable for participants to consider in today's exchanges. The answer can be tied to business objectives as well as technological hurdles. Most exchanges have evolved out of previous efforts by companies to simplify and streamline their procurement processes. Companies such as Wal-Mart and General Electric began moving procurement efforts online several years ago in an effort to cut costs and accelerate the process. To a great extent, today's exchanges are motivated by the same objectives: speed and cost-cutting. To date, most Net Market Makers have not been focused on creating marketplaces that encourage collaboration between buyers and sellers.

One should not underestimate the technical challenges associated with building an exchange either, much less one that can handle complex interactions and negotiations. Today's market makers may be feverishly attempting to add value by offering services such as financing and insurance, but they generally lack the technology to enable buyers and sellers to explore sophisticated business interactions.

On a similar note, one must ask why today's exchanges seem to focus solely on standardized offerings or commodities. Unlike the customized home we mentioned in the beginning of this piece, the purchaser's needs and requirements have no bearing on the actual production of the goods sold on transactional exchanges. Why, one wonders, have no exchanges emerged to enable the trade of customized products and sophisticated services? After all, knowledge-based offerings of this sort represent the most dynamic part of the global economy.

Take the much-discussed efforts of eBay, Monster.com and others to auction off groups of talented technical professionals. The idea of "talent auctions" got much attention when it was first announced in early 1999 that a team of 16 employees from a major Internet Service Provider was willing to leave as a group if it received an acceptably high bid on eBay. Unfortunately, such efforts have not panned out.

What the talent auctions failed to offer was an opportunity for negotiation and collaborative goal-setting. They were premised on the idea that people could be bought and sold the same way you might purchase, say, office furniture. Of course, it's easy to set expectations about the use and value of chairs, tables and desks. People, on the other hand, bring new ideas, abilities and opportunities to a company. It is through a process of negotiation between employer and potential hire that expectations are set and potential value (to both parties) is determined. BtoB exchanges, however, do not presently allow for such complexities.

Even the furniture example deserves further examination. Office furniture companies such as Haworth, Steelcase and Herman Miller now enable their clients to specify and purchase custom configurations that match the particular needs of their work environments. In fact, sales people for these companies often engage customers by using sophisticated multimedia laptops capable of demonstrating countless options and generating quotes on demand. When a purchase is made, the order is immediately sent to accounting, manufacturing and distribution to facilitate rapid turnaround. Could a Web-based office furniture exchange possibly offer a comparable configuration? The answer, quite obviously, is no.

And, finally, why should suppliers wish to participate in exchanges that are inclined to value products on price alone? Such exchanges may eliminate costs for buyers, but they often fail to account for the unique differences of sellers. In fact, they tend to pit sellers against each other in a grueling death-match, driving margins relentlessly down. Transactional exchanges also pit buyers against sellers. Both parties, after all, focus almost exclusively on getting the most favorable prices. In this sense, such exchanges are the antithesis of relationship-based commerce. There is no collaboration – merely a buyer's ruthless search for low prices. What's in it for the suppliers?

The recent announcement that General Motors, Ford and DaimlerChrysler will jointly develop a new exchange to pool their collective buying power is a telling example of this phenomenon. Whether it's admitted or not, the objective of most exchanges essentially is to reduce supplier margins to zero. While buyers – like the auto companies –are likely to wring costs out of the procurement process by squeezing new concessions out of suppliers, it's unlikely that this process will lead to new forms of customer value.

Most likely, the exchange will lead to consolidation among suppliers, favoring large, high-volume, low-cost bidders. It may also benefit a few entrepreneurial product innovators, who find that an exchange makes it easier to get their offerings in front of customers. The exchange, however, will not encourage collaboration between buyers and sellers to develop fuller, more customized solutions to procurement needs.

Most suppliers will see their margins erode as they are compared against other suppliers on an "apples to apples" basis. In some cases, this is perfectly justified. Often, suppliers have relied on low value sources of differentiation such as geographical proximity, high search costs or customer ignorance to remain competitive. The Internet, however, promises to increasingly eliminate such forms of friction. As this happens, companies must demonstrate that they are offering unique value if they are to survive.

Strategies for Supplier Survival

How will companies create customer value that differentiates them in hyper-competitive markets? In the years ahead, competitive differentiation will be inextricably linked to how companies collaborate with their customers, partners and other parties. Companies must build powerful relationships and capitalize on them.

One can expect suppliers to focus on delivering complex and sophisticated solutions that cannot be purchased on today's exchanges if they are to avoid becoming commoditized. As they will (and must) demonstrate, value is derived through interaction, negotiation and collaboration – not just low-cost transactions. High-value differentiation is created through customization – the matching of customer preferences and priorities to complex product-service bundles.

It's nothing new to point out that success can be based on quality (and other factors) as well as price. What's new is that companies must now work even harder to differentiate themselves; the Internet is accelerating the rate at which products become commodities and industries consolidate. The key to survival and success in this new environment is to generate knowledge, leverage new technology and build powerful relationships to create highly differentiated offerings.

Whereas most of today's exchanges are designed to eliminate supply chain costs, emerging net markets will revolve around new revenue generation. And while most of the current exchanges focus on extracting existing value, collaborative commerce is based on the creation of new value. These will become the dominant factors in the BtoB marketplaces of the future. *The most important trends ahead revolve around collaborative, value-based commerce as opposed to antagonistic, transaction-oriented commerce.*

Techno-pundits are fond of speaking of a supposed "power shift," wresting market power from sellers to buyers. This is static, "zero-sum" thinking; it assumes value is a fixed quantity that someone always acquires at someone else's expense. The truth is that both buyers and sellers have an opportunity to thrive in an era of high-velocity, net markets.

That's why the concept of mutual value creation is so critical. Both buyers and sellers now have the opportunity to learn more about each other than ever before. The costs of interaction and negotiation are falling. In the process, they both reduce search costs and enhance the payback on their trading activities. Sellers can more easily determine the value of customers and focus their marketing investments appropriately. Buyers can compare their options more easily to find the best value (a mix of price and quality) for their money.

Even more important, buyers and sellers can now collaborate to create customized offerings that did not previously exist. Through interaction, sellers learn the preferences and priorities of their customers and use that knowledge to create something entirely new – whether it's a portfolio of securities, a customized laptop computer or a complex configuration of office furniture. This enables companies to avoid selling apples against other apple sellers.

Rarely will companies be able to take this route alone, however. Complementary suppliers will need to band together – creating powerful partnerships – if they are to deliver high value solutions and avoid being commoditized out of existence.

Why are partnerships so important? Take Cisco Systems. This networking powerhouse has realized that it can dramatically enhance its effectiveness by sharing information with and leveraging the capabilities of its partners. Indeed, it owns but two of the 36 manufacturing facilities it relies on. Contract manufacturers such as Solectron and Jabil Circuit own the rest.

Cisco has designed its systems and processes to enable the flow of information throughout the extended enterprise. Now, the company perpetually exchanges real-time data with partners regarding demand forecasts, order backlog and inventory. Cisco's deep collaboration with its suppliers and partners enables it to rapidly create and deliver sophisticated networking products without assuming all the responsibilities of manufacturing.

Michael Dell uses the term "virtual integration" to describe this vigorous network of partnerships. Dell's approach, which also relies on the real-time movement of information, combines the agility of a focused, entrepreneurial firm with the coordination of a traditional, vertically integrated one. Like Cisco, Dell Computer blurs the boundaries between itself and its suppliers – sharing information and deepening relationships. Dell depends on suppliers – whether for monitors, motherboards or flat panel displays – to become an integral part of its own production process. Such relationships eliminate inventory, reduce costs and enable Dell to rapidly respond to customer needs.

Indeed, partnerships and alliances are becoming essential to corporate success in most industries. Marriott, for instance, now lets frequent guests earn points that can be used not only for free stays, but for trips on one of 19 airlines allied with the company. Such partnership deals are increasingly common in the travel and hospitality industries. As Marriott sees it, they encourage loyalty by expanding the array of benefits and personalized services it can offer its customers.

It is this web of relationships that will enable enterprises to survive and thrive in the net markets of the future. Partnerships and alliances allow companies to deliver customized offerings by leveraging talents and capabilities that lie outside their own core strengths.

The Promise of Collaborative Commerce

The current frenzy over transaction-based exchanges will eventually die down. Such exchanges will continue to play a significant role in business, but they will not – as some would have it – subsume entire marketplaces. As procurement efficiencies are realized and egregious forms of waste are eliminated, buyers and sellers will once again turn their attention to creating new value. What we need now is new thinking.

The new model of networked, value-based markets is based on the trade of sophisticated products and services as opposed to commodities. Business executives throughout the organization become target customers, not just procurement officers. The transaction process also becomes more powerful. As opposed to simple catalog searches and purchase order deliveries, net markets will enable the rapid issuance of request for proposals (RFPs) and facilitate negotiations around prices and contract terms. Where transaction-based exchanges were static and simple, net markets will be dynamic and complex.

As opposed to discrete transactions, companies will now be able to engage customers and partners in an extended process of collaboration. Where the old value proposition was cost savings, the new value proposition is market expansion.

What makes this possible is the emergence of new collaborative capabilities – intelligent agents and dynamic processes – that facilitate interactions, negotiations and relationships. Agent-based technologies now permit the management of complex trading processes. Some agents enable two-way interactions and help parties negotiate over an extended period of time. Other agents match buyer requirements to seller capabilities. Still other agents manage contracts, projects and leads. They alert market participants to both problems and opportunities.

Take the example of the customized home with which we began this chapter. Despite the complexities associated with collaboration in the building trade, it is possible to create a high value exchange – based on intelligent agent technology – that facilitates complex interactions and relationship building.

One impressive example of this type of approach is now being launched in the United Kingdom. Thebuilding-site.com is a new, networked marketplace for home-builders, suppliers and manufacturers. The site will enable all parties to collaborate more effectively by facilitating the exchange of information and by enabling complex negotiations on the Web.

Builders will benefit from streamlined procurement processes and automated matching of orders and deliveries. Moreover, the service promises greater management control and a clear trail of activity and accountability with all suppliers. Suppliers and manufacturers, meanwhile, receive real- time updates on new building projects, automated alerts of relevant specification changes and immediate warnings of order-delivery mismatches.

Such services can radically enhance the collaborative processes of parties involved in a home building project. But they also demonstrate how companies might be able to overcome the high coordination costs and organizational hurdles that have hindered their ability to effectively collaborate in the past.

One can envision a new brand of partnerships and alliances, driven by customer demand. Just as writers, directors, producers, film studios, casting agencies, movie stars, extras, film crews, production firms and distributors must collaborate in order to create and promote a new movie, companies of all kinds will soon find it necessary to address customer needs through temporary alliances. Much like the many participants in a Hollywood film, it will be increasingly common for companies to join forces to complete a project and then disband when it is over.

In an era of rapidly falling coordination and interaction costs, such models become increasingly attractive not only for multimillion dollar film projects but for sophisticated products, services and solutions of all sorts. The new models, processes and technologies of collaborative commerce take us far beyond the transactional trading arrangements of the present. They help us envision a future in which dynamic relationships – with customers, partners and others – spark the creation of extraordinary new value and wealth.

The Essentials of Collaborative Commerce
Today's transaction-oriented exchanges certainly promise to eliminate costs and inefficiencies. However, there are several elements of value that will matter in tomorrow's net markets. Indeed, collaborative commerce can be distinguished from transactional commerce in various ways:

Dynamic and extended processes. While participants on a conventional exchange are merely focused on a price at which markets will clear and products will move, collaborative commerce involves the integration of *discovery, negotiation* and *support* processes over an extended period of time. Dialogue and interaction are critical. First, customers seek information to understand what suppliers have to offer and suppliers try to determine what offers will appeal to customers. When the parties come together around desirable products and services, they focus on negotiating prices and terms. And, finally, when the deal has been consummated, the focus shifts to fulfillment and support.

Relationship building. Today's exchanges bring buyers and sellers together to make arms-length transactions on a rapid basis. Collaborative commerce, on the other hand, depends on an exchange of information and the development of trust. Through a process of communication and interaction, buyers and sellers jointly create new personalized offerings. The relationship they build becomes a foundation for future interactions and transactions.

Multi-dimensional purchasing criteria. Whereas today's exchanges focus almost exclusively on price, collaborative commerce involves buyers who make procurement decisions based on other factors such as product specifications, service programs and payment terms. Unfortunately, today's exchanges are technically incapable of supporting deals based on such multi-dimensional purchasing criteria. It will take new approaches and new technology to address the limitations of current transactional exchanges.

Multiple suppliers forming sophisticated solutions. Existing exchanges make it possible for a single supplier to sell its products. They do not enable partnerships among multiple suppliers to address complex customer needs. Collaborative commerce is based on the idea that multiple companies can collaborate to provide sophisticated offerings that would not be cost-effective—or perhaps even possible—if they were to be created by just one company.

Knowledge-based offerings. One thing that today's exchanges cannot account for is the unique needs of the buyer. They facilitate the trade of relatively standard products. It is through a process of interaction that deep customer knowledge can be obtained and acted on by a supplier. It is through interaction that a product or a solution becomes personalized and knowledge-intensive. Collaborative commerce enables the creation of such knowledge-based products.

Unleashing the Power of Collaboration for Streamlining Value Chains

"Collaboration" –and, by association, "collaborative commerce"– are popular terms today. But collaboration is certainly not a new concept. Most companies collaborate in some capacity today, and indeed have been doing so for some time (albeit not necessarily well). Consider the supplier-customer relationship, which can be thought of in terms of a continuous lifecycle of engagement, transaction, fulfillment and service activities.[1] Rarely do companies excel in all four, either from a business process or a technology enablement aspect. Indeed, successful companies identify and invest in their core competencies, and outsource or partner for those that are not core. For example, manufacturing-oriented companies are often not good at selling, and "outsource" the function to distributors (channel partners).

According to Webster's, "to collaborate" means "to work together [to achieve a common goal], especially in an intellectual effort." The goal in commerce, of course, is revenue and profit growth, which ultimately stems from customer satisfaction. But companies don't always view their products and services from the perspective of customers. If they did, they would see that their offerings are but singular components of a holistic solution, and would place much more emphasis on their collaboration capabilities. Consider some examples of collaboration with respect to customer-sought aggregated solutions:

- High tech – In terms of solutions, customers often need a combination of computer, storage and network hardware; infrastructure and application software; and consulting, systems integration and training services.
- Financial services – Varying business and investment requirements warrant customized portfolios of multiple financial products and instruments, for which financial planners have long played the role of aggregator.
- Building and property management.
- Telecommunications.
- Media and entertainment.

Collaboration Flavors

Collaboration technologies basically fall into one of two categories:
- unstructured collaboration, which includes document exchange and sharing, shared whiteboards, discussion forums and email (*aka* information collaboration); and
- structured collaboration, which involves shared participation in business processes (*aka* process collaboration).

Chapter 9 - Collaborative Commerce 179

Even though it's sometimes referred to as "collaboration," *process integration* should not be confused with *process collaboration*. *Process integration* involves connecting – in a send-respond fashion – well-defined "internal" (ERP) business processes, which are typically transactional in nature. For example, Company A sends a purchase order to Company B (a function of Company A's purchasing process); Company B sends Company A a confirmation (a function of Company B's order management process). Whereas this type of interaction has been facilitated in the past by fax, email or electronic data interchange (EDI), the modern approach is to utilize the Internet for inter-enterprise process integration. This type of inter-enterprise integration – sometimes referred to as Business-to-Business integration (B2Bi) – is a natural outgrowth of enterprise application integration (EAI), the focus of which was on the intra-enterprise (i.e., "inside the four walls").

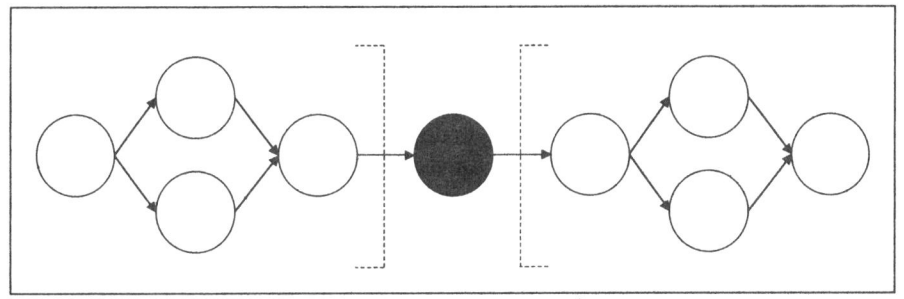

Figure 1. Process Integration

Process collaboration involves two or more parties participating in an iterative, negotiated business process, that process being more relationship than transactional in nature (e.g., coop marketing, vs. a purchase-sales transaction), to achieve a common goal. Indeed, the intended goal of the process is a key factor in determining who does what, and when; which in turn implies that a process collaboration system is adaptive to changing business conditions. Process collaboration typically supports inter-enterprise business processes that heretofore have not been automated, due to the inability (until recently) of technology to support the constant fluctuation of collaborative relationships.

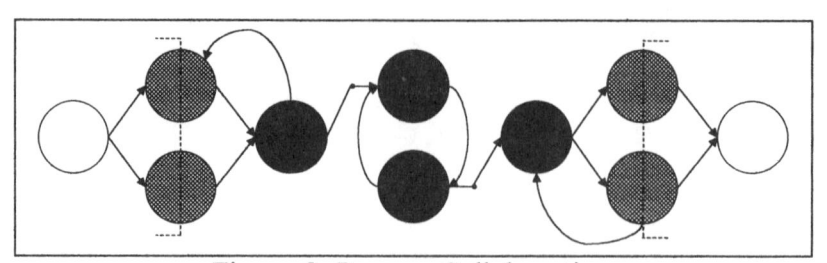

Figure 2. Process Collaboration

Collaborative Functions

Function	Parties	Type	Comments
PLANNING & FORECASTING	S, cP, sP	INFORMATION COLLABORATION	REAL-TIME DATA SHARING (FORECAST DATA AND SALES DATA)
PRODUCT DESIGN	C, S	INFORMATION COLLABORATION	DOCUMENT EXCHANGE COMPUTER AIDED DESIGN (CAD)
STRATEGIC SOURCING	S	PROCESS COLLABORATION	RFX NEGOTIATION, SUPPLIER PERFORMANCE MANAGEMENT
COMPONENT COMPATIBILITY TESTING	sP	PROCESS COLLABORATION	COMPONENT COMPATIBILITY IN SOLUTION AGGREGATION CONTEXT
PRICING	sP, cP	PROCESS COLLABORATION	PRICING IN DEMAND CHAIN OR SOLUTION AGGREGATION CONTEXT
MARKETING	sP, cP	PROCESS COLLABORATION	JOINT/COOP MARKETING (CAMPAIGNS, BRANDING)
SALES	cP, C	PROCESS COLLABORATION	SHARED LEADS, PRESENTATIONS, ITERATIVE CONFIGURATION/QUOTE
ATP (AVAILABLE TO PROMISE)	S	PROCESS INTEGRATION	INSIGHT INTO SUPPLIERS' CAPACITIES/SCHEDULES
MAKE-TO-ORDER	C	PROCESS COLLABORATION	ITERATIVE RFX REQUIREMENTS/ CAPABILITIES ⇒ CONTRACT TERMS
ORDER PROCESSING	sP, cP	PROCESS COLLABORATION; PROCESS INTEGRATION	SPLIT ORDER AMONG SOLUTION COMPONENT PROVIDERS
FULFILLMENT: LOGISTICS	sP, cP, C	PROCESS COLLABORATION	COORDINATION OF DISTRIBUTION RESOURCES
FULFILLMENT: SERVICE DELIVERY	sP, cP, C	PROCESS COLLABORATION	COORDINATION OF SERVICE RESOURCES
INTERNATIONAL TRADE LOGISTICS	cP, C	INFORMATION COLLABORATION	DOCUMENT EXCHANGE (IMPORT/EXPORT DOCUMENTS)
PAYMENT	C	PROCESS	ORDER RECEIPT, INVOICING

SETTLEMENT/ ADJUDICATION		COLLABORATION	
CUSTOMER SERVICE/ SUPPORT	sP, C	PROCESS COLLABORATION	SHARED/SPLIT CUSTOMER SUPPORT FUNCTION BY LEVELS

S: Supplier   C: Customer   cP: channel Partner
sP: solution Partner (provider of complementary product or service, i.e., design partner or service provider)

Supply Chains vs. Value Chains

Old Economy supply chains – typified by discrete manufacturing – are linear in structure, and typically revolve around buy-sell transactions ("I buy from my suppliers, I sell to my customers"). Because the supply chain is spread out linearly, some suppliers can be far removed from the end customer. The value proposition per collaboration to these companies is *visibility*. They benefit by knowing immediately what is being transacted at the end customer end of the supply chain – i.e., the end customer's activities are *visible* to them. Instead of waiting days or weeks (or months!) for that information to flow backwards through the supply chain – with all the potential potholes of erroneous or missing information – suppliers can react in near real-time to fluctuations in end customer demand. Because all members of the supply chain have the same visibility, the supposition is that the supply chain can produce in a more coordinated, efficient manner. Visibility is all about information collaboration, for which XML is the accepted infrastructure vehicle.

In actuality, New Economy supply chains – or "value chains" – structurally resemble a network more than a chain (thus they are sometimes referred to as "business webs" or "market networks"). The implication is that the interaction between members of a value chain extends far beyond the buying of raw materials or components, and the selling of manufactured or assembled products. Members address collaborative issues like, "How do we collectively design and support an aggregated solution?" and "How do we launch new products through complex, conflicted channels?" Moreover, in a value chain structure, no member is far removed from the end customer. Thus, the value of collaboration is more in the form of sharing in the execution of actual business processes.

Many collaboration technology solutions are focused on supply chain *functional* efficiency – e.g., lowering procurement costs –

as opposed to value chain *process* efficiency which ultimately results in market effectiveness:
- increased earnings per share and margins,
- increased revenues and market share, and
- customer satisfaction and loyalty.

Business scientists state that the aggregation of multiple optimized single functions does not necessarily result in overall process optimization. Focusing on a single business function or a single dimension of business relationship (supplier, customer or partner) independently of the others is often self-defeating.

Process Collaboration and Intelligent Agents

Sharing information with suppliers, customers, and partners is one thing; coordinating the activities among them – i.e., value chain synchronization – is quite another. Managing all aspects of a company's relationships synchronously warrants business process collaboration. Offered here is a formal definition of collaboration as it applies to business processes:

> **collaboration**: the sharing of business processes as a set of discrete tasks amongst multiple resources (people, business units, companies), whereby the allocation of those tasks is agreed to beforehand, or can be negotiated in real-time per event rules and resources' capabilities. For example, five companies may have the capability to fulfill an order; the "best" company is selected according to how closely their capabilities meet the goals of the process (e.g., lowest cost, fastest delivery, best service, and minimum warranty).

Intelligent agent technology applies to two terms from the description above: "negotiated" and "best." Agents are small software programs that capture and maintain knowledge about resources' (e.g., employees, partners) capabilities, as well as the condition (state) of the business process. An intelligent agent represents each resource in the network (the value chain) and each task in the process. It's analogous to each country having an ambassador, who represents its respective country's interests, in the United Nations (the network).

Chapter 9 - Collaborative Commerce

Coordinating the actions of these intelligent agents (called "proxy agents") is a "master" process agent. In a value chain, the channel master company is the "master" and its suppliers, customers and partners are resources.

A user initiates a business process through a request to achieve a particular business goal. The request is assigned to a process agent, which selects proxy agents to perform the activities of the business process, according to their capabilities to satisfy the requestor's business goal.

Consider the process of building a house. House building consists of many activities (designing the structure, surveying the site, clearing the land, laying the foundation, framing the house, installing the wiring, etc.), those activities performed by different resources (suppliers). Some suppliers may have capabilities to perform more than one activity (e.g., both design and survey), and their capabilities may be dependent on the certain conditions. For example, a supplier may be able to do the foundation work one week, but is booked on another project the following week; or a supplier is licensed to do surveys in one county, but not another.

In this case, the process agent acts as a general contractor, selecting the best suppliers to perform the tasks of building a house, and coordinating those suppliers so that wastage is minimized or eliminated. Consider the situation where the workers arrive on the site to begin laying the foundation, but there is no cement on site. Because the process agent is aware of the state of the house building project at all times, it can take proactive action to assure that this situation does not occur.

In the enterprise resource planning (ERP) model, workflow definitions consist of tasks (activities), the rules that govern those activities, and roles (the person or company which performs the activity), intertwined in a pre-defined application. The problem with this approach is that if conditions warrant that the tasks or roles change (which often do in value chain partnerships), then someone must change the application. This results in large IT maintenance cycles and costs.

In the agent model, activities, rules, and resources are independent of one another; and are brought together at runtime. Thus, business processes can adapt in real-time to varying conditions. Moreover, intelligent agents have the capability to negotiate with each other – i.e., they may be willing to accept a task assignment under certain conditions. All decisions made by intelligent agents are subject to the conditions of the business process at the time the decision is made. If a condition changes during the course of a business process execution, the agents may renegotiate their participation and alter their decisions.

Think of the house building example. Let's say that the supplier selected to lay the foundation is scheduled for the first week of June. But a storm in the latter part of May pushes the whole project back by a week. When the project resumes, the foundation layers are no longer available; they had committed to another project for the second week of June. In a manual environment, the general contractor would begin calling other foundation contractors he knew, hoping that he could find someone soon who would be available to do the work. In the meantime, the project cost meter is running. With intelligent agents representing all of the resources in a value chain network, the process agent can select the "best" supplier to perform the task, given the time-dependent condition of the project (in this case, delayed by a week).

Summary

The model for competing and winning in the *real* New Economy is value chain vs. value chain.[2] But partnering today is a rigid, drawn out process. To be effective, value chains must be fluid and dynamic. Effective value chains bring together the right subset of partners to respond to advantageous market opportunities. Clearly, the synchronization of those relationships – through agent-facilitated collaboration – is key to success.

References

[1] META Group, "ETFS Lifecycle" 1999.
[2] Morgan Stanley Dean Witter, 2000.

Chapter 10

Portals: Business on the Network Edge

This chapter was originally published in
eAI Journal (www.eaijournal.com) and is reproduced with permission.

Chapter 10 - Portals: Business on the Network Edge

With Barry Morris

In the next few years, commercial Web sites, as we know them, will vanish. As organizations increasingly move to do business on the Internet, their Web sites will evolve into enterprise portals. Ultimately, all organizations will use an enterprise portal to establish their Internet presence. They'll discover that standalone application and integration servers cannot sustain an enterprise portal strategy and will have to exploit service-based application architectures and deploy portal servers.

Some fundamental aspects of enterprise computing will change completely. You'll see no more:

- Web sites, applications, application servers, and operating systems as you know them today
- Status quo —in a business world surviving on the network edge.

No More Web Sites

Web sites – even straight-ahead, high-volume e-commerce sites – don't represent an effective, credible e-business strategy. The reason behind the demise of the Web site lies at the network edge.

Organizations have spent years evolving their information systems infrastructure, which typically one or more operating platforms with some combination of mainframe, UNIX and Windows environments. The infrastructure also typically includes various applications designed to automate business processes. Depending on an organization's sophistication and technical prescience, these applications interoperate to some degree. Finally, the infrastructure contains content, comprising both structured application data and unstructured text, Hypertext Markup Language (HTML) pages and other material.

Meanwhile, the evolution of access technologies continues. Broadband technologies provide an ever-growing pipe to end users, which spurs their appetite for access, which drives the growth in pipe capacity, and so on. A growing variety of appliances, some user-driven and some automated, place ever-greater demands on organizations to furnish information in multiple formats simultaneously. The growth in wireless access technology in particular means that appliances and users can demand information wherever they are, whenever they want.

Infrastructure and access meet at *the network edge*, where organizations are increasingly driven to deliver pervasive, personalized content and commerce. Outside the network edge are billions of Internet devices. Inside the network edge is the enterprise's competitive machinery. Whatever organizations erect at the network edge must be highly scalable, reliable, available and secure all the time.

We're not describing a Web site. Instead, we're describing a new use of the Internet — an *enterprise portal* — designed to meet unique demands placed on an organization at the network edge. An enterprise portal is an Internet site owned and operated by an organization to support its operations. The enterprise portal is a single point of contact and community between the enterprise and all its stakeholders and prospects. Like the popular consumer portals, an enterprise portal organizes various information using indexes and visual presentation.

A company's Web presence is as important to its brand identity, customer perception, and overall performance as its storefronts, selling process and channels. Most enterprise Web sites now contain huge amounts of information, managed by dozens of servers. Enterprise portals will help companies better organize all this information, partly by letting stakeholders create custom views of it.

In addition to information, though, an enterprise portal also organizes tools, applications, and transactions the enterprise provides to employees, customers and other stakeholders. Enterprise portals support customized views of these applications, data, and transactions, as well as access to those resources and external resources such as news and procurement sites.

Enterprise portals are also the platform for active delivery of information and commercial transactions. A customer's view of the portal will contain different resources and data than an employee's view, but a common architecture will provide both.

Access, delivery and personalization are the architectural bedrock. However, enterprise portals will also support linkage between and integration of information and processes — both online and offline — and the provision of new services and products.

Linkage is the interconnection of different applications, data, and transactions to support a user action. For example, linking ordering, inventory status, and credit checking into a single user action may require coordination of three different systems. To accomplish this linkage, the enterprise portal must be able to maintain the user's context, including security, transmit the right instructions and values to each system, and ensure that each operation occurs in the proper sequence.

Integration requires that the portal be able to integrate data from different places and make it work together. For example, a customer care application may pull information from multiple sources, filter that information, and then present it in a single customer screen.

Properly designed enterprise portals create enormous opportunities for organizational effectiveness and agility. They make it possible for companies to explore new business models, products and ways of connecting with important entities. However, poor design, disjointed processes, system outages and botched interactions can destroy these benefits. So, enterprise portals will either distinguish their owners from the mass of Internet commerce sites or damage franchises and brand names built up for years. Success will require careful design, robust infrastructure, and an architecture that can sustain value through rapid changes to portal content and organization.

As enterprise portals become the new standard definition of e-business, organizations will need to provide this level of service and connectivity to stakeholders, or risk damaging their competitive posture.

No More Application Servers

How will these portals be built and supported? Application servers, the application platform of choice today, are insufficient as a portal platform. Instead, organizations will adopt what Gartner Group calls *portal servers*.

Application servers were to late 1990's computing what database servers were to the early 1990's. Just as database servers liberated developers from many of the programmatic responsibilities associated with data storage and management, so application servers make it easier to programmatically isolate business logic into a separate application tier. Application servers, components and the Java programming language are highly complementary, and each has contributed to the others' popularity. Application servers are useful for function-rich Web sites, and even for low-end consumer portals, because they provide a rich container for new application logic. However, enterprise portals are far more demanding than this.

For example, enterprise portals require extensive integration of enterprise applications on various platforms. This integration needs to be non-intrusive, standards-based, both synchronous and asynchronous in nature, and driven by a flexible process modeling and workflow mechanism. Additionally, enterprise portals require extremely feature-rich Web-facing capabilities. Portal implementers will need features such as personalization, access control and management, and content management. They'll want to be able to expose portal content to various client devices.

Application servers are good at supporting business logic, but not at application integration, content management or any of several other important enterprise portal functions.

As more organizations realize the importance of back-end integration to their portal strategies, application server vendors have begun to bolt integration capabilities onto their standard application server offerings. This is a misguided approach to portal construction that ultimately won't let developers keep pace with the nature of Internet application development. The approach ignores the fundamental imminent change in application architecture — that application servers will become *portal servers*.

Portal servers provide organizations with all the development, deployment and management functions they need to build effective enterprise portals. They offer an application platform, integration platform and Web-facing platform. They provide the combined functionality organizations need to build and deploy enterprise portals.

Portal servers are more than a loose collection of application server, integration server and Web development technologies. They're designed from scratch to supply what Gartner Group calls "front-end to back-end integration via composite-applications-oriented solutions."

No More Applications

Applications today, whether they're intended for mainframes or Java 2 Platform, Enterprise Edition (J2EE) application servers, tend to be built as distinct, single systems. These applications may be designed to interact with other systems and may even support standard distributed application architectures, but they're islands nonetheless. Integrating the islands is a difficult, expense task.

For an e-business to succeed, its applications must readily integrate and interoperate with other applications on other platforms and other environments. They must become what Gartner Group calls *composite applications*. This is the definition of e-business computing. Today's application architectures don't easily meet these criteria. We must begin to build applications in an entirely different way to leverage the benefits of enterprise portals and the Internet.

The next generation of applications will be designed from the ground up to interact and collaborate with other systems. A new approach to application development — one that relies on a *services-based* application architecture — will make this possible. More than ever, we'll build applications using components. These components will present themselves as a collection of services, operating in a context in which discovering and invoking services occurs in a standard manner.

These services will be entirely independent of underlying Application Program Interfaces (APIs) and component models. The services will also be location, language and platform independent. They'll reside and interconnect on the Internet-standard transport, Hypertext Transfer Protocol (HTTP). They'll communicate using the Simple Object Access Protocol (SOAP), which works similarly to Remote Procedure Call (RPC) technology.

Services-based architectures are familiar to organizations that employ Common Object Request Broker Architecture (CORBA) the Object Management Group's standard for platform- and language-independent application interoperability. However, the typical CORBA developer is a software engineer writing C++ applications. For mainstream application developers, services-based architectures represent a different approach to application design and implementation.

Microsoft, with its .NET strategy, is promoting services-based application architectures to application developers. These architectures are at the heart of Microsoft's strategy. That strategy envisions "constellations of computers, devices, and services that work together to deliver broader, richer solutions [where] computers, devices, and services will be able to collaborate directly with each other. Businesses will be able to offer their products and services in a way that lets customers embed them in their own electronic fabric."

Applications built around what Gartner Group calls *e-services* and Microsoft calls *Web services* will feature:

- business services that involve both new functionality and re-capture existing application functionality
- front-end services providing portal access to various users at various clients.

Expect that these applications will involve an enormous variety of data. Today's application developers are often concerned with database-centric transactions. Many application server vendors respond by focusing on their Online Transaction Processing (OLTP) capabilities. But enterprise portal users will need access to more than database data. With exposing the entire enterprise to a heterogeneous audience as adesign goal, enterprise portals will support applications concerned with mixed and often unstructured data. Accordingly, developers of services-based applications will focus primarily on *interactions*. Certainly, these interactions may subsume traditional transactions, but they'll also involve unstructured data and business logic.

You can expect that:

- These applications and their services will involve transactions and interactions that transcend machine, application space, and even enterprise boundaries.
- SOAP will provide the communications protocol for these services and Internet-wide computing generally.
- These services-based applications will have to accommodate various client devices and, on each device, various customized and personalized interfaces.
- Users will expect each application's front-end services to accommodate their unique needs.
- One or more standard *e-business platforms* will provide a vast collection of standardized services.

No More Operating Systems

These new services-based applications will require an underlying e-business infrastructure designed to support such applications and the enterprise portals that contain them. Whereas once the terms *infrastructure* and *operating system* were largely synonymous, the coming e-business infrastructure is entirely operating system independent. In fact, operating systems have already become less important, and as enterprise portals increasingly drive end-users' computing experiences, operating systems will become entirely irrelevant.

The Internet represents the triumph of computing standards. The e-business platform will be entirely standards-based, with support for:

- Extensible Markup Language (XML), the well-known language that's both human- and machine-readable — with support for content modeling, content management and application data storage and manipulation — and that easily interoperates with existing Internet technologies.
- SOAP, authored by Microsoft, IBM, IONA and others, which provides an open network protocol supporting invocation of application functionality across the Internet. SOAP opens the door to the device-, platform- and language-neutral service-based application architectures that will change the way applications are designed and deployed.
- Universal Description, Discovery and Integration (UDDI) proposed by IBM, Microsoft and Ariba, begins to solve the problems inherent in bringing together e-businesses — each with its unique processes, collection of automation technology and services — made available to customers and prospects. UDDI provides a universally available, standard means for unique entities to describe and promote themselves on various dimensions.
- J2EE, Sun Microsystems' specification for large-scale distributed Java systems, which is intended to provide a standardized, services-rich platform for building enterprise Java applications.
- .NET, Microsoft's vision for the future of the Internet, which provides a device- and platform-neutral architecture on which you can build and deploy application services across the Internet and make them available to various clients.

Because Internet applications demand it, the e-business platform will be tremendously scalable. It must be constructed on technology that can scale quickly, both in volume and function. It cannot be device dependent, nor can it deliver poor performance to scale.

Given that it must support composite applications, with their substantial back-end services and concomitant application integration, the e-business platform must provide support for synchronous and asynchronous transactional event/message paradigms.

With composite applications running on top of it, the e-business platform must provide a service-based, location-transparent architecture for systems and application components. Developers from several backgrounds and disciplines, using several programming languages, will rely on the e-business platform to solve various challenges. This means the platform must provide programming personalities for native XML, Enterprise Java Beans (EJB) J2EE, mainframe programs such as Customer Information Control System (CICS), Information Management System (IMS), COBOL and PL/1, CORBA and Component Object Model/Distributed Component Object Model (COM/DCOM).

Enterprise portal applications will present a dizzying variety of services and functionality to a diverse population of end-users. Developers will need some application features and services and not others. The e-business platform must allow for this and provide options for service, including security, distributed transactions, management, load balancing, and fault tolerance.

Application developers using XML and Java, who have no particular .NET- or CORBA-like experience, will particularly appreciate the e-business platform. With its ability to expose existing back-end applications and other enterprise resources as services, it will ease the transition into services-based architectures and portals.

No More Status Quo

The Internet changes everything. Organizations are rapidly gravitating to enterprise portals that become the vehicle by which they expose enterprise processes to customers and partners at the network edge. Enterprise portals will be built and deployed in a new kind of container, a portal server. Portal servers will provide developers with business logic, application integration, and portal access in a controlled development and deployment environment.

Executing in these environments will be composite applications that conform to a services-based architecture. In these applications, both new components and existing applications will present themselves according the services they can provide. Developers will work to assemble the services they require to meet a particular composite application need. Finally, underlying all this will be an XML-native e-business platform, providing a standards-based infrastructure and a set of enterprise services for all the layers and devices above it.

Chapter 11

Adaptive Strategies for B2B Marketplaces

With Biri Singh

A Value Chain Approach

The emergence in the past several years of B2B marketplaces has led to widespread speculation on their eventual impact as entities for conducting business. The true value of a B2B marketplace lies in its ability to integrate with and capitalize on the value chain of a particular industry or defined market – meaning it must enhance the existing structure and processes of the market that it serves. As businesses seek new ways to create and manage their processes, B2B marketplaces offer the potential of cost savings and new revenue opportunities.

The most beneficial solutions are ones that focus on integrating the entire value chain (both supply and demand) while leveraging past investments in technology. These solutions will improve processes related to sourcing, manufacturing, and selling – benefiting all areas of the value chain. They will integrate suppliers and buyers with the supply chain and incorporate purchasing and selling processes with public and private marketplaces.

Current solutions are marked by an inability to communicate easily across and between departments and systems. This leads to problems such as inefficient product development, significant manual intervention with the systems, and low customer retention. These problems stem from:

- Lack of an approach by solutions providers to solve problems of the enterprise as a whole
- Lack of tools to allow for all types of buying and selling, including multi-parameter negotiation, auction, reverse auction, RFP, RFQ, bid/ask, etc.
- Lack of a platform to facilitate integration to legacy systems and best-of-breed components that increase the efficiency of the entire organization
- Outdated technology or technology that does not conform to technical standards, thus increasing the effort to install and maintain the systems

Efforts to address these problems with ERP, CRM, and SCM systems have solved pieces of the problem, but they fail to address these root causes. The benefits of online B2B e-commerce lie well beyond simply procurement and automated customer relationship management; they come from better collaboration, increased sales, and reduced expenses throughout the entire value chain. The ability to participate in B2B marketplaces, both public and private, will allow companies to eliminate inefficiencies in the value chain thereby better managing current business and creating new business opportunities.

Value Chain – Pain Points and Opportunities

The value chain refers to the process companies go through to source, manufacture and sell their products and services, adding value to the raw materials (or inputs) to deliver a needed good or service to the marketplace.

> ***Source*** refers to the processes required to locate vendors, determine products and prices available, purchase the products and receive them into the company.
>
> ***Manufacture*** refers to the processes required to turn the inputs into the value-added outputs the company is going to sell.
>
> ***Sell*** refers to the processes required to market, sell and deliver the goods and services.

The value chain is often marked by inefficiencies and disconnects that increase the expenses and reduce the revenue for a company, thereby preventing it from recognizing the maximum value for its shareholders. What is required is a single platform that can integrate business systems and processes to enhance the existing value proposition of a company, enabling it to continue to grow into the future. This integrated solution would:
- Automate and facilitate off-line relationships
- Enable the company to take advantage of the benefits of public and private B2B marketplaces
- Preserve the value proposition of the company
- Decrease internal IT costs while providing a scalable, flexible solution
- Reduce administrative costs by 50% - 70%[1]
- Significantly improve processes while reducing inventory
- Reduce expenses while increasing revenue.

Building B2B Marketplace Strategy

As companies seek to develop a B2B marketplace strategy, several issues must be addressed. At a minimum, the strategy must include a vision, a flexible architecture plan, and an understanding of what defines success. Key decisions must be made around building or participating in a marketplace, taking existing off-line relationships into an on-line environment, and assessing potential channel conflicts arising from this new level of customer access, to name a few.

The steps to create the strategy that an enterprise must consider include:

Decide how to participate. First, consider the type of B2B marketplace that is right for the enterprise. This decision is driven by business and competitive strategy. B2B Marketplaces represent another channel for doing business, on both the sourcing and selling sides of the value chain. Hence, the enterprise should apply evaluation criteria and metrics similar to those utilized to define the organization's approach to other channels. As a result, the B2B marketplace decision should represent the perspectives of all relevant stakeholders within the organization.

Build on an open platform. No matter what B2B marketplace format is selected, it is clear that building on an open, scalable, standards-based platform is paramount. It positions the enterprise to promptly respond to ever-evolving function, feature and technical requirements —ultimately helping the enterprise maintain its competitive advantage.

Leverage existing infrastructure investments. The long-term benefits of a B2B marketplace go far beyond trading. The enterprise must think about the ultimate integration of existing SCM, ERP and CRM systems into the B2B marketplace infrastructure. Ideally, functions such as ordering, service request tracking, inventory checking, transaction monitoring, and payment processing should all be included and therefore planned for as part of the strategy. While the integration will take time, it is important to recognize the competitive advantages of this approach and plan for it today.

Consider the buy-side implications. *It's not just about getting the cheapest price* —B2B Marketplaces represent a host of benefits in addition to attractive pricing. While it is true that in some cases (e.g., commodity products) B2B marketplaces may drive prices down, participants also benefit from the opportunity to trade based on other factors such as delivery time, service, support and quantity. In addition, they provide a tremendous opportunity for process-related cost savings and online collaboration for product development and supply chain management, which build upon already strong relationships.

Consider the sell-side implications. *B2B Marketplaces create opportunities to de-commoditize products* —B2B marketplaces are essentially new playing fields, where differing levels of value added services (such as delivery timing, shipping types, quantity categories, and service agreements) are now associated with commodities. These services allow vendors to differentiate themselves and de-commoditize their offerings, generating greater value.

B2B Marketplaces can reduce cost of sales and distribution —B2B Marketplaces are essentially a new distribution channel for suppliers. Utilized effectively, they can reduce the cost of sales and distribution, improving margins.

Know the competitive landscape. Before an enterprise builds a B2B marketplace or selects a B2B marketplace to participate in, it is imperative that a thorough analysis of the competition be performed. A thoughtful approach to examining the competitive landscape will provide the enterprise with needed perspective on its B2B marketplace position.

Establish success metrics. The ultimate goal of B2B marketplace participation is to increase revenue and decrease costs, by leveraging the host of new opportunities created by B2B marketplaces. Prior to launching a B2B marketplace, the enterprise manager must define some parameters for measuring achievement.

Build the case for the B2B marketplace. With a clear picture of the current B2B marketplace landscape, the enterprise can begin to build a B2B marketplace plan. Below is a basic checklist for enterprise managers to follow when developing a B2B marketplace strategy.

Conduct a competitive review to determine:
- What are competitors doing in this space?
- Which B2B marketplace formats have they selected and why?
- Are these formats successful?
- How long will that success continue?
- What impact the competition's presence will have on your business?

Define your strategic positioning.
- What results do you want the B2B marketplace to deliver (e.g., expand supplier base, streamline supply chain or access new trading opportunities)?
- What position do you want to take in the B2B marketplace landscape?

Select market model(s).
- What B2B marketplace format or combination of formats best meets your objectives?
- What kind of flexibility do you require to adjust for market changes?

Define B2B marketplace development parameters. Parameters include objectives, scope, timing, expected results and associated cost.

Establish success metrics. Measure the performance of your B2B marketplace initiatives by monitoring specific indicators of success.

Budget. Define the budget for development and maintenance, tying investments to expected returns.

Build. Leverage existing technology to develop a B2B marketplace. Utilize best practices information and proven B2B marketplace technologies available today.

Launch and Evaluate. Continuously evaluate performance and adjust success metrics as the market matures and changes.

Technology Considerations Behind B2B Marketplaces

One of the difficulties in conducting business online is the ability to translate offline business processes into terms that a computer can understand and execute. Using procurement as an example, automation has been applied to the process in many enterprises, but it is often inefficient. People use procurement software without really knowing how the online procurement process works or how the software was configured to function. When a user interacts with a procurement system, he or she must conform to the way the system works, since the system rarely functions in precisely the same way the business has traditionally worked. Essentially, when seeking to transform traditional business practices into online processes, there is a disconnect between the system and the user who has the domain knowledge of the business.

When businesses change, business processes like procurement must also change. However, given the way software exists today, businesses can only change up to the point that the software allows – which, typically, isn't very much. Users are therefore constrained to work the way the software has been developed. The common solution to this problem has been to extend the life of the software by piecing it together with other software to accommodate the new requirements, but this solution is not elegant, and often further convolutes already confusing user processes.

Rather than design software that simply meets current business requirements, enterprises must use a more forward-focused approach, and demand a design strategy that builds in flexibility to accommodate change as business needs change and technologies advance.

Delving into the technical aspects of a B2B marketplace, it becomes apparent that two primary areas need to be addressed —the domain knowledge and the enabling, through technology, of behaviors based on that domain knowledge. The enabling aspect requires a "knowledge engine," which is discussed in greater detail later in this chapter. Many of today's applications simply address the automation of business processes and don't take the context of the process into consideration. A much larger issue, however, is how to allow B2B marketplaces to have an understanding of the products and services being exchanged and the attributes that represent them. In other words, the system has no concept of what constitutes domain knowledge, so it cannot differentiate between the terms used in a petroleum exchange as compared to those used in a shipping exchange. Although the domain knowledge of each of these B2B marketplaces differs drastically, the application of the domain knowledge and the enabling of behaviors based on that domain knowledge are very similar in successful public and private marketplaces.

Recognizing these critical design shortcomings in the e-business software available today, it is worth examining the causes of these problems, and suggesting design improvements, which can result in a dynamic, adaptive software foundation that can resolve these issues. The discussion will examine 1) the concept of domain knowledge and how it can be expressed and understood by computers, 2) the importance of following standards as a way to provide for an evolutionary transition into the future, and 3) how logically combining the two can result in a fully flexible environment which conforms to any business model.

A New Model-based Approach to e-Business Platforms

Domain Knowledge. Domain knowledge constitutes every facet of a business —products, customers, suppliers and the rules and relationships that govern how they interact with one another. Domain knowledge includes a full understanding of what takes place when a buyer sends a purchase order and a supplier sends an invoice. It is the entire collection of structured information that is passed back and forth between businesses and the business rules that are enforced during the transfer of that information.

In the traditional business enterprise, this domain knowledge is the collective experience and intelligence of the business' employees. It includes that information that is documented in the form of policies and procedures or best practices, that which exists in the form of repetitive, daily tasks and routines, and that knowledge which exists only in the minds of experienced workers. Because domain knowledge is so widespread, considerable effort is required to consolidate it and translate it into information the automated system can use. Inside a B2B marketplace, domain knowledge is expressed as market rules and terminology, and the relationships between those terms that drive B2B marketplace transactions.

Within a B2B marketplace, there are many categories of domain knowledge which must be defined in order for the system to replicate offline business processes online; including, but not limited to, products, participants and market behavior in the industry.
- Products and Services —each product or service being exchanged must be described concisely, using attributes that fully define each item and differentiate it from other offerings.
- Participants —the traders, buyers and sellers, and any other users, including the market makers and administrators, must be fully defined and differentiated.
- Market Terms —business transactions that are central to the market, such as invoices, purchase orders and shipping or-

ders, must be defined in terms of the behavior that must take place to complete each transaction.

Encapsulating and defining domain knowledge inside the system requires an understanding of the concepts of taxonomy and ontology. Webster's Dictionary includes this definition of taxonomy:

> **taxonomy** \Tax*on"o*my\ (-m[y^]), n. The laws or principles of classification.

In the context of a B2B marketplace, the term taxonomy refers to the attributes of the goods and services that are being exchanged. For example, the taxonomy of a brick would be size, shape, color and weight. For a trader, the taxonomy may be name, telephone number and address. The taxonomy is just one element of domain knowledge.

Additionally, the products, participants and market terms require a categorization of attributes; that is, a way to represent each component and the relationships between components.

Webster's definition of ontology is:

> **ontology** \On*tol"o*gy\, n. That department of the science of metaphysics, which investigates and explains the nature and essential properties and relations of all beings, as such, or the principles and causes of being.

For the purpose of building a B2B marketplace, the ontology defines the relationship between the attributes. It describes how the taxonomy is applied, so that the information can be utilized by processes such as workflow, matching and optimization.

This information is derived from the structure of the business model and from the business itself. For instance, a purchase order has specific attributes or contents, such as purchase order number and date. Similarly, each product included in the purchase order has its own attributes, such as color and size. Finally, the market participants that create or accept the purchase order have attributes associated with them, such as name and telephone number. These attributes are associated with each component in an agreed upon format. When represented collectively, these components and attributes form a logical structure that can be translated into terms software can use. Standards exist that can optimize the translation of this domain knowledge into electronic data, and these standards apply throughout the entire system including at the granular level. These standards are discussed in greater detail later in this chapter.

Thus, the critical information for these components —products and services, participants and terminology — is captured within a taxonomy and an ontology to create the main body of the businesses domain knowledge:

> Taxonomy + Ontology = Domain Knowledge

But there is a final aspect of domain knowledge, which has not yet been addressed — the business rules that govern the way business is conducted in an organization and within a B2B marketplace. Declaring and enforcing these rules is a challenge, but nonetheless a very important part of the B2B marketplace equation. The ultimate goal is to define business rules in such a way that they can be 'combined' with the basic domain knowledge and implemented wholly in a single equation. In this way, all domain knowledge, products and services, participants and market terms along with business rules, can be expressed in a universal format and utilized simultaneously in a transparent manner as shown in Figure 1.

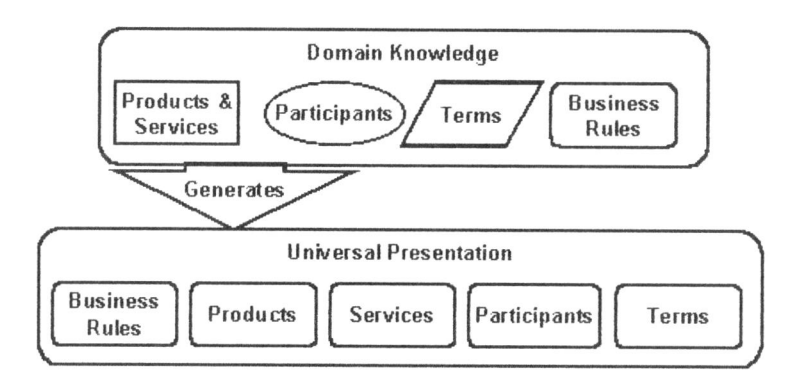

Figure 1. Domain Knowledge Generated into a Universal Representation

Business Behavior. What differentiates industries, and the companies within those industries? At the most fundamental level, it is the domain knowledge, including the business rules, that define and govern how these businesses operate. By capturing this domain knowledge electronically, a company can provide for flexibility and efficiency as the business grows and changes. But how can this be automated when each market and business works differently?

With the concepts of taxonomy and ontology in mind, we turn our focus to the behavior part of the equation. If a knowledge engine could be developed for various behaviors, and those engines designed to function based upon the domain knowledge stored in the environment, then the software would react differently according to the information available in the knowledge repository as illustrated in Figure 2.

Domain Knowledge + Knowledge Engine = Desired Results

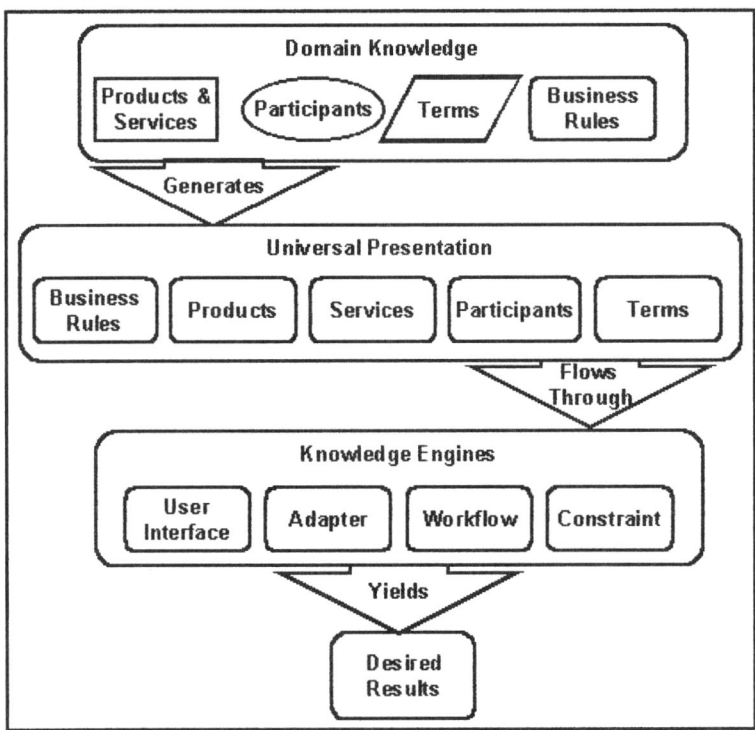

Figure 2. Domain Knowledge Transformed by Knowledge Engines

Chapter 11 - Adaptive Strategies for B2B Marketplaces 209

If the domain knowledge is expressed in a universal format understood by the knowledge engines, then different engines can be called on at any point in a given business process in order to obtain the desired behavior. These engines correspond to distinct areas of functionality, such as satisfaction, optimization and workflow.

Likewise, domain knowledge could change from business to business, but the same knowledge engines can perform their tasks regardless of business or industry. For example, if a company operates a public or private home builder's supply marketplace and it decided to add steel products to its current wood offerings, the company could update the domain knowledge repository, without making changes to the knowledge engines. And as the business requirements change, knowledge engines could be substituted without altering the domain knowledge. The two aspects of the online business remain separate, although they work together to accomplish the business functions desired.

The key here is that the domain knowledge and the knowledge engine, which acts upon the domain knowledge to deliver the expected behavior, are stored separately in the run-time environment. In this way, the same software can be used across every industry and still work as it should based on that business' or industry's needs. This is a very different concept from conventional systems, where the domain knowledge and behavior are laced together in a program or in a single business object, requiring a custom approach for every business and every industry.

A New Approach. It is possible to build a system to meet the needs of a specific marketplace that contains both the domain knowledge and behavior embedded through programming. However, such a system would not be easily extended. Any small change in the domain knowledge would require an intense system-wide modification to alter the information and all objects that initiate actions based on that changing information.

However, by physically separating the domain knowledge from the behavior components (knowledge engine) of the system, either can be changed without impacting the other. Changes required to the domain knowledge would not necessitate modifications to the knowledge engine. To change the behavior of the environment, the knowledge engine could be substituted or updated, without impacting the domain knowledge. By designing the system in this way, the software is also made extensible to other industries and businesses, because it is no longer "hard coded" for one business environment.

Standards. The conformance to industry-accepted standards is one additional ingredient essential to this new model of application development. The good news is that the software industry has recognized the need for standards and many new standards are being developed for digital commerce. Unfortunately, a great deal of overlap and confusion exists due to the emergence of so many different standards.

Over time, we expect a few superior standards to become dominant. While no one can predict with complete accuracy how technology will evolve, recognizing the necessity for industry-accepted standards will result in smart decisions today, minimizing difficulties tomorrow. It is important to research and identify leading technological standards to ensure a competitive advantage in the future, and to avoid becoming constrained by a process or technology that will be obsolete down the road.

Some examples of today's dominant standards include:
- XML — Extensible Markup Language — A flexible way to create common information formats and share both the format and the data on the Internet, intranets, and elsewhere
- RosettaNet — XML-based vocabulary for the exchange of electronics domain knowledge
- WfMC — Workflow Management Coalition – Standard for software terminology, interoperability and connectivity between workflow products.
- BTP — Business Transaction Protocol – Standard for collaborative information
- BPML — Business Process Modeling Language - A meta-language for the modeling of business processes, providing an abstracted execution model for collaborative and transactional business processes based on the concept of a transactional finite-state machine.

A quick examination of programming languages reveals that, while many are in use today, only Java meets the true requirements for new, Internet-based applications. Advanced applications do more than use the Net as a communications protocol. They require the Internet as a truly global, distributed computing environment in which to operate. Within Java, J2EE is the most stringent standard available for enterprise-level software in a distributed environment. J2EE was developed with native constructs specifically for the Internet, and is recognized throughout the industry as the standard programming language for a heterogeneous environment.

From a B2B marketplace perspective, the following recommendations can be made:
- XML is currently the best format available for data, since it contains not only the data itself, but also the format for its representation. It should be used to capture domain knowledge.
- J2EE is the most adopted Java standard for enterprise-level software in a distributed environment. It should be used to develop knowledge engines.

Today's standards are not all-encompassing. They are typically technological standards for data format and communication, not semantics or domain knowledge. By combining technological and semantic standards, solutions become extensible to any specifiable area of business. In the end, there will be a standards "ripple effect," with additional standards being developed for specific, new purposes.

How to Implement The New-Model in a B2B Marketplace

The concepts of separating business knowledge and business behavior allow for greater flexibility and extensibility. They can be applied to a B2B marketplace in the following manner.

Market Dictionary. Domain knowledge can be captured and stored in a Market Dictionary, an XML-based document where the B2B marketplace operator, either public or private, creates a set of core descriptions that include every parameter unique to the B2B marketplace —every product, attribute, user, order, offering, transaction and match. The Market Dictionary also contains the business rules that govern the transaction activity within a B2B marketplace.

By using a Market Dictionary, the B2B marketplace operator has enormous flexibility to edit, extend and customize the domain knowledge according to the specific needs of the enterprise or industry. This ensures that business rules do not have to be hard coded into the application; rather, the application references the Market Dictionary, which is easily amended and expanded. As a

B2B marketplace grows and adds new products, services and participants, the Market Dictionary will support this growth and continue to provide a seamless integration.

Universal Business Objects. Under the conventional model of development, creating the business logic in business objects is a labor intensive process. Most often today, domain knowledge is captured by creating business objects for core business functionality and extending those objects for each specific environment, which requires additional programming. A high-level business object is created to represent a product and for each business or industry, new business objects are created to represent each specific domain or business process.

For each separate implementation, a business object would be extended to represent the correct product attributes. This is a relatively simple task for indirect procurement goods, such as office supplies, but much more difficult for direct procurement products, since they are more specific and sometimes configurable. For example, a #2 pencil can vary only slightly from its core representation to a specific need in a given industry. It is a simple product, and very few of its attributes are open to change. However, across industries, most products are extremely different, and product attributes vary widely. Very few products would overlap the steel industry and the food industry, for example, so every core representation is new and different. At this point, extending core business objects to meet the needs of these very different industries would become extremely time consuming to develop and to maintain.

A better method of implementation is to automatically generate these business objects with the domain knowledge and business rules contained in the Market Dictionary. This approach can make the system simpler to develop and to change. The XML document(s) from the Market Dictionary can be used as the input data to automatically create the entire set of required business objects, meaning that the same core systems could be used for steel, food, petroleum or even services. The industry or type of business does not affect the functionality of the software.

When changes or additions to the Market Dictionary are completed, new or updated business objects are automatically generated, making the new information and business rules available throughout the system. No hard coding is required. This process

Chapter 11 - Adaptive Strategies for B2B Marketplaces 213

makes it much easier to manage a developing or growing marketplace.

What facilitates this process? A Business Object Generator with the intelligence to create the required objects, whether they are static, like products, or dynamic, like business rules, to enforce trader spending limits. The resulting system is not "static" or "pre-defined." Rather, the Business Object Generator creates a dynamic, adaptive environment that allows changes to be propagated automatically throughout a B2B marketplace.

Figure 3 illustrates how the Market Dictionary feeds the Business Object Generator, which in turn creates the required business objects. The Market Dictionary defines business objects according to increasingly specific parameters. An example of a business object, a laser printer, is outlined below. The printer attributes are defined and stored in the Market Dictionary.

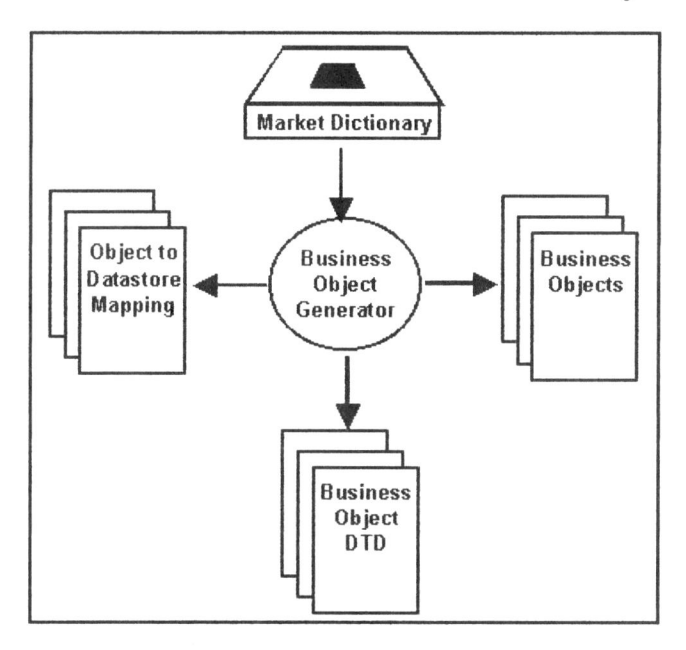

Figure 3. Market Dictionary and
Business Object Generator

The object is categorized by attributes such as market_type "Printer," attribute name "resolution," type "integer," market_types name "Laser Printer," and so on. Once the attributes are set, the B2B marketplace operator can set up constraints to further define the business object. All printers have a certain resolution, which can be represented by a number. In this case, Laser Printer is a type of printer. The laser printer in this example allows for two types of paper and therefore has constraint values of "A4" and "Letter" assigned to it. Notice that at each successive level, a more specific criterion, in the form of a constraint or attribute, is set for the business object.

The actual business object is created at runtime. Once the business object is defined according to the rules of the B2B marketplace, it has all of the required technical characteristics of CRUD – create, retrieve, update and delete – and therefore can be used in the generation of queries. This would allow users to perform queries, such as a search for all laser printers that accommodate A4 paper. Business objects can also be saved for future use.

Knowledge Engines. To this point, we have covered the concept of domain knowledge, and have shown how it can be captured in the Market Dictionary and automatically converted into a universal format as Java business objects. This allows both the market terms and business rules to be processed by a knowledge engine, which emulates the desired business model.

In business, this process is applied in scenarios where the B2B marketplace is the core business model, and a transaction engine is the core application of the B2B marketplace. We can follow the business process external to the software and peer into the transaction engine to see how the desired results are carried out.

Constraint-based Satisfaction Engine. By their nature, B2B Marketplaces are constraint-based satisfaction mechanisms. This means that the suppliers who have offerings to sell and buyers who desire to make purchases have certain constraints which must be satisfied in order for a purchase agreement to take place.

Using a building supplies marketplace as an example, let's suppose that the attributes for products to be exchanged are those listed in Figure 5.

```
Attribute 1:  Building Supplies
Attribute 2:  Wood
Attribute 3:  Ply Wood, Particle Board
```

Chapter 11 - Adaptive Strategies for B2B Marketplaces 215

| Attribute 4: 4x8 sheet-½", 4x8 sheet- ¾", 4x8 sheet-1" |
| Attribute 5: Price |
| Attribute 6: Quantity |

Figure 5: Sample Attributes From a
Building Supplies Market Dictionary

A supplier may come into the marketplace and want to sell sheets of ¾" plywood for at least $15 per sheet to a pre-approved list of buyers, in minimum quantities of 500 pieces. The constraints from this sell offering include the combination of Building Supplies, Wood, Plywood, ¾" sheet, Price and Quantity where Price is $15 or greater and Quantity is 500 or greater.

A buyer from the pre-approved list may be willing to buy the product with those attributes from an exchange, auction or negotiation provided that Price is no more than $16.25 and the supplier has 500 pieces. The constraints from this buy offering include the combination of Building Supplies, Wood, Plywood, ¾" sheet, Price and Quantity where Price is $16.25 or less and Quantity is 500 or greater.

Furthermore, if the B2B marketplace is a public exchange, the market operator may wish to impose a constraint that only orders that have a total value of at least $5,000 are filled. This constraint is configured prior to any offerings in the marketplace, but is enforced at the time of the matching.

Across the B2B marketplace, we have product attributes and business rules that encompass the participating entities in the B2B marketplace, the buyer, the supplier and potentially a market maker. These rules are enforced within the constraint-based satisfaction engine. Once the sell offering has been made in this scenario, the engine determines all of the matches that satisfy the constraints and returns the applicable results.

Another way constraints are used is to emulate the various types of transactional mechanisms, such as fixed price, auction, reverse auction, RFQ/RFP, bid/ask and exchange. If a supplier wants to sell products or services through an auction[2], he simply submits the offering as an auction. The same engine will handle the process, but to set up conditions that are appropriate for an auction, it will apply a constraint on time. For example, it could set a five (5) day limit on the transaction, and award the transaction to the buyer with the highest priced entry. For a catalog[3], the supplier places a constraint on the price. And for an exchange, a real time matching of the requested attributes determines when transactions between buyer and seller can be fulfilled. Price, in this situation, would be an attribute, but it would be open to negotiation.

Simplicity is the key to this model. Regardless of the trading mechanism being implemented for each transaction, the underlying components —the satisfaction engine (knowledge engine) and the product attributes (domain knowledge)— exist once. The same software is used to deliver multiple transaction types, and requires only a modification of the rules of the transaction to emulate the desired behavior of diverse types of trading mechanisms. This is a completely different concept compared to systems that require separate software applications for each type of trading mechanism. The following scenario illustrates this point.

A buyer wants to conduct a reverse auction[4] for a product, but desires to directly negotiate with the three lowest bidders. To accomplish this, most systems would require two different software applications, one for reverse auction and one for direct negotiation, or one package that has two underlying modules, one for each task. In either case, the buyer would be required to first initiate a reverse auction for the desired product, and then, with the field of potential suppliers narrowed to three, end that transaction and create a direct negotiation with each of the three suppliers. Even if the processes are integrated, meaning multiple modules in the same system handle each part of the transaction, a transformation of the data and business rules would be required in order to complete the transaction.

However, using the new approach described in this chapter, where the domain knowledge is separate from the knowledge engine, the domain knowledge remains in its universal format throughout the transaction lifecycle, allowing for the process to be automated, and allowing it to occur as one core transaction. This eases the burden on the users and streamlines the transaction, making the market more efficient. If a solution is based on constraints applied to the same underlying data, one transaction would accommodate the user's requirements, which shift as the transaction lifecycle progresses.

Here's how the process works. First, the buyer initiates a reverse auction negotiation, making it available to the open market or a subset of the open market for a specified amount of time. Once the lowest three bidders are identified in that time period, the transaction can continue, but shifts to a direct negotiation until the final supplier is selected. Constraints in this scenario include the initial time limit during the reverse auction, and any constraints the buyer placed on the offers of the final three suppliers to direct negotiations with them.

Conclusion

Successful B2B marketplaces will be defined by their ability to address the complete value chain and adapt to change. As companies define their B2B marketplace strategies, they should create their plans and select software that not only meets today's business needs, but also future business requirements, evolving business models and an ever-changing technological landscape. The software framework described in this chapter ensures that current and future investments in marketplace software can be leveraged as offline business processes are moved online, as well as when business requirements and marketplace models change, which they certainly will.

References

[1] Harvard Business School Case Study, AT Kearney, Aberdeen Group
[2] Traditional Auction - Sellers initiate auction by posting item(s) for sale and buyers place bid. Highest bidder wins.
[3] Fixed Price Item - Offering that has no negotiable parameters, with the exception of purchase quantity
[4] Reverse Auction - Buyer posts request for items to purchase and sellers specify price and quantity they can supply. Winner determined by allocating total quantity among lowest bidder.

Chapter 12

B2B Integration: The Message is the Medium

With Scott Blackburn

The Promise and Challenge of Business Integration

There is no longer any doubt that the Internet is reshaping the business landscape. Over 92% of CEOs and members of top management agree that the Internet is profoundly transforming the global marketplace. They also agree that tremendous competitive advantages will belong to those companies that are quick to harness the power of the Internet to facilitate business processes. The vision is dramatic and exciting —businesses exchanging mission-critical information in real time, with trading partners around the world, over every conceivable network, including value added networks (VANs), wide area networks (WANs), virtual private networks (VPNs), and the Internet.

Information integration within companies and across trading communities will reduce costs and radically boost productivity. Real-time information flow will allow companies to respond quickly to the movements of a highly demanding global marketplace. With the Internet incorporated into a network strategy, companies will be able to expand their networks rapidly to encompass new partners, new customers and new markets.

Creators of B2B trading exchanges, whether they are a dot-com startup, an industry consortium or just a single company, face similar growth paths. Whether the service is a closed network such as a buying consortium or an open-to-all online marketplace, the goal is the ability to host real-time, completely secure, automated business processes. These new ways of performing common business processes, such as placing an order or tracking a document can be made manageable and reportable end to end across entire value chains.

Achieving the benefits of B2B trading exchanges, however, is not as easy as it may seem at first glance. Chris Pacitti, venture capitalist at Austin Ventures, explains that the magic does not just happen, "Everybody thought you could throw up these exchanges and they'd work flawlessly. But it's difficult to link with manufacturers and the buy side, so the better ones have to figure out how to crack the code."

Building and managing exchanges that truly add value depends upon how easily, swiftly and securely, private information can be exchanged — and how scalable the facility is in this regard. Many first generation e-markets ignored this requirement until it was too late.

Unlike B2C commerce, B2B relies on complex applications to run the business. Configuring supply and purchase applications to operate without human intervention requires an extremely high level of integration of buy and sell side systems with back office management systems including order fulfillment processes, supply chain management, logistics, invoicing and reconciliation.

Data needs to be translated into the correct formats for the systems of the multiple participants and passed seamlessly and securely. Business processes of the participants must be aligned. For example, PC resellers must maintain different product return procedures for each distributor or direct manufacturer with whom they do business. In order for more and more commerce to take place electronically between companies, one would think that businesses need to agree not only on standard data formats and interfaces between computer systems, but also on common processes to achieve common business outcomes. Due to the ever-increasing number of standards and new technologies, there will be no complete agreement.

Of course integration is already the nightmare of IT departments across the world. According to the British research organization, Ovum, many organizations estimate that 30 to 40 per cent of IT budgets are eaten up creating integration interfaces, protocols and other procedures to link various systems. Moreover, the code referred to in the Ovum report refers in the most part to software that is written within companies, for use behind the firewall, where process change and IT standardization come under the control of a single management team.

Business-to-business commerce, on the other hand, requires integration between companies. The parties in a trading community — all of whom will no doubt have implemented systems differently — need to agree on common ground for integrating their disparate technologies and information systems.

The alternative is for each organization to develop different means of communication with each trading partner, a massive duplication that will consume skills, resources and precious time. As more and more participants join the exchange with more incompatible systems and data formats, the complexity multiplies.

Aberdeen Group analyst David Alshuler elaborates, "All the diversity inside the firewall grows geometrically when you add trading partners. Integration is the dirty back end of all e-business."

Companies need to build strong digital relationships with their suppliers, trading partners and B2B marketplaces. But while it is easy to determine the business case, executing a business-to-business digital strategy is a daunting challenge. The mantra is integration, integration and integration — integration of data, integration of business processes, integration of workflows, integration of computer applications, and integration with legacy systems of the company and those of suppliers and trading partners.

The implementation of business process integration (BPI) systems is one of the major goals of organizations in all sectors as companies strive to create stronger links with all of the other organizations in their value chains. Business-to-business integration must be "any-to-any" —any kind of data, shared across any application, or hardware platform. BPI systems must tie into existing infrastructure environments including electronic data interchange (EDI), enterprise resource planning (ERP) and supply chain management (SCM). They must handle greater volumes of business-critical data across an ever-widening trading community. Legacy systems alone are a monumental challenge as companies need to continue to support their existing intranets and extranets as well as new Internet commerce systems. A company must manage its intranets, extranets and Internet connections simultaneously, inside and outside its firewall. Sound complicated? It is.

To take on the challenge of business process integration, companies need a secure and reliable integration infrastructure for mission-critical commerce applications. The infrastructure must provide for the transparent exchange of information with suppliers, trading partners and customers. It must reliably and securely exchange data internally and externally via the Internet or other networks. It must allow end-to-end integration, and provide message delivery across multiple systems that may be applications, databases, clients or servers. The infrastructure must respond to high demand with scalable processing power and networking bandwidth. The infrastructure must serve as the integrator, transformation engine, and transaction infrastructure for both digital market makers and traditional brick-and-mortar businesses that want to leverage the Internet for mission-critical commerce.

Because guaranteed delivery of messages is absolutely critical, the heart of the infrastructure must consist of an industrial strength messaging backbone with the capability to adapt to a variety of reporting subsystems, data encryption and authentication tools. Because the business events that trigger action in digital commerce are delivered to the participants as messages, Message Oriented Middleware (MOM) is essential for providing the quality of service needed in B2B communications.

The digital marketplace's complex trading environment is flooded by events that generate messages that, in turn, drive transactions. For example, the arrival of a file might require a batch job to run, while the arrival of a message might trigger a database transaction. Another example, the arrival of a form via the Web, might result in accessing an application and delivering a reply in the form of a pager or e-mail message. The infrastructure must synthesize and process events by defining and managing the business processes that need to be activated when certain events occur. Only by being able to handle numerous types of business events, can effective and comprehensive integration occur. What is needed is a comprehensive infrastructure that delivers total business event management as shown in the figure below.

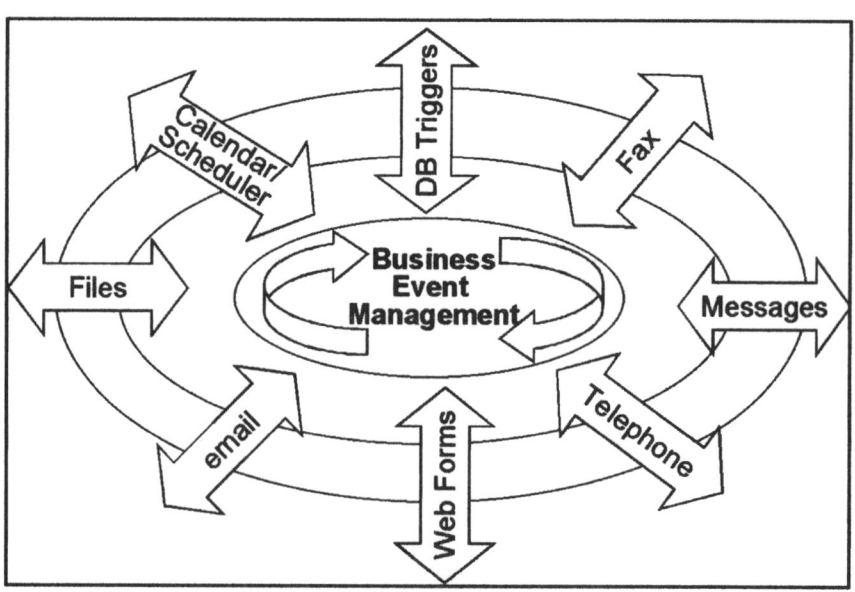

Business Event Management

XML and Standards: Necessary but Not Sufficient

The eXtensible Markup Language (XML) holds great promise for creating a business language understood across the Internet. XML is a meta-language, a language for defining other languages. Several XML "vocabularies" have been defined as standards in many industries. Each vocabulary represents a set of messages that make up business conversations to initiate and consummate business transactions. Examples of these vocabularies include cXML and ebXML.

One high level XML standard goes beyond industry vocabularies and sets forth a specification for Universal Description, Discovery and Integration (UDDI). If successful, UDDI will enable companies to find each other on the Internet and understand how to do business together both at the personal level and the software level. According to the UDDI organization, UDDI's aim is to allow anyone to discover businesses worldwide that offer the exact products and services needed. Companies will register the products and services they offer for others to discover. UDDI is also a building block that will enable businesses to quickly, easily and dynamically find and transact business with one another using their preferred applications.

UDDI will help business partners find each other, communicate what it is that they do and what systems are used to drive the business. Although UDDI provides a powerful standard for helping business partners find each other, it does not go the final step of providing the technology to actually conduct business.

In its current form UDDI does not provide a transaction engine capable of any-to-any integration. For firms to reap the full potential of UDDI's standards, they must be able to integrate with a variety of technology and software platforms. Otherwise what remains is a powerful and compelling vision without the muscle necessary for execution. Imagine the frustration of the architects designing the Golden Gate Bridge if no one ever showed up with steel and concrete. Standards are necessary but not sufficient. An integration infrastructure is still needed so that companies can plug in and participate in e-marketplaces and other business-to-business exchanges without overhauling their existing software.

A Comprehensive Integration Infrastructure

Most of the traditional file and data-transfer products of today do not provide incremental and scalable solutions. They also fail to provide a migration path to real-time, transaction-based distributed applications that will be deployed in the future.

Data-transfer mechanisms are usually limited to point-to-point transfers of a single file or a series of files between one source and one destination. In some instances, if a data transfer fails at any point, the entire transfer session must be re-established and started again. In most cases, no facility exists for intelligent recovery, checkpoint restarting, load balancing or assured delivery in the event of network or other system failures. For information that is mission critical, "most of the time" performance is not good enough.

Conventional data transfer solutions suffer from several performance limitations. By and large, they are connection oriented, they are not modular and they lack restart and recovery capabilities. They also lack central monitoring and administration facilities and provide limited workflow application integration.

A comprehensive business-to-business integration infrastructure must include essential characteristics that are not available with Internet technologies and protocols alone. These characteristics allow corportions to offer their trading communities the full facilities needed to conduct business in real-time across an entire supply chain.

Any-to-Any Data Translation and Transformation. An integration infrastructure includes data translation and transformation services that permit communication between trading partners using different standard or proprietary formats. For example, an EDI purchase order from a buyer can be converted to an equivalent XML document format suitable for a given supplier.

Connectionless Communication. The integration infrastructure must operate independent of network or system resources. It must not require the systems involved in the transfer of data to be in active communication when data-transfer is initiated. As a result, programs exchanging information do not have to be available at the same time. These asynchronous communication facilities are essential because a given participant in a value chain cannot expect that all other participants' systems are available at all times. The real world of commerce simply does not work that way.

Guaranteed Message Delivery. The integration infrastructure must protect the enterprise against catastrophic data loss with assured message delivery. The infrastructure must provide failsafe delivery of critical data by using either persistent messaging or automated end-to-end recovery, even during network and system-level failures. The infrastructure must use checkpoint restart technology to automatically recover from network or system failures, thus eliminating the need to retransmit or reprocess entire files. This saves time and reduces the burden on system and network resources.

XML Standards Support. The integration infrastructure must support a wide array of information formats including XML in order to accommodate existing and emerging standards. XML is becoming the language of digital business and will become increasingly important. XML standards have already emerged in many industries and cross-industry standards will be essential to the networked e-marketplaces of the future.

End-to-End Business Process Management and Monitoring. The integration infrastructure must enable the execution and management of business processes across the supply chain, monitoring transactions and business from events end to end, while logging and reporting problems and exceptions.

Bullet Proof Security. The infrastructure must support mutual authentication and encryption, and have the ability to support non-repudiation through the use of public key technology.

Flexible Application Integration. The infrastructure must include software to streamline and automate data and application integration across disparate hardware platforms and network protocols. Custom and packaged application programming interfaces (APIs) must be adapted quickly to the infrastructure. This allows a number of standard and proprietary data formats including XML and EDI-based business objects to be transported over the infrastructure. It must provide integration points for accessing data in databases, file systems and ERP systems.

High Performance Transport. Comprehensive compression services are needed that can embed, multi-platform compression technologies that conserve precious network bandwidth. The infrastructure must be capable of parallel operations so it can process multiple data transfers simultaneously and broadcast data (including multiple files) using multiple channels. It must permit dynamic routing to optimize network availability and overall performance.

Reliablity and Scalablity. The infrastructure must be designed so that it is robust and scalable. It must grow and adjust with natural enterprise expansion, or with the consolidation resulting from mergers, acquisitions and corporate re-engineering. Within any of these environments, infrastructure services must be implemented in single or multiple configurations, providing scalability as throughput requirements grow. The architecture should handle the integration needs of virtually any size or type of organization, handling peak and non-peak loads.

Auditability. The integration infrastructure must provide extensive audit trails for all activities for each host participating in the transfer of information. Audit facilities allow administrators to diagnose and perform analysis on anomalies that may arise during the distribution of information.

Integration with Non-Internet Based Networks and Protocols. The integration infrastructure must not be restricted to the Internet. For example, it must enable truly global commerce by accommodating existing EDI systems over value added networks. It also must support alternative communications networks and protocols, such as extranets, VPNs and WANs.

Service Management. Because the integration infrastructure links a company to its entire trading community, the infrastructure must manage all the trading partner connections, as well as data and business object mapping.

Infrastructure Implementation. The implementation of the infrastructure must meet or exceed the quality of service standards employed in the internal networks of major corporations. These typically include scalability, redundancy, disaster recovery and high bandwidth availability.

These features combine to provide the managed network services that organizations demand if they are to integrate their information systems with those of their trading partners throughout the supply chain. These are the critical components for any company requiring a mission-critical infrastructure capable of blending the best of the Internet with the best of legacy networks already in use.

Getting There

Companies wanting to implement an industrial-strength integration infrastructure need to analyze their requirements and internal capabilities. They can buy relevant software and build their own infrastructure or they can turn to a managed infrastructure service. The choices have significant consequences.

To date, companies engaging in business-to-business commerce have relied largely on VANs or other dedicated links handling EDI transactions. These traditional solutions continue to be deployed in the market and for many companies will likely hold a strategic role for years to come. But these conventional outsourced networks present significant challenges:
- By handling only limited kinds of business data, they contribute little to a reporting structure intended to provide a comprehensive view of business operations.
- Designed primarily for batch transactions, they offer little support for the real-time business process integration that will be essential in the digital marketplace.
- Their service and transaction costs will be viewed as more and more expensive as the Internet emerges as a cost benchmark.
- They are relatively expensive and complex to implement making it difficult to expand or change networks in response to market shifts.
- Because of their high-end system requirements and relatively high cost of compliance, they are generally inaccessible for smaller trading partners.

Many new software products have been developed to integrate disparate business systems over the Internet. Most of these point solutions are web-centric, making them inadequate for the full range of enterprise requirements:
- Few are designed to promote absolute business integrity and operational scalability as the Internet begins to move a high volume of "bet–your–business" data.
- They lack point-to-point connectivity, security, and reliability features required for trusted, mission-critical integration.
- Most run over the Internet in native mode. Today's Internet cannot guarantee the security of the networks or the fulfillment of high-volume business transactions.

- They do not integrate with data from other networks, such as VANs, WANs, and VPNs. The ability to connect with multiple networks is essential to trading communities that want to leverage existing technology investments such as EDI.

Companies in the process of moving their critical data to the Internet need an "industrial-strength" alternative to native Internet message transport. Companies are naturally reluctant to relegate their high-volume, mission-critical communications to the Internet environment due to ongoing concerns over security and reliability of message transport in this medium.

Consequently many turn to providers of electronic trading networks (ETNs) for enhanced Internet-based network and messaging services. As online trading networks expand their reach and the number of Internet market makers continues to grow, so will the need for managed trading services that allow organizations to reduce time to market and the overall development, deployment, maintenance, and help desk costs associated with their integration infrastructures.

Successful business-to-business trading communities will lead to continuous streams of innovation. But along with each new innovation comes the need for more and more sophisticated integration among community participants. Having built an initial foundation for high volume transaction capabilities and security, a B2B community faces the new challenge of rapidly adding new applications and services to further streamline participants' business processes. With the support of a strong electronic trading network, B2B communities can overcome the complexity and gain proven and tested integration facilities to guarantee transaction integrity regardless of the volume of transactions or complexity of the trading community. Marketplaces, public or private, can move swiftly to a position of high volume and tight integration, achieving sustainable competitive advantage.

Chapter 13

Bringing Visibility to the Extended Supply Chain

With Chris Stone and Justin Steinman

Providing Critical Information to the Networked Economy

Today's supply chain consists of a complicated web of suppliers, assemblers, shipping and logistic firms, sales and marketing channels, third-party customer support firms, and other business partners linked primarily through information networks and contractual relationships. For these entities to work together effectively, an infrastructure service is needed for collecting, analyzing, and distributing information about transactions across the extended supply chain. "In-the-Net" analytics services can leverage existing information networks to provide dynamic, holistic views across the extended supply chain and allow users to "drill down" into detailed analysis about supply chain activities.

In-the-Net analytics services can simplify business reporting and analysis by providing supply chain data on-demand from within and outside the enterprise. The service detects supply chain delays before they impact customer shipments, finds new sources of supply on-the-fly across multiple vendors and marketplaces, provides visibility into customer buying habits across multiple distribution channels, and assists customer service staff in pinpointing and acting on potential customer service problems.

Because end-to-end supply chains are not owned by a single enterprise, a trusted third party is needed for reconciling order, shipment, and billing data among trading partners, helping to prevent disagreements resulting from mismatched information. Integrated on-demand information across the supply chain helps businesses adapt quickly to market changes and new opportunities.

The third party infrastructure service complements and extends the existing information networks of enterprises, value-added networks (VANs), and private transaction networks that need the business efficiency gains possible through improved supply chain visibility.

Businesses Need On-Demand Insight into the Extended Supply Chain

The extended supply chain provides an aggregate view of business processes from both the demand and the supply side. A supply chain links buyers, sellers and all of the intermediary and third party business partners in a seamless but dynamic grouping. This framework allows organizations to improve process transparency and to get the right products to the right place at the right time.

Supply chains are rapidly evolving into complicated webs of suppliers, assemblers, shipping and logistic firms, sales and marketing channels, third-party customer support firms, and other business partners, linked primarily by information networks and contractual relationships shown in Figure 1.

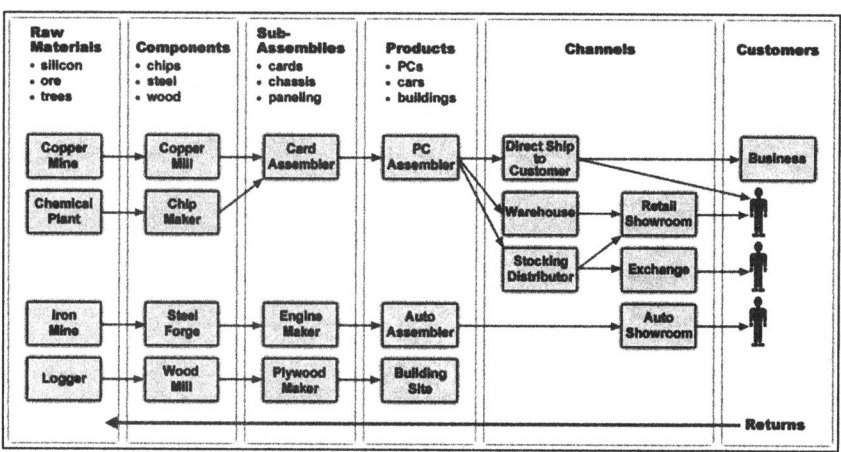

Figure 1. The 21st Century Business Model: A Complicated Flow of Goods and Materials

Global communications and transportation networks have taken proximity out of the business equation, allowing new efficiencies:
- Businesses can sell to customers around the world.
- Materials, components, and services can be sourced from wherever the best price and quality can be found.
- Just-in-time inventory practices and direct-to-customer shipments are minimizing physical inventories.

- Build-to-order manufacturing allows fine-tuned responsiveness to customer demand.
- At the same time, the increasing complexity and velocity of the supply chain creates new problems:
- Accountability across numerous business partners becomes harder to measure. ("Who dropped the ball? Who even knows?")
- Management's view of business processes can become fragmented, making it difficult to identify further opportunities for efficiency gains.
- Supply chain reporting often comes from many sources and after the fact, reducing the capacity for timely and effective action.

In this environment, proactive management requires new information and tools that can provide on-demand insight across and into these increasingly complicated supply chains. This demand has given rise to a new class of software – Supply Chain Event Management.

Adoption of Virtual Business Models

The fundamental nature of business is changing due to the increased reliance on outsourcing and business partnerships, both of which replace traditional vertical integration.

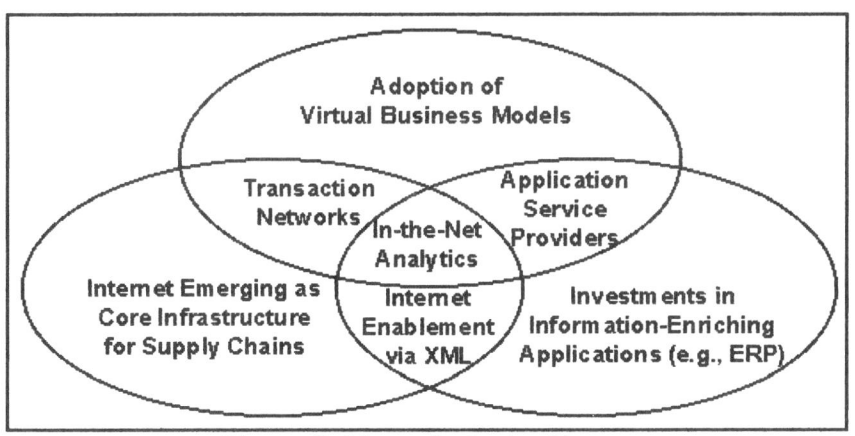

Figure 2. Macro-Industry Forces Shaping the Networked Economy

Outsourcing of many traditional business functions allows a tighter focus on core competencies and differentiators and provides greater flexibility to move quickly in the face of changing markets and new opportunities. New infrastructures and on-line business communities – in the form of industry-sponsored and vertical market private trading networks – are increasing trading opportunities and efficiencies. Private networks allow companies to gather all of their suppliers in one place and share information freely to improve quality and lower costs. But each buyer can have multiple communities of suppliers, and each supplier will belong to multiple buyer communities. The ability to manage a global web of business partnerships is emerging as a critical core competency.

Investments in Information-Enriching Applications

Over the past several years, organizations have made large investments in ERP (Enterprise Resource Planning) systems and data analytic solutions to understand better their business metrics, patterns, and trends. As virtual business models take hold, much of the most important business information – such as channel inventory levels and supplier delivery schedules – now resides outside the core enterprise. Effective management now requires access to information residing on information networks that lie outside the core organization.

Internet Emerging as Core Infrastructure for Supply Chains

The Internet is emerging as the core unifying communications infrastructure for inter- and intra-business communications. Technological advancements in Internet-based VPNs (virtual private networks) and extranet technologies have allowed companies to overcome proximity, cost, and access limitations so they can get closer to their customers and partners. Security advancements in the form of enhanced firewall technologies, PKI (Public Key Infrastructure), and SSL (Secure Socket Layer) have allowed for increased confidence in the Internet as the unifying communications network for business.

Today, organizations are making investments in "Internet-enabling" components to improve their information networks that are not yet Internet-friendly. XML (eXtensible Markup Language) is emerging as an industry-standard for exchanging transactions across the Internet. Enterprises and private transaction networks are rapidly adopting Internet technologies and infrastructures to improve the speed, quality and accuracy of their Internet commerce.

In-the-Net Analytics Bring Visibility

Adoption of virtual business models creates a need for on-demand information across large and complex supply chains – where critical information is spread across many organizations and systems. Investments in information-enriching applications have captured business metrics but have failed to present that information in a coherent and impactful way. The Internet now provides a unifying communications infrastructure for moving information from where it resides to where it's needed. XML provides a common format for collecting information from many sources into an integrated picture of an entire supply chain. Convergence of these macro-industry forces creates the need for "in-the-Net analytics," the on-demand, integrated information that organizations need to thrive in the networked economy.

Information networks are the glue that binds supply chains together. Global supply chains and distribution channels, custom production, build-to-order, just-in-time inventory –these characteristics of 21st century competition can be realized only through the instantaneous global communication available through information networks. On-line order taking, credit card transactions, EDI (Electronic Data Interchange), and EFT (Electronic Funds Transfer) are replacing postal mail and fax. Business processes are increasingly managed by software systems used for order processing, financial management, inventory control, manufacturing control, and CRM (Customer Relationship Management).

In many cases, customer shipments now consist of nothing more than a few electronic records spread across multiple information systems – directing various inventory transfers or assembly operations as shown in Figure 3. In some cases, for example travel reservations, the *only* item that is exchanged is information.

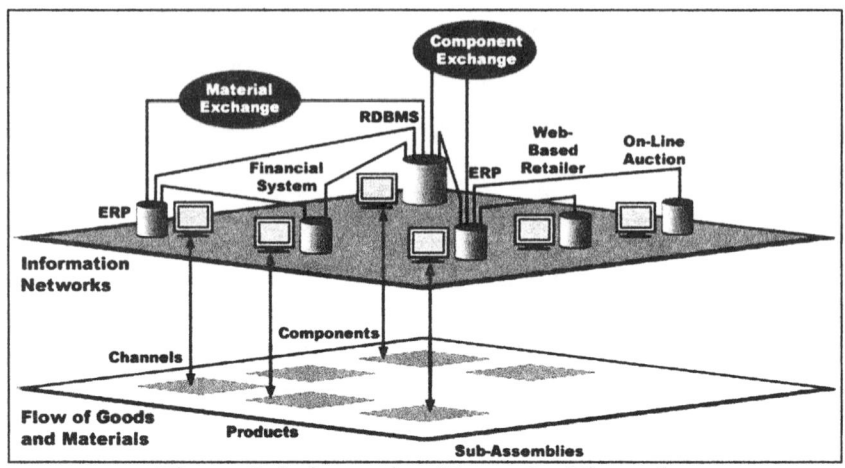

Figure 3. Information Networks Direct the Flow of Goods and Materials Through Supply Chains

Seeing Problems Before Your Customers Do

Virtual businesses gain many advantages, including global supply chains and customer bases, lower inventory costs, the ability to deliver custom products to meet the needs of each individual customer, and the ability to move quickly in response to changing market conditions.

But these benefits come at a price. Along with complexity comes increasing fragility and more opportunities for things to go wrong. Most of the time, everything works – orders flow, components are assembled into products, shipments are delivered to customers, bills and funds move, and information networks collect and distribute information.

But when things go wrong, it's quite likely that a company's customers are the first to notice. In the networked economy, where each customer order is a "work-in-progress" spread across multiple vendors, a final product may not come together until it arrives at a customer's door. Unfortunately, nobody may notice a delayed or partial shipment until it reaches (or doesn't reach) a customer's doorstep. When the customer calls to complain, it may be very difficult to have the information available to either identify the cause of a problem or find a remedy.

Bridging Information Gaps

At the heart of the problem is the supreme irony: *we are awash in information, but at the same time, we see less.* To date, most software systems have focused on individual links in the supply chain – managing internal production and inventories, collecting and reporting on sales transactions, and exchanging transactions with direct vendors and customers. Each system does a good job at what it's supposed to do: managing its corner of the universe and providing information to the division it supports. Problems arise when information held by one system is needed by another one. One system may see a trend, such as a growing backorder early in the extended supply chain – but there's no way to use that information to increase production or predict delays in customer shipments further up the chain.

The networked economy has triggered a revolution in the way companies collaborate and trade. It has increased the amount of information available to buyers and sellers and shortened the time for purchase decision making. But in large part, on-demand information about "in-the-Net" e-commerce transactions is still unavailable. The price, availability, supplier, and product transparency that businesses dreamed would arrive with business-to-business commerce remains elusive. Many businesses are still relegated to their monthly or quarterly reconciliation reports to gather information about the efficiency of their commerce models.

The challenge is bridging the gaps that keep information from reaching the places where it is needed most. Meeting this challenge requires visibility into the extended supply chain.

To succeed in today's economy, a business must manage a web of vendors and customers in a way that ensures prompt and timely delivery of customer orders – while having little direct control over much of its supply sources, assembly lines, logistics chain, or distribution channels. To do so requires a coherent, integrated picture of all supply chain-related information, originating within and outside the organization, across a business' entire supply chain.

What is needed is the right business information at the right time so that companies can make intelligent and informed decisions. Companies wanting to tap this critical information require an infrastructure for collecting, analyzing, and distributing information about supply chain data and inventory levels across an entire supply chain.

Having the right information, at the right time, makes it possible to:
- Detect supply backlogs and find alternate sources before customer shipments are delayed.
- Avoid lost sales due to out-of-stock channels.
- Avoid high levels of obsolete product inventory.
- Maximize efficiencies across the entire extended supply chain.
- React quickly to changes in market conditions.

As shown in Figure 4, an in-the-Net analytics service provider collects XML-translated copies of business data from multiple points along the supply chain using the Internet as a communications medium. Data collection does not interfere with the ongoing operation of information networks controlling the flow of goods and services through the supply chain; rather, the service provider copies supply chain transaction data and then runs analytics on that data to provide insight into the supply chain.

The in-the-Net analytics service provider analyzes, transforms, and presents information dynamically, filling the existing void in on-demand supply chain analytics. The service simplifies the reporting process – making it easy for a supply chain executive to view detailed reports through the familiar user interface of a standard web browser. Dynamic, holistic views across the extended supply chain allows users to "drill down" into detailed analysis about specific transactions. Data can be exported to spreadsheets and other common desktop applications to perform user-defined analyses. XML-enabled applications can access data on-demand across the Internet directly from the service provider.

The infrastructure service complements and extends the existing information networks of enterprises, VANs, and private trading networks that each want the business efficiency gains possible with detailed analytics. Subscribers benefit from all the advantages of an outsourced service: low up-front investment, rapid deployment, minimal impact on staffing requirements, reliable service at low operating costs, and ongoing support and upgrades.

Chapter 13 - Bringing Visibility to the Extended Supply Chain   241

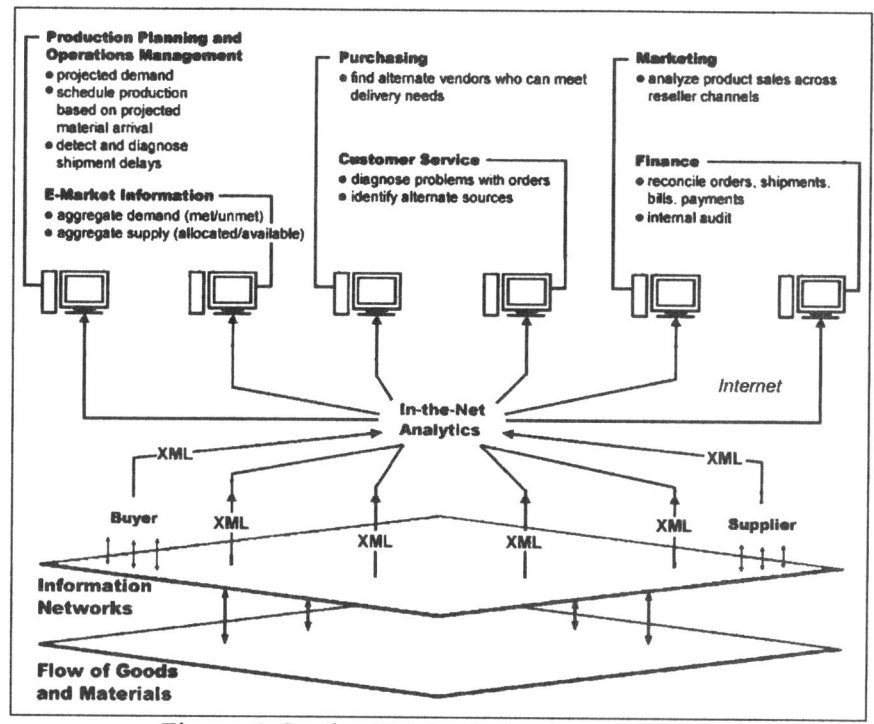

Figure 4. In-the-Net Analytics Leverage and
Extend Existing Information Networks

Improving Businesses Processes

Information can be viewed and organized as needed to address the new management challenges facing businesses in the networked economy. In-the-Net analytic services help improve business processes by:

☑ *Keeping Goods Moving:* In today's just-in-time world, it is no longer possible to rely on physical inventories as buffers against unforeseen events. In-the-Net analytics provide the early warning needed to detect and resolve inventory and delivery problems before they impact the flow of goods. The analytics provide visibility to inventory levels at suppliers, and visibility to inventory in-transit – as well as how long it takes to get there and why.

☑ *Managing Supplier Performance.* In-the-Net analytics quantitatively track s the performance of suppliers – who delivers

on-time, who delivers partially, who has the best invoice accuracy – so that a company can identify the best trading partners and give them the majority of their business.
- ☑ *Measuring Channel Effectiveness:* In-the-Net analytics helps a business keep track of their customers' buying habits – who's buying what, when, and through which channels – across increasingly more complex channel mixes.
- ☑ *Providing Customer Service:* Customers are coming to expect instantaneous, web-based information about their orders. In-the-Net analytics can help assemble the information needed, across the supply chain, to answer the seemingly simple question, "Where is my order?" In-the-Net analytics can help customer service representatives not only explain a delay, but also provide an alternative option, such as shipping a partial order or finding an alternate source for a back-ordered item.

A Secure, Reliable, and Trusted Information Source

In-the-Net analytics services collect supply chain data at its point of origin, where it is true and trusted. Locally-installed software must encrypt data before it leaves customer sites. The analytics service provider must also use strong computer and operational security measures to protect sensitive data.

Subscribers must retain ownership and control of their proprietary transaction data even while it is stored at the service. Data is made available only to those individuals specifically authorized by the owners of the data. Subscribers can define, in detail, what information is collected and stored, and what data and reports different employees, business partners, potential customers, and others can access –all through a simple, web-based interface.

A number of critical services can only be performed by a neutral and trusted third party:
- ☑ Provide complete and trusted information on-demand, about orders, shipments, invoices, payments, and credits. Mismatched information need no longer be a source of disagreement when resolving problems or reconciling transactions across trading partners.
- ☑ Monitor SLA (Service Level Agreement) thresholds, providing the same trusted and unambiguous data to both buyer and seller.

☑ Serve as an intermediary for aggregating data anonymously, allowing a trading community to assemble sector-specific metrics and indices.

Industry Examples

The following examples illustrate some of the ways in which in-the-Net analytic services can play a pivotal role in diverse businesses.

Industrial Manufacturer Example
Problem: Supplier Rationalization.
Goal: Identify the best suppliers based on their performance.

The networked economy has created a wealth of supply options. Companies have more trading partners than ever before as geographical boundaries disappear and more suppliers are competing for the same business. The industrial manufacturer is faced with the very real problem of determining who is the best supplier. Oftentimes this determination is made solely on price. But rarely is the best supplier also the cheapest supplier. Savvy purchasing managers need to look at such factors as on-time delivery, order fill rate, average delivery time and cumulative inventory turns when deciding with whom to do business. As a trusted third party, with access to detailed transaction records, an in-the-net service provides the necessary analysis to make these decisions.

Figure 5 shows how an industrial manufacturer could use a scorecard to evaluate its suppliers.

In-the-Net analytics helps a business to:
☑ Identify supply chain bottlenecks and inefficiencies to prevent problems and lower costs
☑ Gain a complete picture of its supply chain by looking at data from inside and outside the organization
☑ Evaluate supplier performance using a neutral third-party service
☑ Measure suppliers using quantitative metrics based on the actual transactions taking place between parties
☑ Track and reconcile purchase orders, shipments, partial shipments, returns, acknowledgments, invoices, payments, and credits across multiple trading partners.

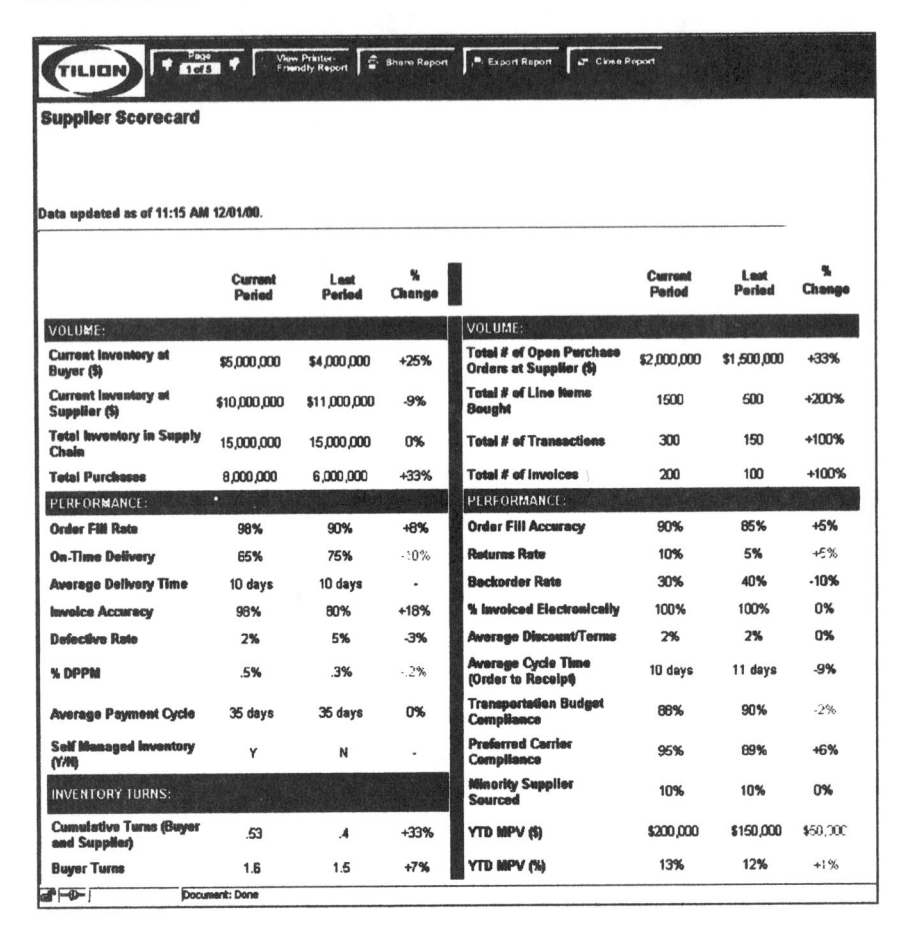

Figure 5. Monitoring Supplier Performance

High-Technology Manufacturer Example

Problem: Optimizing complicated distribution channels.
Goal: Minimizing channel inventories while maintaining availability of products to customers.

In today's world, orders arrive from many sources. Some orders flow through a direct sales force. Other orders arrive by phone, through both company-operated and third-party phone centers. Yet other orders flow through on-line channels: web-based order sites, on-line auctions, group buying services, product exchanges, and EDI. And some orders are immediate, such as

Chapter 13 - Bringing Visibility to the Extended Supply Chain

automatic channel replenishment to maintain agreed upon inventory levels.

Product assembly and delivery have also become more complicated. Some products must still be stocked on retail shelves for immediate delivery to walk-in customers. Product must also be stocked at shipping centers to support overnight shipments through phone and web orders. At the other extreme, some products must be built-to-order and then shipped directly to customers – from both company-operated and subcontractor assembly facilities.

Keeping track of inventory items has become more complicated. Ownership of a memory chip may remain with its supplier until it is incorporated into a specific built-to-order product for a specific customer. A product may change ownership several times as it moves from manufacturer, to distributor, to retailer, and possibly to a secondary market.

Inventory management presents a difficult challenge as manufacturers, their suppliers, and their reseller channel partners strive to meet two contradictory goals:

- ☑ Maintain sufficient inventory to deliver product when and where needed.
- ☑ Minimize write-offs of slow-moving or obsolete items.

At best, it is possible to achieve an optimum balance, where inventories at each location across all distribution channels are held at the lowest possible levels while still allowing customer orders to be filled on-demand. Figure 6 illustrates how in-the-Net analytic services can help meet the challenges of optimizing complicated channel mixes.

In-the-Net analytics can provide the information needed to manage complicated channel mixes and deliver up-to-date information, on-demand, to all of a company's distribution channel partners:

- ☑ Complete, accurate, and timely information allows better prediction of customer buying habits, providing more accurate replenishment of channels. Inventories can be kept low while still ensuring that the right product arrives at the right place as needed to fill customer orders.
- ☑ Slow-moving items can be detected quickly – allowing them to be redirected into more effective channels or allowing production to be cut before inventories build up.

☑ Specific products can be found quickly – across all channels – permitting quicker responses to back orders and special orders.
☑ Open boxes and other returned items can be more quickly directed to receptive secondary markets.

In-the-Net Analytics provide on-demand access to up-to-date transaction data. Manufacturers and channel partners can:
- acquire on-demand visibility to inventory throughout the supply chain
- gain insight into customer buying habits and channel performance
- identify mismatches between production, inventory, demand
- identify slow moving items
- reconcile orders, shipments, and bills across channel partners
- track secondary market demand for older products and open-box merchandise

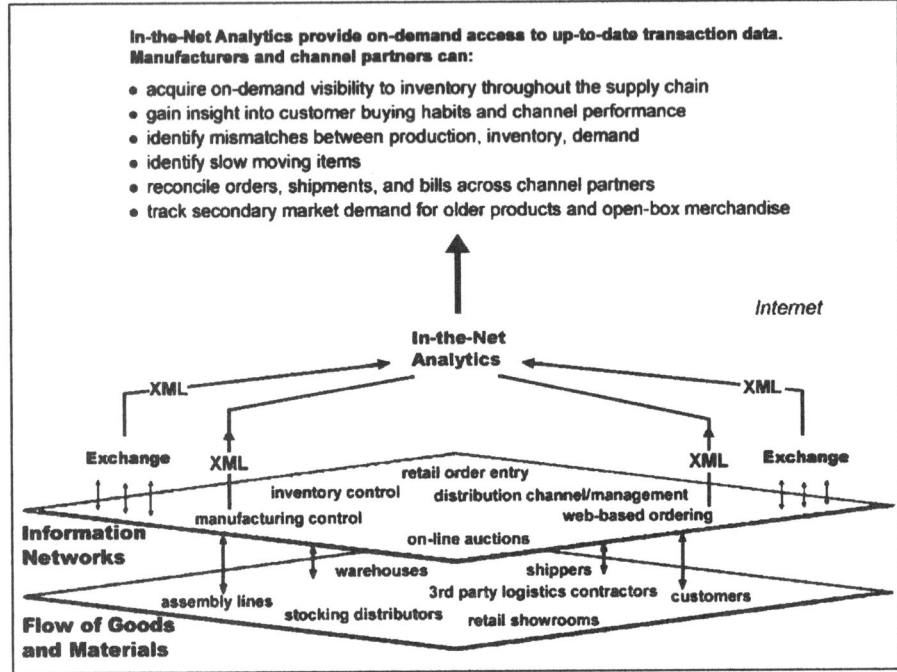

Figure 6. Managing Complex Distribution Channel Mixes

In-the-Net analytics can provide all channel partners with a shared view of commerce metrics – simplifying reconciliation of financial transactions, despite multiple changes of ownership of many inventory items. Analytics help a company optimize the flow of goods through its channels and streamline the flow of information between and among channel partners. In-the-Net analytic also helps a company find alternate sources of supply on short notice.

In-the-Net analytics can assemble supply and vendor data across multiple sources, making it easier to:

☑ Identify immediate sources of supplies to meet critical short-term needs – pulling together supply information from divi-

sions within a business, inventories across the supply chain, shipments in progress, vendors, and materials exchanges.
- Gain visibility to inventory levels at suppliers and contract manufacturers.
- Evaluate a broad spectrum of sources to optimize price, availability, quality, and reliability.
- Track critical market conditions that may influence purchasing decisions such as rises in spot market prices that may suggest locking in a long-term price.
- Create and track mutually agreed upon standards and SLAs for measuring supplier performance.
- Predict aggregate demand across an organization – allowing purchasing departments to buy in larger quantities and negotiate from a stronger position.

Building Contractor Example

Problem: Keeping job sites working while minimizing material costs.

Goal: Making sure that raw materials and components are where they're needed, when they're needed, at the lowest possible cost.

Organizations must constantly adjust their flow of raw materials and component parts – continually making trade-offs among conflicting goals:
- Keeping production moving at optimum efficiency requires a steady flow of raw materials. High inventories reduce the risk of idle people and machines, but they incur carrying costs and the risk of overstocks that must be disposed of later.
- Obtaining the best cost for a raw material requires volume purchases at the risk of over-purchasing.

Erring one way or the other can be extremely costly. In today's "just-in-time" business world, even a small out-of-stock condition of a critical item can have widespread ramifications. A rejected shipment of raw materials can delay receipt of components from a vendor. One delayed truckload of girders can idle a construction crew and its associated heavy machinery.

Complicating matters further is the range of parallel purchasing activities that may be occurring.

Multiple divisions of the same organization – each using their own ERP system – may order the same low-level components. One job site may have a critical out-of-stock condition, while another site may be laden with the needed materials. The organization may be paying a much higher price than necessary because multiple divisions are ordering the same item, in low quantity, from different vendors, or even from the same vendor. In-the-Net analytics can provide the information needed to optimize the flow of materials.

In-the-Net analytics allow companies to determine the entire cycle time for orders –how long it takes for an order to be fulfilled from the moment it is generated and all of the stops that it makes along the way. With this information, a company can:

- ☑ Detect delays in raw material and component shipments before they jeopardize production — giving an organization time to reschedule equipment, reassign construction crews, reroute material transfers, or find alternate sources.
- ☑ Identify changes in material demand in time to increase or decrease orders.
- ☑ Locate overstocked inventories that can be reallocated or discarded.
- ☑ Spot trends – such as increasing shipment delays from a key vendor – before inventories are depleted.
- ☑ Identify unacceptable cycle time delays and work proactively to solve those problems before they cost money.
- ☑ Reduce costs and overhead associated with trying to locate goods in-transit.

Transaction Network Example
Problem: Maintaining a competitive position.
Goal: Adding new capabilities quickly and at low cost.

Transaction networks are quickly emerging as critical intermediaries for networked commerce. Value-added networks (VANs) are rushing to move their operations to the Internet. Meanwhile, a new generation of companies are creating private communities on the Internet where buyers can build a community of suppliers. In addition to speeding up the procurement process, these marketplaces are helping to lower prices and mediate business processes among multiple trading partners.

The growth of these transaction networks has been so rapid that the network-makers have had a difficult time deploying their transactional infrastructures. At the same time, these networks are driven to continually add new functionality and services in order to maintain a competitive position. An in-the-Net analytics infrastructure service can provide a transaction network with an easy means of obtaining supply chain analytics to help the network-maker understand its own market dynamics and to deliver

Chapter 13 - Bringing Visibility to the Extended Supply Chain 249

a new high-value service to its participants. In-the-Net analytics are the next step up the value chain for the transaction network.

A third party analytic service provides a way for a transaction network to offer advanced analytic services to their customers. By installing a small piece of data collection software allows a transaction network to feed XML-translated data to the service provider. The service provider can then produce a variety of analytic reports that the network provider can resell to its participants – providing value to its customers, enhancing its competitive position, and gaining a revenue source. Figure 7 shows some of the ways in which in-the-Net analytic services can help transaction networks deliver new value to their participants.

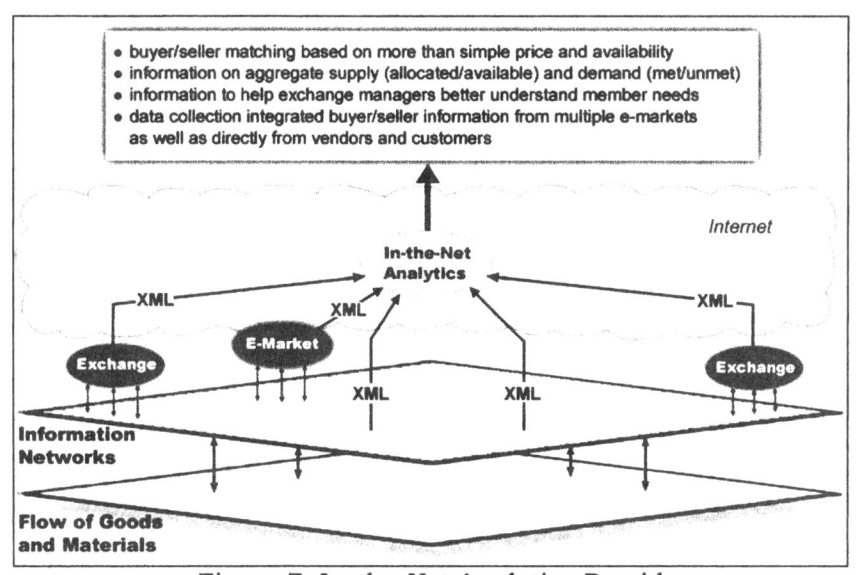

Figure 7. In-the-Net Analytics Provide a
Unified View of Activities in the Transaction Network

Price and availability alone are incomplete metrics for matching buyers with sellers. Quality metrics, ability to meet delivery timetables, and reliability are as important. By forwarding transaction data to an analytics service provider and then reselling those analytics as part of the network services, a transaction network can provide its participants with a variety of enhanced services:

- Buyers can identify vendors who meet a complicated mix of metrics –not just price and availability– including delivery, back orders, return rate, and damage rate.
- Buyers can access aggregated supply-side data – such as the total volume of a specific product that can be sourced via the network for immediate purchase.
- Sellers can access aggregated demand-side data – such as the total demand for a specific product within the network or VAN.
- Sellers can identify themselves to potential clients using metrics that go beyond price and availability.
- Potential network participants can preview the supply and demand characteristics of an network to identify whether or not there is a fit.
- Using the same raw data, in-the-Net analytics can provide network managers with detailed information about how participants are using the network – allowing the managers to fine-tune the service offerings to better meet participants' needs.

Putting It All Together

In-the-Net analytics leverage and enhance existing information networks to provide critical information to the networked economy. In-the-Net analytics meet the emerging need for on-demand insight into complicated supply chains. A trusted third party analytics service can provide an infrastructure for collecting data from multiple companies and systems across the supply chain, analyzing the data, and then distributing analytic reports over the web to complement and extend the capabilities of existing information networks.

With companies today competing on the strength of their supply chain, optimizing the end-to-end supply chain is a strategic business requirement. But a company cannot optimize what it cannot see. Because visibility is the cornerstone of supply chain optimization, companies that want to excel in the networked economy will adopt in-the-Net analytics now.

Appendix A Backgrounder:

Prelude to the Digital Economy: The Dot-Com Crash of 2000

"Any sufficiently advanced technology is indistinguishable from magic."[1] — Arthur C. Clarke.

Irrational Exuberance.

In January, 1999, @Home bought eXcite for $6.7 billion the same month that Ford bought Volvo automotive for $6.5 billion.[2] Meanwhile, Amazon.com's market cap reached $25 billion in December 1998, topping J.C. Penney and Kmart combined — believe it or not. What's really going on here? Arthur C. Clarke, distinguished author of science and fiction including *2001: A Space Odyssey*, says ideas often have three stages of reaction. First, "it's crazy and don't waste my time." Second, "It's possible, but it's not worth doing." And finally, "I've always said it was a good idea." Did everyone finally think that the Internet was a good idea and that it would bring magic to Wall Street?

The Dot-Con Game.

In one his usual insightful columns, "Tech stock boom was a legal con game,"[3] Mercury New's Technology Columnist, Dan Gillmor crisply described what had happened to the e-gold rush. "The technology boom has been called the largest legal creation of wealth in the history of the planet. Maybe so, but that's not the whole story. As the events of 2000 have shown, it's also been the greatest legal con game of all time."

"I stress the word ``legal'' — even though we're likely to learn in coming months and years about significant criminal activity accompanying the tech-stock bubble that began deflating last April."

"The violations of law will be the exceptions. They will only highlight the uglier truth. As commentator Michael Kinsley has pointed out in another context, the real scandal is often what's legal."

"This time, countless investors lost vast amounts of money in technology investments. Yes, they were greedy. They bet stupidly, even blindly, as suckers tend to do when they join a stampeding herd."

"So yes, to some degree, they conned themselves. But they had plenty of help. A daisy chain of entrepreneurs, venture capitalists, Wall Street investment bankers and stock brokerages pulled off something unprecedented. They transferred almost all risk into the public markets."

"The people with the least amount of information were sold the most speculative investments. The sellers were insiders who fully understood the reality."

"In older days, venture capitalists took big risks. They'd invest in start-up companies, hoping to hit an occasional home run to make up for the losers. If a portfolio company did go public or get sold, their payback would be many times the original investment, because they'd have bought in at pennies per share."

"In older days, investment banks looked carefully at companies before taking them into the public markets or selling follow-on offerings, asking about mundane things like reliable earnings. Equity analysts did serious homework on the companies they followed. For about 18 months to two years, everything changed. The Internet mania swept away common sense and old-fashioned ethics."

"At the heart of the mania, as always, were kernels of truth. Technology was plainly changing the economy. Early risk-takers had gotten incredibly rich, and so had some late-comers who had truly great new ideas or who bet on market momentum. Investors wanted a piece of the action. The ones who hadn't joined the stampede began to feel like suckers. That was the most dangerous time."

"I don't know if the venture capitalists and investment banks created the craze, but they definitely fueled it. Hype, not profits, took over. Analysts became little more than shills. No deal was too crazy to make. No company was too speculative to take public. In a market like that, there was almost no risk for the early investors and investment banks. They could sell anything, and they did."

"What this meant, though, was that public investors were now taking the kind of risks that venture capitalists had borne just a few years earlier. Yet the public investors were buying shares that were far more expensive than the VCs were ever willing to touch."

"The journalism profession bears a share of responsibility for the debacle. Journalists served more as stenographers than skeptical observers while technology executives, public-relations people, market "analysts" and other self-serving participants in the con talked up the New Economy and insisted that some fundamental laws of economics had been repealed."

"We celebrated the 21-year-old billionaire of the week. We raved about companies with tiny revenues and no prospect of earnings as the harbinger of a new world, when the newly rediscovered reality was firmly rooted in old truths."

"One headline last year asked, evidently with a straight face, 'Does P/E Matter Anymore?' Think about that. This was asking if earnings mattered. Of course they do. Investors don't put money into enterprises unless they expect to make money at some point. Some companies get sold before they make a dime. Some investors sell their holdings to greater fools. Yet actual profits from running businesses do matter eventually, because they are the basis of business."

"I don't doubt for a second that technology will ultimately lead to massive and, for the most part, positive changes in our economy and society. We're already feeling some of the beneficial impacts. Nor do I doubt that technology-related investments are smart in the long run. What I don't know is whether the current crop of companies, with a few exceptions, will be the long-range survivors in a revolution that is just beginning."

"Capitalism is all about risk and excess. People make money on new ideas, and others follow. Markets get saturated and business cycles turn down. People lose money. Just as a stopped clock is precisely accurate twice a day, markets hit equilibrium briefly on the way up and the way down, because investor sentiment is a blunt instrument. The overall trajectory trends up, but the market oscillates and always will."

"The losers in the debacle of 2000 are part of the capitalist system. So are the winners, who made their money from greater fools. In a world where shame still had meaning, the participants in that cynical gravy chain would contemplate the carnage they helped engineer. They might even hint at regret. I'm not going to hold my breath."

Where did all that loose cash come from, anyway? An unprecedented 49% of American households today own stocks, either directly or through mutual funds and 401(k) plans, compared with just 4% in 1952.[4] Each payday, more and more cash was pumped into public markets. It was automatic, a kind of perpetual motion machine, but that is sure to change.

IT analysts were right there in the middle of the e-hype fray. Not only did they make wild crystal ball projections, once one of these projections hit the streets, they were quoted as "the source" and the truth by all who would anchor their next round of stories in such "facts:" ... "so and so predicts the B2B market to grow to $7 trillion by 2004" and the like.

In one of her usual entertaining and insightful talks to a national convention, Maryfran Johnson, the no-nonsense editor-in-chief of Computerworld described the IT analysts predictions' as ice hockey sticks.[5] Draw a graph, label it as you like (B2C, B2B, e-marketplace, e-whatever), start the growth curve flat and let it jump off the chart.

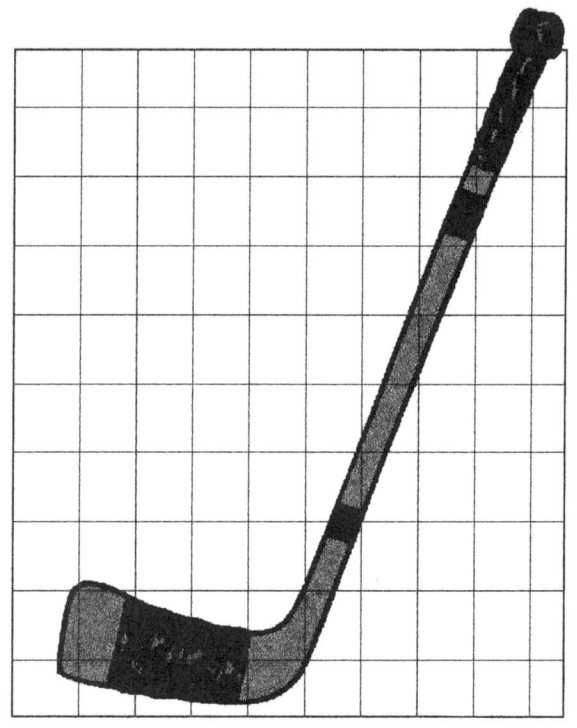

Figure 1. Maryfran Johnson's Depiction
of Analysts' Predictions

The results of what really happened, instead of estimates and predictions, came rolling in as early as January, 2000 when Boston investment banker, T. L. Stebbins, forecast that a stock crash loomed. Stebbins is an "old school" investor who has more than three decades of experience at the Boston investment firm of

Adams, Harkness & Hill. Just as Alan Greenspan had described the irrational exuberance of the stock market, Stebbins described some of his firm's Internet investments as "irrational," based upon nothing more than hype and a desire for quick profits. Stebbins does not buy the idea of a "new investment paradigm" where market soars into the stratosphere. Even without year end hind sight, he foretold of a crash just around the corner to more than 100 attendees at a MIT Enterprise Forum seminar.

"The market is as fragile as I've seen it in 35 years. The end will come with a bang. I think the first quarter will be great for our business, and then everyone should run for the hills."[6] Stebbins nailed it.

In late February, 2000, at an e-commerce boot camp on the New Economy organized by the Round Table Group, Professor Mohan Sawhney, of Northwestern's Kellogg School compared venture capitalists to teenaged girls, "once one has a certain kind of handbag, they all have to have one." He went on to discuss the succession of e-business fads, from portals, to B2C, to B2B. The fads can collapse without warning, he noted, leaving small investors out in the cold. "We saw what happened last fall to all those B2C stocks; B2B's demise is just around the corner. Please do not start a plain-vanilla B2B market maker today," he pleaded back then. "Party's over."[7]

The news reports were widespread starting in April, 2000, after the financial markets had digested the dismal performance of the dot-com e-retailers during Christmas 1999. These virtual "catalog houses without print" had capitalized on the mystique of radical Internet business models, but the financial markets rapidly climbed the learning curve. They did their due diligence and began to ask, "Where's the business beef?"

CNNfN's Staff Writer Catherine Tymkiw filed this exemplary story, "Pets.com, whose sock puppet "spokesman" was popular enough to be sold in toy stores. Eleven months ago, the online retailer spent millions on Super Bowl ads. In November, its revenue paltry, its stock price decimated, Pets.com folded. Like the California Gold Rush of the 1840s or the Dutch Tulip Bulb Craze of the 1600s, the Internet mania showed all the signs of a market bubble. It popped.

(Source: Pets.com)

This was also a year when staid investments became sexy — and sexy turned staid. Sysco (SYY: Research, Estimates), the food distributor, outperformed Cisco Systems (CSCO: Research, Estimates), a kind of proxy for the growth of the Internet. Bonds did better than stocks."[8]

All year, bankruptcies, cash famines and layoffs were announced —for the B2Cs starting in April, followed in short order for the e-procurement B2Bs, and then on to B2B e-marketplaces exemplified by rising star, Ventro. A provider of leading B2B marketplaces, the company dumped two of its highly touted ventures, the Chemdex life sciences and Promedix specialty medical products marketplaces. The company's Board of Directors determined that it was in the best interest of shareholders to shut down both Chemdex and Promedix in an orderly manner. As a result, Chemdex and Promedix initiated significant layoffs beginning December 31, 2000, to be completed no later than March 31, 2001.

As the public markets closed down 2000, mighty B2B and electronic marketplace commerce providers were not immune to reversals. Ariba, which has held up better than its peers, had a 52 week low of $43 a share, down from a high of $183. Commerce One's 52 week low of $18 was down from a high of $165; FreeMarkets' 52 week low of $17 was down from $370; PurchasePro is hovering around $9, down from $87; and VerticalNet is just under $4, down from $148.[9]

Meanwhile, priceline.com stock sat at $1.19 the day after Christmas 2000, down from a peak of $162 in April 1999. Net Perceptions develops software that helps online and offline retailers (such as CDNow, Lowe's, Mattel, Kraft Foods and J.C. Penney) analyze customer data and develop targeted marketing based on customer behavior. The company went public in April 1999 at $14 a share and saw its stock rise toward $60 last winter. Shares closed the day after Christmas 2000 at $1.78.

Dot-coms announced a record 8,789 job cuts in November 2000, a 55 percent increase over October's record total of 5,677 layoffs. It was the sixth consecutive month of increases, according to international outplacement specialists at Challenger, Gray & Christmas. But that's not all. Christmas 2000 pushed the records to new heights, a 19 percent increase or 10,459 workers in December. From January through June, dot-com job cuts totaled 5,097. That figure was six times as high, rising to 36,177, for the period between July and December. This year, 41,515 positions were trimmed from 496 companies. Among the categories, Internet-services companies such as consulting, financial and information-service companies such as Scient (25% layoffs) and Viant

Appendix A - The Dot-Com Crash of 2000

who bill themselves as companies that build digital businesses for the world's leading corporations, led the job cuts with 19,535, followed by retail dot-com companies with 9,523.[10] Even grimmer, 20 percent of the companies in the original survey have gone out of business. This headline provides a glimpse into Internet speed in reverse gear, "How Scient helped Verde.com go from launch to bankruptcy in less than 60 days."[11]

As venture funding and stock market valuations dried up the *New Economy* scoreboard began tallying losers. The following is a sampling of those that have gone out of business:

Toysmart (Disney backed)	Red Rocket
Furniture.com	Living.com
Toytime.com	Babytime.com
Foofoo.com	Digital Entertainment Network
Violet.com	Craftshop.com
Garden.com (throwing in the trowel)	hSupply
StartUpStreet.com	HomeGrocer.com
MotherNature.com (vitamins)	AdMart
Bizbuyer.com (business marketplace)	Babygear.com
Productopia (price-comparison service)	Eve.com (cosmetics and beauty aids)
TheMan.com	Hardware.com
Streamline.com	ShopLink.com
WebHouse Club ($300m burn rate)	SpinRecords.com
Reel.com (video rental, $90m burn rate)	Freei Networks (free Internet service)
Auctions.com	eSeated.com (restaurant reservations)
Gazoontite	FleetScape.com (trucking)
iVendor	Pandesic
UrbanDesign.com	Mylackey.com
Desktop.com	Bid.com
Pets.com	More.com (drug retailer)
Surfbuzz	Epidemic Marketing

Many other Web-related companies that remain in business have announced substantial job cuts to trim their expenses and

260   The Death of "e" and the Birth of the *Real* New Economy

conserve cash. The following is a sampling of the companies that have laid off workers:

Drkoop.com ($19.87 - $.18)	EMusic.com
Salon.com	CBS Internet unit
Oxygen Media	APBnews.com
Kbkids	AltaVista
Skymall	Quepasa.com
Amazon.com ($113 - $14.87)	Petstore.com
Beyond.com ($11.68 - $.12)	PlanetRx ($154 - $1)
FreeRide.com	MyPoints ($98-$1.12)
Net Perceptions ($67 - $1.43)	Razorfish ($57 - $1)
MedicaLogic/Medscape	Learn2.com ($9.50 - $.37)
Stamps.com ($90 - $2)	Drugstore.com ($55 - $.78)
Scient ($134 - $1.81)	Viant ($64 - $2.96)
WebMD (1,100 layoffs)	Kozmo.com

Sources,[12] (numbers in parentheses are 52 week stock highs and lows as of Year End 2000)

Why, there was even a new web site, dotcomfailures.com that not only chronicled what's happening blow by blow, but also advertises "demotivational posters" and Despair, Inc. calendars at thinkgeek.com. Oops, stop the press, dotcomfailures just went belly up![13]

Welcome to the ghost towns of the e-gold rush and the penny stocks of 2001 and beyond. With the NASDAQ down nearly 50 percent at year end from its high in March 2000, the worst annual performance for the index since its inception in 1971, and the first loss in a decade for the Dow Jones, it's no wonder the folks at BankruptcyData.com predicted that 2000 would be a banner year for bankruptcies. The site reports filings from dot-bombs. And for those who fancy dot-bomb tracking, try (www.thecompost.com), Upside.com's Dotcom Graveyard (www.upside. com/graveyard), eCompany Now's Failed Dotcoms, or TheStandard.com's Flop Tracker which keep tabs on new-economy companies that have gone belly-up.

Appendix A - The Dot-Com Crash of 2000 261

Figure 2. Thinkgeek.com's 2001 Calendar

What does all the Y2k dot-bomb news mean? For answers, we turn to Chapter 1 and let the journey begin.

References

[1] http://www.acclarke.co.uk/a6.html
[2] http://cnnfn.com/hotstories/deals/9901/28/deals_wrapup
[3] http://www0.mercurycenter.com/svtech/columns/gillmor/docs/dg121700.htm Copyright © 2000 San Jose Mercury News. All rights reserved. Reproduced with permission. Use of this material does not imply endorsement of the San Jose Mercury News.
[4] This Time It's Different, Time magazine, January 8, 2001 VOL. 157 NO. 1, http://www.time.com/time/magazine/article/0,9171,93322,00.html
[5] Maryfran Johnson, Keynote, AITP National Conference, Tampa, Florida, April 2000.
[6] Investment Banker's Forecast: Stock Crash Looms, http://boston.internet.com/news/article/0,,2001_283401,00.html
[7] Fortune, March 20, 2000, http://www.kellogg.nwu.edu/ext_rel/clipping/000320f.htm
[8] Catherine Tymkiw, Wall St. ends a tough year, CNNfN, December 29, 2000, http://cnnfn.cnn.com/2000/12/29/markets/markets_newyork/
[9] http://qs.cnnfn.cnn.com, stock quote lookups.
[10] http://news.cnet.com/news/0-1007-200-4045861.html, *Data show dot-com job cuts increased during December,* Chicago, December 27, 2000, http://www.msnbc.com/news/508245.asp
[11] http://www.soundbitten.com/verde_c.html
[12] a. Rachel Konrad, *It's been a miserable spring for the new economy,* CNET News.com June 23, 2000.
    b. http://news.cnet.com/news/0-1006-200-4235320.html?tag=st.ne.1002.bgif.ni
    c. cnnfn.com stock quotes.
    d. http://www.upside.com/graveyard
    e. http://cnnfn.cnn.com/2000/11/16/technology/shutdown
[13] Sandra Swanson, "Oh, The Irony: Dotcomfailures.com Bites Dust," *Infoweek,* Septermber 14, 2000. http://www.techweb.com/wire/story/TWB20000914S0010

Appendix B
Backgrounder:

The Pillars of Digital Commerce

"Someday soon you will look into a computer screen and see reality. Some part of your world - the town you live in, the company you work for, your school system, the city hospital - will hang there in a sharp color image, abstract but recognizable, moving subtly in a thousand places. This Mirror World you are looking at is fed by a steady rush of new data pouring in through cables. It is infiltrated by your own software creatures, doing your own business."[1]
—David Gelernter, Department of Computer Science, Yale University.

The Advent of "e"

Imagine being the CEO of Barnes and Noble and picking up the Wall Street Journal in July 1995. Grabbing the phone and calling his CIO, the CEO demands to know, "Who is this Bezos?" Today we know, of course, that it was Jeff Bezos, the CEO and Founder of Amazon.com books, "earth's biggest bookstore." The amazing story of Bezos' virtual bookstore teaches many lessons from the business battlefront of today. Out of nowhere and totally unheard of in the book industry, this digital bookstore turned an industry up-side-down, using blitzkrieg tactics. What happened here was more than creating a web site. An *intelligent and ubiquitous digital business* was conceived and implemented globally. *Its system is its business, its business is its system.*

The company represents a competitive form not seen before on the business landscape and not possible prior to the ubiquitous, interactive communications network, the World Wide Web. Shattering traditional value chains in the book-selling industry, Amazon.com opened thousands of virtual bookstores in its first months of operation. These virtual bookstores are independently operated by people and organizations (Amazon calls them Associates) that create web sites in their specialty fields and seamlessly interoperate with Amazon.com using the Web as the backbone.

The many tasks needed to establish a virtual bookstore are handled digitally. Once established, intelligent software agents notify the virtual bookstore operators and individual customers of new books relevant to their interest. Thousands of activity and sales reports are available on the Internet for Associates to access anytime, any day without a drop of ink. Meanwhile, digital sales clerks gently suggest to customers browsing a particular book that others who have bought the book also bought these other titles - a little reference selling.

Amazon's high-tech site is also high-touch. It delivers more information than the shopper of a real bookstore can find as real shoppers are limited to what's on the limited shelf-space and reviews and comments simply do not exist while perusing a shelf of books.

When it first opened for business and true to the notion of the *virtual corporation,* Amazon.com did not need physical book stores or warehouses - why, they didn't even need books since wholesalers like Ingram were used to fulfill orders. They competed with information and knowledge-based information systems and outsourced the rest of the business to the industry's value chain. Over the initial years, Amazon has refined its business model, understood the long term viability of pure net plays without brick and mortar resources, and added modern warehouses and distribution centers to its asset base. Amazon learned that it would be neither the brick and mortar retailer nor the pure net play e-tailer that would dominate. Instead, it would be the click and mortar corporate form that maintained competitive advantage as the Internet became mainstream in the business world.

While many companies are contemplating the *future* of electronic business, Amazon.com does it *now* and makes it seem easy. But if it's so easy, why isn't every business *just doing it?* Proper recognition of the true nature of the challenge is the foremost obstacle.

Today's forward thinking CEO recognizes the challenge of electronic commerce as a strategic business issue, not just one more technical issue to be delegated to the IS department. Although a company may have reengineered its *internal* business processes over the past decade, and perhaps painfully installed an ERP system to bring efficiencies to the back office, electronic commerce is about reengineering *outward-facing* processes:

- ☑ industry process reengineering versus business process reengineering (IPR Vs BPR),
- ☑ redefining industry boundaries,
- ☑ inventing new industries,
- ☑ repositioning,
- ☑ disintermediation (cannibalizing supply chains), and
- ☑ reintermediation (establishing new marketspaces on the Web).

It's about 1-to-1 marketing, segmenting a single customer instead of segmenting mass markets. It's about outsourcing customer service to the customer himself. It's about relationship marketing and building digital communities. It's about honoring the customer not as king, but as dictator who is but one mouse click away from turning his back on you. This is the stuff with which CEOs, not technologists, must grapple.

The transition to the emerging digital economy will not happen overnight, and there will be many skirmishes, misfires, and changes of direction along the way. Surprise attacks will shake industries, ála Amazon.com's "hello, Barnes and Noble," and E-Trade's "hello, Charles Schwab." Pioneer Electronics did something in May 1998 it had never done before and began selling directly to consumers. Not wanting to alienate its network of 1,200 dealers and 15,000 stores it left out those products they carry, at least for now. Why even risk alienating them? Pioneer had to in response to competitors.

Meanwhile GM is bringing to the Web its response to Auto-by-Tel and Carpoint with consumers going online to configure and price its vehicles without bypassing dealers. Instead the sites will direct customers to the nearest dealer and let the haggling begin. Stories such as these appear with greater frequency as we step across the threshold to the digital economy.

IT departments have a new customer, the marketing department. While traditional IT has been inward facing, handling the affairs of the back office, successful marketing requires outward, customer-facing, real-time, "killer applications." *Information systems had to shift their focus and capabilities from keeping records in the back office to greeting customers in the front lobby!*

Marketing itself has witnessed a shift in focus from the *product* to the *customer.* Customers want products made just for their specific needs. As the Internet gives companies the capability to personalize offerings and shift from mass production to mass customization, marketers must know the needs of their individual customers, not the needs of huge market segments.

Remember the Sears mail order catalog? Sears had information about addresses where it could mail its catalog, but, due to the technology of the time, not the intimate details of its customers' buying behavior. The new capability to harness information technology to drill down below the demographics directly to the behavior of individual customers has far reaching implications for companies that do not want to go the way of the Sears catalog.

The business processes and workflows of commerce are today essentially human phenomena. People are adaptive problem solvers and can deal with new situations "on their feet" and handle incomplete, inconsistent information in real-time, usually making good business decisions based on judgment gained from experience. This is precisely what computers must be empowered to do in digital commerce. Thus the challenge of electronic commerce is to capture the information and knowledge in people's heads and place it in computer systems.

Like people, the computer systems that operate in the digital economy must be knowledge-based, adaptive and continue to learn from experience. Sound like Buck Rogers? Not really. Adaptive, reactive, and reflective task knowledge is the essence of a field of computer science known as distributed artificial intelligence (DAI), popularly known as intelligent agent technology. It is one of the most rapidly advancing computing technologies. When codified into digital software agents, the task knowledge once isolated to a human specialist becomes available to an entire workforce, assisting the customer service representative at the call center, suppliers, trading partners, the salesman in the field and the customer himself with intelligent customer self-service.

The company that masters electronic commerce is the company that will master its industry in the emerging digital economy. Such mastery is not an end game, it is a continuing and unfolding process. *Agility* is the byword of success — an agile business empowered by agile information systems.

Due diligence is in order since the software needed to power digital worlds that mirror the real world are not yet mature, although most of the pieces are available from new and established software companies. Evaluating and partnering with the emerging electronic commerce software vendors should be a top business priority. Distributed architecture, open standards, and the appropriate use of agent technology are the key criteria for selecting commerce vendors, platforms and frameworks.

The Pillars of Digital Business

To understand what we want computers and our software vendors to do for us in the realm of electronic commerce and digital business, we can begin by looking at the real world of commerce. A successful digital business strategy begins with building on the existing market spaces in which a given company operates.

Figure 1 shows the three pillars of electronic commerce that stand on the foundation of an existing market space: electronic information, electronic relationships, and electronic transactions.

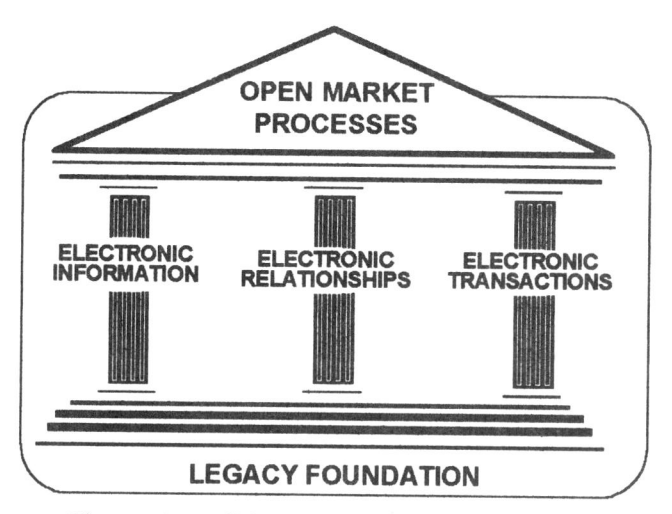

Figure 1. Building the Digital Corporation

The *electronic information* pillar is, at least initially, the easy part. The Web is a global repository of documents and other forms of multimedia. Everyone can be a publisher of information with as little as a HTML enabled word processor, a free file transfer program, and a $19 a month account with an Internet service provider. Product and service information is easily accessed and displayed anywhere, anytime, giving the smallest of businesses a "Web presence." Forrester Research reported that by the end of 1996 about 80% of Fortune 500 had established Web presence compared to 34% in 1995.[2]

Displaying a company's products in an electronic catalog, however, can become complicated quickly. For example, an auto parts store that puts its catalog on the Web, will overwhelm the customer who must navigate the 40,000 or so awkwardly coded part numbers carried by even the smallest of auto parts stores. And that's not all. The customer needs to know if the part is in stock. If not, is the part available from the store's jobbers or wholesale distributors? Is the part available for restocking and, if so, when? Parts are can be substituted, and quite often they are superseded by newer parts.

Existing information must be translated into appropriate formats for the Web: HTML, XML, GIFS, JPEGS, RealAudio and so on. Tools for accomplishing such content publishing can be as simple as FrontPage or Powerpoint. Managing the content is the challenge, often requiring specialized document management and searching software.

Electronic catalogs are major endeavors, especially when the content one company wants to display comes from suppliers using different formats and data as well as in-house content. And, who wants to see an entire catalog? Most customers will only want the parts relevant to them and in the order they wish to view the information.

Catalog management can become quite complex, especially when catalogs are *virtual*, combining information from several sources into a consolidated, normalized catalog that can be extended, inspected, resequenced and subsetted. Making the right information available to the appropriate entities is another issue. Wholesale prices, for example, need to be available to retailers, but not to consumers. Thus catalogs need to know who is looking at them and reveal only authorized information.

Sherif Danish and Patrick Gannon's book, *Building Database-Driven Web Catalogs*, provides an excellent discussion of the sate-of-the-art, and describes the need for Marketing Product Data Management Systems to synchronize engineering, marketing, operations, and ERP systems so that CD-ROM, Web, print and custom catalogs maintain integrity and synchronization. The need for real-time updates to aggregated catalogs along with the need for configurator systems that can build a product on the fly indicate that sophisticated processes, not just data, are essential to web catalogs of the future.

Search engines are of course important, but catalog information, to be effective, should be "pulled" by the customer to match individual preferences. This personalization capability requires profiles, a sensitive subject. Profiling is a hotly debated privacy issue, and to address the issue standards such as the Open Profiling Standard (OPS) are beginning to emerge. Profiling can be intrusive, using those little "Cookies" on the computer's hard drive. Nonintrusive profiling can be accomplished in ways to insure privacy. Click streams can be captured, maintained, and analyzed on the e-commerce host system or "trusted" third party intermediaries can use their software *proxies* to ensure anonymity on the Web — a service sure to be vital to the widespread acceptance of e-commerce.

As this discussion reveals, there is much more to the electronic information pillar of e-commerce than simply publishing content. Dynamic publishing of information can require many tasks and intelligent decisions to be made in real-time. The use of intelligent software agents will be essential to handling these many tasks of creating, maintaining, and delivering content on the Web. And software agents will be needed to allow the user to intelligently navigate and interact with the information glut. While the graphical user interface (GUI) was a boon to personal computing by allowing direct manipulation of objects on the screen, task *delegation* (to software agents) is the next big step needed in user interfaces, helping people filter through the information glut. Further, it is not just people that must interact with electronic catalogs. The computer systems of suppliers, customers and trading partners must as well.

To be successful in e-commerce, a company must master the central pillar, *Electronic Relationships.* Building a site and hanging out a shingle on the Web, does not mean they will come. First and foremost traditional means of customer acquisition such as advertising, promotions and public relations do not go away. Once people are attracted, a Web site must create the "buzz," much like Amazon.com has done in the book selling business. The site must be innovative, add value, provide information and interaction not otherwise available and create forums for opinion-building activities. In short, the site must build *community* and become the "port of entry" for commerce.

Before it went bankrupt for non-Internet reasons (management difficulties), Fruit of the Loom (FOL) understood this concept when it built its ActiveWear e-commerce site and pioneered the notion of coopetition (cooperating with its competition) on the Web. It wanted to become the port of entry in its industry where everyone would come to transact business, tell their stories and display their wares.

FOL positioned itself as the preeminent cybermediary by using its e-commerce systems to not only host its own site, but to provide its expertise, software and hosting to its distribution chain. Even the smallest mom-n-pop FOL distributor could have a sophisticated site with all three pillars of e-commerce, thanks to FOL, without having to acquire hardware, ISP services or software. And the distributors were not restricted to handling FOL products only. Customers could buy Hanes underwear from these distributors using the complete facilities of FOL. FOL exemplifies the business nature of e-commerce issues. Industry *positioning* was a well thought digital strategy developed by business executives, not programmers.

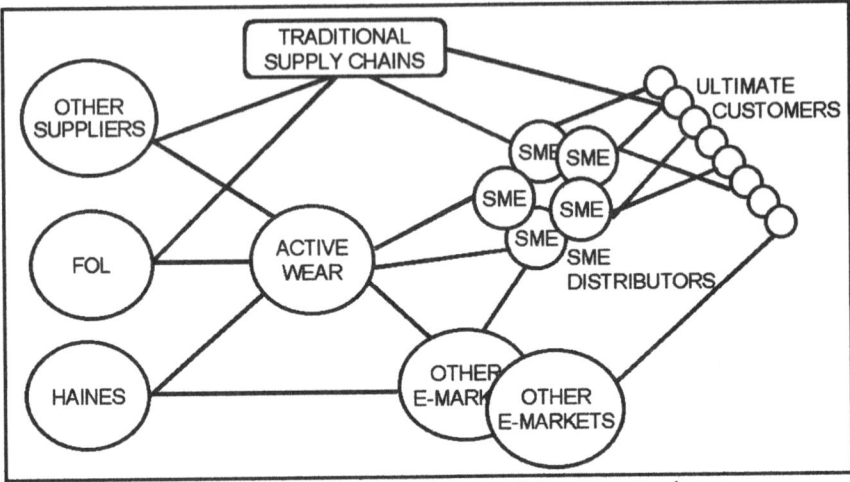

Figure 2. Market Positioning and Restructuring Using the Internet

A business-to-consumer Web site must not only get customers to come, it must get them to come back, and come back regularly because it is so important to them. This "stickiness" is the essence of e-commerce. Unlike the mass media of print and broadcasting, the Web is an interactive medium. Interactive tools for building electronic relationships can be a simple as opt-in email. More advanced tools include list servers, news groups, bulletin boards, chat rooms, and in the future, virtual spaces may become commonplace such as those developed by ActiveWorlds.

Two choices are available for determining customer interest: having the customer provide profile information or having the system analyze a user's activity trails through a Web site. Such profiling processes can allow personalization and information filtering. Collaborative information filtering can be used to connect people with similar interests, can enable opinion making and, using advanced techniques such as artificial neural networks, uncover *tacit* information.

Analysis of consumer buying behavior will become increasingly important as 1-to-1 marketing gains momentum on the Web and as autonomous software agents offer the potential to intelligently mine for buying patterns from vast pools of customer information. Intelligent agents are a natural for customer data mining and can help to avoid the market researcher's computer "query from hell" as well as uncover patterns humans would likely miss.

While data mining provides an opportunity for reflective, usually off-line, analysis of buying behavior, real-time profiling is essential as well. Forgetting about the Web for a moment, companies such as Catalina Marketing allow the supermarket clerk to print coupon offers directly targeted to the customer at the checkout lane, in real-time, at the point of sale based on the current shopping basket. Such pinpoint profiling accuracy in real-time is the key to marketing, adding value to individual customers, and cross-selling. Building customer relationships depends on both deep analyses of historical customer information and up-to-the-second real-time data — the winning combination for e-commerce.

Customer relationship management (CRM) is not just computer based. In fact the most important medium for CRM is today's call center, and companies that operate call centers should look to the knowledge and experience they have gained with this function to serve as the foundation for building electronic relationships. The integration of traditional call centers and Web-based customer service is inevitable. The two technologies will be integrated via Computer Telephony Integration (CTI) using IP telephony, integrating these customer "touch points." Such moves are essential to e-business customization strategies and provide an evolutionary path for users of such hybrid systems. Companies embracing the Web for CRM should include their call center team as cornerstone players in their initiatives.

The capability to handle *Electronic Transactions* is the third and least mature pillar of e-commerce. Perceived and real obstacles have to be overcome before electronic transactions become a widespread means of consummating binding contracts and making payments. Back to the Forrester report mentioned above, only 5% of the Fortune 500 companies with Web presence handle transactions on the Web in 1996. The major barriers include security on the Internet, lack of accepted standards for authentication and payments, non-repudiation, and general fear and uncertainty by consumers. Several commercial standards and offerings have already appeared including Secure Electronic Transactions (SET) for credit cards.

Business-to-business incarnations of electronic commerce have grown more rapidly than business-to-consumer forms, in part due to the widespread use of traditional Electronic Data Interchange (EDI) in large corporations. Currently, most electronic commerce transactions such as retailer to consumer are simple: browse a catalog and make a selection, then make a payment using a credit card. This kind of "see-buy-get" transaction in no way is reflective of the complex and nested transactions of real commerce.

Transactions in the real business world are often long lived propositions involving negotiations, commitments, contracts, floating exchange rates, shipping and logistics, tracking, varied payment instruments, exception handling and termination or satisfaction.

Commercial transactions have two phases, *construction* (information collection involving catalogues and brokerage systems to locate sources; agreement leading to terms and conditions through negotiation mechanisms; and engagement resulting in the "signed contract") and *execution* (configuration involving deployment across the group of participants in the transaction; service execution in context of the higher level contract and management of exceptions; and termination involving validation and closing the contract across all participants). Termination may be very long lived as contracts may include ongoing service agreements with online customer service delivery and other aspects of overall customer relationship management. In the world of digital commerce, traditional transactions are replaced with long lived, multi-level collaborations.

In a joint white paper of the Object Management Group and CommerceNet, Gabriel Gross, President of Centre Internet Europeen, summarized the current state of electronic commerce applications as "mainly limited to two functionalities: cataloging on one side and payment facilities on the other side. The [current] electronic commerce world is in practice a lot less sophisticated than real world commerce where several levels of interaction can take place between a potential client and vendor, and several levels of intermediaries can act or interfere."[3]

What happens when e-commerce matures to reflect the real and complex world of multi-seller, multi-buyer commerce? The real world of e-commerce will require building digital simulations of real world open markets. As shown in Figure 1, *Open Market Processes* provide the capstone for an enterprise wanting to build information systems capable of participating in the emerging digital economy. Such an open market is illustrated in Figure 3. Gross explains, "... an open electronic market infrastructure will act as the foundation of an ecosystem where *actors* will be able to join in and play the roles they want. The roles of the individual actor will depend on the situations, on the other actors he is faced with, or on his motivations of the moment."

Figure 3. Open Digital Markets

A given actor may play *multiple, simultaneous, and dynamic roles*: customer (the one who pays), consumer (the one who receives), merchant (the one who gets paid), and provider (the one who delivers). And there is more to these basic roles when considering the roles of broker, aggregator, referral service and other forms of intermediation along with the supporting roles of the banker, credit card provider, shipper, insurer and other third parties.

Open market processes require interoperation of computer applications and consistent protocols and formats for information interchange. The complexity of building such "virtual commerce places" mandates a distributed computing paradigm based on *standards* if there is to be any hope of interoperability.

Without consistent business semantics, processes and workflows cannot be shared across multiple, distributed, and disparate businesses. Sound complicated? It is.

Standards must address two facets, standard data definitions and standard task knowledge. The eXtensible Markup Language (XML) will likely revolutionize the data aspect and is discussed further in Chapter 6.

The *task* knowledge needed for such inter-enterprise activity (adaptive business processes and workflows) overwhelms today's software paradigms. The use of intelligent agent technology which is based on task level knowledge and knowledge sharing standards such as a simplified version of the Knowledge Interchange Format (KIF) will be essential to the future of open digital markets. Collaborative multi-agent systems are central to building open, digital commerce places as illustrated in Figure 3. The figure shows several enterprises convening around a commerce transaction and shows the multiple simultaneous roles of Enterprise A (for example, as a merchant and provider).

Trading process models being developed for electronic commerce are fundamentally the same as traditional commerce processes. Core processes include pre-sales and sourcing, order placement, supply chain management, settlement and post-sales support. *Coordination* of these processes is essential and pioneers in developing open markets turn to coordination theory such as that being researched at MIT's Sloan School under the direction of Dr. Thomas Malone. Coordination is also at the heart of designing and building multi-agent systems. The collaborative working arrangements and processes of today's real commerce will eventually be simulated in the knowledge-based software of open digital commerce.

Tilburg University's Infolab summarizes the complexity of doing real commerce electronically, "Although e-commerce aims at supporting the complete external business process, including the information stage (electronic marketing, networking), the negotiation stage (electronic markets), the fulfillment (order process, electronic payment), and the satisfaction stage (after sales support), currently, e-commerce is hampered by:
- ☑ closed (self-contained) markets that cannot use each other's services
- ☑ incompatible frameworks that cannot interoperate or build upon each other
- ☑ a bewildering collection of security and payment protocols

☑ use of inadequate techniques to model business requirements and enterprise policies."⁴

Strategy must recognize and navigate the many pitfalls and obstacles. Companies cannot, however, wait until the ultimate commerce systems are in place. Instead, they must act now to harness the current best of breed technologies, and evolve increasingly robust business models as the technologies evolve.

What Electronic Commerce Really Is

According to the Association for Electronic Commerce, a simple definition of e-commerce is "doing business electronically.⁵" Sound fuzzy and ill-defined? It is. According to this definition, using the telephone to conduct business is e-commerce. In large corporations e-commerce is often equated to electronic data interchange (EDI) where structured messages representing standard business forms are exchanged over private networks.

In everyday usage the terms Internet commerce or I-commerce, Web-commerce, digital commerce and e-business are often interchanged with e-commerce, sometimes leading to academic arguments. In his article, "E-commerce? E-business? Who E-cares?" Walid Mougayar, the founding chairman of CommerceNet Canada explains, "In a nasty little intramural squabble, some analysts and online businesspeople have decided that E-business is infinitely superior as a moniker to E-commerce. That's misleading and distracts us from the business goals at hand. The effort to separate the E-commerce and E-business concepts appears to have been driven by marketing motives [IBM circa 1996] and is dreadfully thin in substance. Here's the important thing: E-commerce, E-business or whatever else you may want to call it is a means to an end. The objectives, as with IT, are to improve or exploit unique business propositions — with the focus now being the online world. Worrying about the definitions of those words, or about which is superior to the other, or about which is a subset of the other, is a silly little inside-the-beltway argument.⁶"

So, depending on who is asked, e-commerce will have a wide variety of definitions and even differing names. This may not be such a not bad thing, because vague definitions and various names help to keep our thinking open.

The industry consortium, CommerceNet, provides sharper focus with their definition, "E-commerce is the use of internetworked computers to create and transform business relationships.⁷" CommerceNet elaborates, "It is most commonly associated with buying and selling information, products, and services via the Internet, but it is also used to transfer and share information within organizations through intranets to improve decision-making and eliminate duplication of effort. The new paradigm of e-commerce is built not just on transactions but on building, sustaining and improving relationships, both existing and potential."

Regardless of the e-label, the Internet provides an infrastructure for extending a company's inward-focused, unique business processes to customers, trade partners, suppliers and distributors with new, outward-facing applications. The interconnections make it possible to do things in ways not previously possible by eliminating time and distance. More importantly, and unlike the telephone and fax, *the Internet connects people and computers not only with each other, but also with the information base with which they work.*

Opportunities and challenges permeate the enterprise affecting R&D, engineering, manufacturing and production, supply chains, marketing, sales, and customer care. Because it reaches directly into these core business processes that are the lifeblood of the enterprise, digital commerce is a mission-critical business issue. *Because the Internet provides real-time connections on both the supply and demand sides of a company, nothing less than a digital enterprise will be able to thrive in the digital economy.*

From this perspective, it becomes clear that digital commerce is not something a corporation can just go out and buy. Neither is it based on speculation, but rather on the experience of a growing number of companies that already are using the Internet to streamline their business processes, procure materials, sell their products, automate customer service and create new wealth. The Internet is turning industries upside down and forcing enterprises to refocus their information systems from the inside out.

The Importance of the Business Model

Simply "porting" a brick and mortar business model to the Internet will most likely fail. What's needed is a recognition of how the Internet can change the customer experience, and that change is not always appropriate —the Internet does not always change the basic value proposition. For example, the retail trades distinguished between convenience and specialty goods. Convenience goods are the basics of life —groceries, banking, and other commodities that people want to acquire while spending the least amount of time and effort. Specialty goods, on the other hand, are highly valued and only complete information will satisfy the consumer in making these infrequent, but more highly valued buying decisions. The distinction between convenience and specialty buying does not go away with the advent of the Internet. In the process of buying aspirin and buying prescription drugs, the activities are essentially different — the commodity versus the specialty good.

And, even with, let's say, a book selling scenario, if the Internet is to make a difference, the online store must offer more features and functionality to delight customers, or customers will go to their nearest brick and mortar bookstore with its expensive designer coffees and relaxing reading areas. Selling prescription drugs on the Net had better offer the consumer something better than the bulk buying programs that are already automated. Express Scripts, Merck-Medco, PCS and giant pharmacy benefit managers (PBM's) dominate the bulk prescriptions business. Watch out PlanetRX and Drugstore.com.

As reported in "After the Gold Rush," "Rather than join up with some new Internet enterprise, those PBM's decided to 'go it alone" on the Web, convinced that what mattered was not what a customer sees on a computer screen but "the complicated processes behind the screen — processes that Merck-Medco had already perfected. While Drugstore.com thought the Internet would be 'disruptive' to Merck-Medco and others, it was actually 'sustaining' in that it enhanced the older company's competitiveness. Drugstore.com's second mistake was cramming. If you look at Drugstore.com you will find the same products you would find at a regular drugstore —the same model as a terrestrial drugstore, but they have moved it online. Contrast this, the study suggests, with uncrammed Reflect.com. It enables the customer to customize their own brand of personal care products. It provides customers with an experience that is unique to the Internet. It permits customers to do things for themselves that only a cosmetician could do for them in the past. The customer is always asking: 'Is the new way better than the old way?' It rarely is." [8]

Just because we can do something on the Internet does not mean that that something will work. Quality and convenience still count as sustainable differentiators. Customers know the difference. Only the hyper-efficient and hyper-effective business models will win in the digital world of business.

References

[1] Gelernter, David, *Mirror Worlds: or the Day Software Puts the Universe in a Shoebox...*, Oxford University Press (1991).
[2] Economist, May 10, 1997
[3] Stephen McConnell, Editor, *The OMG/CommerceNet Joint Electronic Commerce White Paper*, July 27, 1997.
[4] http://infolab.kub.nl/general/e-commerce.php3
[5] http://www.eca.org.uk/
[6] Walid Mougayar, "E-commerce? E-business? Who E-cares?" *Computerworld*, 11/02/98.
[7] http://www.commerce.net/resources/pw/chap1-9/pg2.html
[8] http://www.washingtonpost.com/wp-dyn/articles/A21863-2001Jan20.html

Appendix C
Backgrounder:

Business Fundamentals for the 21st Century

Business Fundamentals for the 21st Century

How do business fundamentals change when the whole world can share a common information system? How will these fundamentals shape the transitions to the digital economy?

As the business world emegres from the euphoria and then crash of the dot-com craze, industry analysts and pundits have already changed their slogans and acronyms —from, B2C to P2P (path-to-profitability) and from time-to-market to time-to-reason. The past four or five years will be characterized by business historians as "Euphoria, Alarm and Reason."

As the Internet continues its climb into the mainstream of business it will impact business fundamentals in many ways. When it becomes possible to connect any-to-any and all-to-all, some interesting things start to happen.

Kevin Kelly, founding editor of *Wired* magazine, has defined a new law for the value of relationships in the digital economy. Kelly concludes that the value of the Internet increases faster than Bob Metcalfe's formula of n^2, where n is the number of people connected. Metcalfe's law is based on single-point connections between two people. The Internet enables multiple simultaneous connections among customers, suppliers and trading partners, making the value of relationships not just n^2, but n^n.[1] Kelly's law and the following new fundamentals of the digital economy provide a starting point for mastery in 21st century business:

1. The Customer Becomes a Dictator
2. Mass Customization Supercedes Mass Production
3: Business Becomes Ubiquitous
4. Relationship Management Becomes Holistic
5. Customers and Trading Partners Become Virtual Employees
6: Digital Corporations Achieve Hyper-efficiency
7. Only the Transactions of the Economy Move to the Net
8. Competition Becomes Value Chain Versus Value Chain
9. Digital Markets, the New Middlemen, Reduce Friction
10. Operational Requirements Become 7x24
11. Cycle-Times are Slashed
12. Branding Still Counts
13. Pricing Becomes Dynamic
14. Inter-Organization Design is a Really Big Challenge
15. A New Kind of Software Powers the Digital Corporation

1. The Customer Becomes a Dictator.

Information is power. Authoritarian societies rely on one-way, hierarchical information flows, where information flows down, from one-to-many. Democracies rely on matrixed forms of communication that provide many-to-many information flows.

Up until the introduction of the Internet in industrial societies, information flowed in one direction, from the producer to customers in a one-to-many fashion. The Internet, on the other hand, provides many-to-many connections among customers. The Internet turns the producer-consumer relationship upside-down with the balance of power going to the customer, laying the foundation for the Customer Age.

What is the first thing that most people do when contemplating a major purchase such as a new car or computer? They start asking around. They contact their friends and colleagues who have relevant experience and information. With the Internet, they can ask the whole world.

A fully informed consumer is one of the basic tenets of pure competition, and the Internet makes it practical to obtain and share information in ways never before possible. Knowledge is power, and the Internet has created a more fully informed customer who, in turn, has wrested power from producers. In recognition of this fundamental shift, marketing expert Regis McKenna explains, "It's about giving customers what they want, when, where, and how they want it.[2]"

A hallmark of the industrial age is that manufacturers mass produce goods and push them to market, controlling information about their products through the mass media with advertising and public relations. This form of commerce is called supply-push. The Internet flips the coin to demand-pull. And the more information customers gain, the more demanding they become. Caveat Venditor (seller beware).

2. Mass Customization Supercedes Mass Production.

As control of markets and economies shifts from the producer to the consumer, companies must use the interactive capabilities of the Internet to customize their offerings, one customer at a time. Build-to-order is the secret of Dell Computer's success.

When a company interacts electronically with customers, buying behavior can be analyzed so that the company can customize its product and service offerings to the individual customer. This is the essence of the one-to-one marketing revolution.

Customization provides value to customers by allowing them to find solutions that better fit their needs and by saving them time in searching for their solutions. Personalization is a cornerstone for building a customer-driven company. The Internet allows a company to greatly enhance the buying experience through value added services such as collaboration, building communities-of-interest, and multimedia renderings of complex product information. Providing a personalized, enhanced buying experience is essential to any future business strategy.

3. Business Becomes Ubiquitous.
The railroad, the automobile and the Interstate highway system all changed the business landscape and the economy. Now, the Internet changes "what we do," and "where we do it."

On the Internet a company can conduct business everywhere, all the time. The Internet can eliminate the barriers of time and location in operating a business.

Not only can the Internet make company information available worldwide, it can distribute an enterprise's business rules and processes in real-time. All the information, business processes and control needed to transact business can flow friction-free anywhere, anytime to customers, suppliers and trading partners. The Internet enables a multitude of connections between customers, suppliers and trading partners: process-to-process connections between servers, browser-server connections and a growing number of network-savvy information appliances that can plug-and-play on the Internet (e.g. cell phones, pagers, palm tops, WebTV, fax) – all the current and future business touch points.

4. Relationship Management Becomes Holistic.
Customers and suppliers interact with a company through many media: email, fax, telephone and computer-to-computer communication. These same touch points equate to new sources of customer information. Increasingly rich customer information, in turn, allows a company to analyze customer buying behavior and customize its offerings to individual customers.

More importantly, a holistic approach to relationship management can optimize the lifetime value of each customer. It's not the individual sale of a product to a customer that matters. With the cost of new customer acquisition, no customer is more important than an existing customer, and the lifetime value of each customer must be carefully managed. That requires a complete view of all customer interactions, including sales transactions in the marketing department and complaints received by the call center. Daily, weekly and quarterly sales statistics were the key to mass marketing; tacit information regarding the overall company experience by each customer is key to mass customization. The Internet provides a powerful new tool to return to the more intimate relationship of the mom and pop grocery or hardware store down the street in days past.

In the past, with a few exceptions such as the insurance giant USAA, each form of customer communication remained with the department that handled that form of communication: the call center handling telephone inquiries or the mail center handling postal mail. When a letter reaches USAA in its San Antonio or Tampa offices, it doesn't go past the mail room. Instead it is scanned and incorporated into a shared information base available to any employee that interacts with the customer in the future. By capturing customer interactions and coding them as bits, a complete view of the customer replaces the fragmented view available in most companies. Further, access is made available to the mobile workforce regardless of device or location. The USAA agent has access to complete information at the scene of an accident or standing in the aftermath of a hurricane.

The Internet introduces yet another and most powerful touch point. Customers will no longer tolerate being bounced between department to department or being trapped in a touch tone maze trying to interact with a company. Integrating all customer touch points to obtain and maintain a complete view of each customer is the key to maximizing the lifetime value of customers.

5. Customers and Trading Partners Become Virtual Employees.

The Internet can provide double leverage when it comes to perhaps the most critical business function, customer service. By implementing a self-service paradigm, the costs of customer service can be cut dramatically while increasing the quality of customer care.

Today's reality is often a frustrated user who must navigate call center menus that lead to intolerable on-holds or, finally, a human who abruptly tells the customer to call another number in another department. Automating customer service through a single enterprise access point or portal can put the customer in control of navigating the company's service resources.

While giving the customer greater control, labor costs can be slashed since the number of customer service representatives can be reduced as a result of outsourcing customer service to the customers themselves. Or, more likely, customer service representatives can use their time making out-bound marketing and customer satisfaction calls.

Just as it is with gasoline stations today, an increasing number of customers will go to the self-service lane on the information highway. Self-service allows the customer to do for themselves, potentially yielding greater satisfaction and reduced cost.

And it's not just after the sale that customers can be put to work as employees, in this case, doing the work of the sales engineer or representative. Automated tools can assist the customer in the buying process: calculating monthly payments or configuring a custom PC.

Chat rooms and discussion groups can afford the opportunity for customers to share their product or service experiences with others during either buying or service activities. A potential buyer can learn from the experience of others who have been interested in, bought, and used a particular product or service.

These interactive capabilities are especially useful for buying specialty goods where purchasing decisions have many dimensions and involve multi-step processes. By providing calculation, configuration and collaboration tools, a company can create communities-of-interest where consumers go first to become informed about purchasing decisions and seek help in using a product.

In business-to-business markets, product configurators, computer-aided design (CAD) systems, and collaborative problem-solving tools can bring dramatic productivity increases to the design, development, and procurement of complex products and services. Large-scale and complex projects can be transformed by sharing product specifications, bills-of-material and production schedules across many suppliers and trading partners in real-time. As bandwidth increases, the use of virtual reality technologies will no doubt be used to further enhance both consumer and business buying experiences and after sale support.

Companies that recognize the self-service paradigm will gain significant competitive advantage. They will put their customers and suppliers to work as virtual employees.

6. Digital Corporations Achieve Hyper-efficiency.

Physical inventories have always been a major cost component of business. The classic goal of inventory "turn" can be dramatically enhanced by linking to suppliers in real-time. In his new book *Direct from Dell: Strategies That Revolutionized an Industry*, Michael Dell explains, "Inventory velocity has become a passion for us. In 1993, we had $2.9 billion in sales and $220 million in inventory. Four years later, we posted $12.3 billion in sales and had inventory of $233 million. We're now down to less than eight days of inventory and we're starting to measure it in hours instead of days."[3]

The Internet provides a multitude of opportunities for radically reducing the costs of designing, manufacturing, and selling goods and services. A company must take advantage of these opportunities or find itself at a significant competitive disadvantage.

Over the last decade, business process reengineering (BPR) led to new levels of internal efficiencies in Global 2000 corporations. Around the globe, companies networked their internal computers to eliminate duplicate business processes and paper handling. Companies must take their reengineering efforts to the next level by encompassing what is external as well as their internal operations. They must extend their supply chain management systems and optimize their operating resources using the Internet. Competing against hyper-efficient companies and supply chains enabled by the Internet will become increasingly difficult.

7. Only the Transactions of the Economy Move to the Net.

Except for purely digital products like software, information and music, logistics and physical distribution remain as the other side of the digital commerce coin. Dennis Jones, VP and CIO of FedEx explains, "What often gets lost in discussions about Internet commerce and the digital economy is the physical aspect of doing business. The Internet has engendered a feeling that anyone can start up a Web site to sell widgets, and instantly they're worldwide marketers. To succeed in Internet commerce, we believe a company has to be as effective in the physical world as they are in the electronic arena. The ability to move information around the world at the speed of light is a great enabler of commerce, but it breeds a corresponding need for the physical goods. The information network needs a physical network."[4]

8. Competition Becomes Value Chain Versus Value Chain.

Because the Internet gives the customer greater visibility to supplier information, it's not just your company anymore. As markets become more and more transparent, customers can find and get the total solutions they seek: the right set of products and support services delivered at the right price, time and place.

Customers in both business and consumer markets want complete solutions. For example, buying a home requires many ancillary resources such as a mortgage, title and property insurance and appraisals. By aggregating many and diverse resources in a complete value chain around a complete solution, companies can gain significant competitive advantage. But they must change their thinking from the products and services they now provide, and focus on the bundles of solutions their customers need to fulfill their requirements – a plane ticket is not a vacation.

In the digital economy, where total customer solutions are demanded, it's not Sears competing against J. C. Penney, it's Sears' value chain competing against J. C. Penney's value chain. It's Home Depot's value chain competing against Lowe's value chain. The customer-driven value chain is paramount in determining the winners and losers in the digital economy.

9. Digital Markets, the New Middlemen, Reduce Friction.

Contrary to all the talk of disintermediation, middlemen are not dead in cyberspace. Middlemen have always added value in distribution channels providing warehousing, logistics, shipping and other economically valuable services. But traditional brick and mortar middlemen cannot rest on their laurels. To succeed in the digital economy, they must add new value through providing information and aggregating services not previously available. Companies such as the huge PC wholesaler, Tech Data, were early adopters of the Internet and played a leadership role in setting new standards and processes for their industry by becoming a founding board member of RosettaNet in 1998.

RosettaNet is a non-profit consortium of major information technology, electronic components and semiconductor companies working to adopt common business processes to advance IT supply chain interaction worldwide. These standards form a common e-business language (the organization's name was adopted from the ancient Rosetta stone), aligning processes between supply chain partners on a global basis.

When brick and mortar Tech Data joined RosettaNet in 1998, the Fortune 500 company generated sales of $7.1 billion. By the end of 2000 the click and mortar middleman had generated sales of $17 billion and reported record earnings. Rather than be disintermediated, Tech Data harnessed the Internet to become a super-intermediary.

On the other hand, when intermediaries do not truly add value, demanding customers will eliminate them. For example, American Airlines' Travelocity was originally designed so that travel agents would still add value by being the means of delivering the ticket. Consumers who represent the travel community perceived little value in this arrangement, and the travel agent was disintermediated from the consumption process.

Cybermediation is critical in business-to-business markets. With the diversity of industrial and business goods and services, searching for the right vendor with the right product specifications and ancillary supporting services can be a daunting task. Including pure net plays such as the recently established electronic marketplaces and B2B exchanges, the intermediary that can bring together diverse suppliers and customers and provide them with information unavailable elsewhere will win the middleman game of the digital economy. GE's Trading Process Network (TPN) is an early pioneer in this marketspace and, like its competitors, must keep running hard to stay ahead of the game of adding compelling value and growing business-to-business communities.

10. Operational Requirements Become 7x24.

It's no longer 9-to-5. Doing business on the Internet means 7x24x365 operations and no holidays. Because the Internet can make a company ubiquitous, digital commerce must follow the sun, greeting markets as they arise each day in Tokyo, then Hong Kong, and later in Riyadh and Johannesburg, then London, New York and on to San Francisco.

The good news is that a digital workforce labors around the clock without demanding overtime pay. The sobering news is that Internet-based systems require availability and reliability that can be achieved only through much effort and investment.

Not only must an e-Commerce system be technically reliable, it must also be dynamically scalable so that it can withstand the onslaughts of traffic that are frequently associated with breaking news and product announcements. Even without a stampede, speed is important. In a report released in July, 1999, Zona Research reveals that "Slow download times at online shopping sites could place at risk as much as $4.35 billion in U.S. e-commerce revenues each year. Analysts estimated that online shoppers would wait up to 8 seconds for a site to download. The sales risk crosses all types of sites. For example, an estimated $3 million may be lost monthly due to slow securities-trading sites.[5]" The effect of slowdowns is multiplied many fold when real-time business-to-business traffic is taken into account.

Researchers at MIT responded to the availability and reliability challenge and started Akamai Technologies. Through advanced network management technologies, Akamai optimizes performance, delivers broadcast-caliber streaming media, and provides interactive application services for content providers the likes of Yahoo!, CNN Interactive, and Apple Computer. In short, Akamai eliminates Web congestion by transforming the Internet from an inconsistent transport medium into a high-performing network.

The non-stop, mission-critical nature of e-commerce demands non-stop systems and network assets. Redundancy, scalability and fail safe must be built into all components of e-commerce systems and the platforms on which they run.

11. Cycle-Times are Slashed.

In some cases, lag time from product development to market availability can be reduced to near zero. In fact, Microsoft and other software manufacturers reach their markets prior to complete product development. Customers use their products before they are actually released. Beta versions of software products are downloaded free by customers. The result is that the customer actually becomes involved in product development. Because people prefer what they already know, the customer gets hooked on the Beta version of a product, and it takes just one micro-step to convert Beta users to paying customers. Time-to-market is no longer a competitive advantage; it is a competitive necessity. Through collaborative product development and knowledge sharing, cycle-times can and must be successfully managed.

But speed is not everything. Many dollars were thrown at dot-com startups whose primary competitive advantage was that of first mover. The lessons learned from the crash of the dot-coms include that speed is not everything. Without the ability to perform, speed means first to crash and burn. The "revenge of the BAM's" has seen traditional "brick and mortar" (BAM) companies scream past their upstart dot-com competitors. While the dot-coms were faster, the BAM's could actually deliver as they came on stream in digital markets.

The ability to sense and respond with a solid value chain is the key to success. The ability to deliver and to change in response to market realities is what counts. The ability to change is now more important than being first.

12. Branding Still Counts.

The notion of "branding" is a cornerstone of business. Consumers turn to brand names and often pay a premium in so doing. Why? It's because of trust. Trust is built over time with consistency, quality and service.

When shopping for a computer on the Internet, cost may be the foremost requirement. But if the best price is offered by John Doe's Computer Shop, the consumer may hesitate before entering a credit card number. Although John Doe's Computer Shop may use the same secure credit card server as CompUSA or Best Buy, the consumer may take the price hit to go with a trusted brand name.

New entrants into digital markets can build a brand in cyberspace as did Amazon, but brand acceptance and loyalty must be earned over time. A first mover had better be the most convenient, cost-effective, informative, simple, secure and reliable resource available. These are the ingredients of building loyalty and ultimate trust that result in successful branding.

Word travels instantly through electronic communities and reputations can be made or destroyed with the click of a mouse. Without strong branding, a given company will likely be reduced to a commodity provider, competing with ever shrinking price points and margins.

Because branding on the Internet is as essential as branding in the traditional business world, established brick and mortar companies have significant advantage. They bring an established brand to the table.

13. Pricing Becomes Dynamic.

When time is eliminated in the supply and demand equation, pricing dynamics change radically. Whether dealing in commodities or premium brands, in either business-to-consumer or business-to-business marketspaces, pricing policy is a core part of business strategy. Pricing strategies must adapt to the realities of

Internet market mechanisms which are becoming increasingly real-time and global.

Fixed pricing is a relatively new concept in the world of commerce. Ancient markets certainly had no price labels on their products or shelves. Bargaining and supply and demand conditions set the price of each transaction.

Today, the Coca Cola company is testing a vending machine that sets the price of a can of Coke based on the weather – customers must pay more on a hot, dry day. Such notions of dynamic pricing would not work without real-time supply and demand information.

Pricing, however, will not be the only component of the buying decision. Availability, perceived quality, and service still count, but dynamic pricing strategies are vital to successful marketing plans. Still, whether dealing with a premium brand or commodity, pricing policy, a major component of overall business strategy, must be increasingly dynamic as a result of the market transparency wrought by the Internet.

14. Inter-Organization Design is a Really Big Challenge.

The need to optimize entire value chains, collaboration and knowledge sharing are paramount. The entire chain becomes a community of knowledge workers who are able to work together and learn from each other, despite being scattered around the globe. Wishful thinking, however, will not bring about information synergies in a value chain. Governance and control are obvious challenges.

Forming inter-company teams that can perform well together is a difficult proposition. It represents the same class of problem encountered with all star sports teams. Sports teams exemplify *team learning* where total team performance is greater than the sum of the performances of the individual players. That is why teams "jell" during the season to create something extraordinary. But when the all star teams are formed at the end of the season, the collections of individual stars produce less than optimal teams. All-star teams are often clumsy. They have had too little time for team learning.

15. A New Kind of Software Powers the Digital Corporation.

Competition in the digital economy is about information and knowledge. Computer systems should likewise be about information and knowledge. Informate, not automate, is the appropriate term.

Corporations need a computing paradigm to match the digital business paradigm, for in the digital corporation the underlying information system *is* the business. The underlying information system must be:

- ☑ *Open* to reduce the friction of integrating new customers, suppliers and trading partners' information systems,
- ☑ *Agile* enough to thrive on change,
- ☑ *Intelligent* enough to manage overwhelming complexity,
- ☑ *Engineered* for rapid manufacture of new applications
- ☑ *Ubiquitous* so that they may be used by anyone or any computer, anywhere,
- ☑ *Intuitive* so that they can be used by humans with minimal or no training, and
- ☑ *Knowledge Based* to enable customer self-service and design collaborations among trading partners.

Current software development methods, tools, and architectures have hit technical and information walls when it comes to meeting these requirements. In addition, they overwhelm the ability of users to assimilate diverse information. As such, these tools and techniques will not advance us much past our current position with respect to our ability to develop the necessary information systems in a timely and cost effective manner.

Just as corporations turned to the ERP vendors like SAP to acquire complete platforms capable of driving complex enterprise-wide systems, companies will turn to the software industry to acquire complete platforms for electronic business. The move will be from ERP to CRP, from enterprise resource planning to "commerce resource platforms." The CRP, however will be far more intelligent and sophisticated than ERP systems of the past if they are to meet the requirements listed above. New players from the university research community are likely to play a key role as the demand for intelligent software becomes ever more pressing.

The new business fundamentals for the digital economy provide a framework for developing business strategy and should be central to senior management thinking as they prepare their companies for the ride ahead. The Internet provides a completely new infrastructure for a whole new way of conducting business and competing.

References

[1] Kevin Kelly, *New Rules for the New Economy: 10 Radical Strategies for a Connected World,* New York: Viking Press, 1998.
[2] McKenna, Regis, *Real Time.* Harvard Business School Press, 1997.
[3] Michael Dell and Catherine Fredman (Contributor), *Direct from Dell: Strategies That Revolutionized an Industry,* Harperbusiness, 1999.
[4] Dennis H. Jones, "The New Logistics," in *Blueprint to the Digital Economy*, McGraw Hill, 1998.
[5] David Lake, Slow sites cost vendors billions, CNN Interactive, July 9, 1999, from The Industry Standard, http://www.cnn.com/TECH/computing/9907/06/slowsite.ent.idg/

Appendix D
Backgrounder:

Understanding ebXML, UDDI and XML/edi

Appendix D - Understanding ebXML, UDDI and XML/edi

With David R. R. Webber and Anthony Dutton

Introduction

Extensive and accelerating amounts of work are being devoted to providing practical implementations and technical specifications to enable the deployment of open, interoperable e-business interactions. The work is particularly focused around utilizing the W3C XML syntax and the Internet as the underpinning technologies.

In this context, the ebXML initiative[1] is developing specifications to enable a single global electronic marketplace based on an open public XML-based infrastructure. The goal is to enable the global use of electronic business information in an interoperable, secure and consistent manner by all parties. A primary objective of ebXML is to lower the barrier of entry to electronic business in order to facilitate trade, particularly with respect to small- and medium-sized enterprises (SME's) and within developing nations. The ebXML initiative is sponsored by UN/CEFACT and OASIS[2] and is an open public initiative with now approaching two thousand participants.

The Universal Description, Discovery and Integration (UDDI) initiative by contrast was started by IBM, Ariba and Microsoft about five months ago as a means to create an implementation of their technologies that deliver the underpinning for the interoperation of net market places and integrating business services using the Internet. UDDI[3] is based around the concept of standard registry services that provide Yellow, White and Green Page business-centric functionality. The UDDI focus is on providing large organizations the means to reach out to and manage their network of smaller business customers. The biggest issues facing UDDI are ones of acceptance and buy-in from businesses themselves, and implementation issues of scalability and physical implementation.

By contrast the XML/edi Initiative[4] was start three years as a grass-roots initiative to promote the use of XML for e-business. The XML/edi Vision includes the concept of the Fusion-of-Five: XML, EDI, Repositories, Templates and Agents to create next generation e-business. The ebXML and UDDI work represent embodiments of the XML/edi vision and as such we need to understand how far this work has come, and how much further is needed to fully deliver on the promise of XML and e-business.

ebXML

In order to make sense of the technical architecture for ebXML is it important to first understand the conceptual thinking behind the initiative. From the outset the technical architecture team approached the project from the standpoint of business workflow, selecting the objects common to many business processes, such as address, party and location. With the advent of XML it was now easier to identify and define these objects with attributes (data) along with the functions that could be performed on those attributes. A cornerstone of the project was allowing these objects to be reused so that ebXML could provide for the means to unify cross-industry exchanges with a single consistent lexicon.

It is important to realize, however, that the role of ebXML is not to replicate the reliance on electronic versions of common paper documents such as purchase orders, invoices, tender requests and to offer up and develop such implementation examples. Instead the ebXML specifications provide a framework where SME's, business analysts, software engineers, and other organizations can create consistent, robust and interoperable business services and components seamlessly within an integrated global e-business market.

The actual architectural model of ebXML uses two views to describe the relevant aspects of all business interactions.[5] These two views stem from early work on OpenEDI by UN/CEFACT, and are part of the *UN/CEFACT Modeling Methodology (UMM)*.

The first view is the Business Operational View (BOV), which addresses the semantics of business data transactions, and associated data interchanges. The architecture for business transactions includes operational conventions, agreements and mutual obligations and requirements. These specifically apply to the business needs of ebXML trading partners.

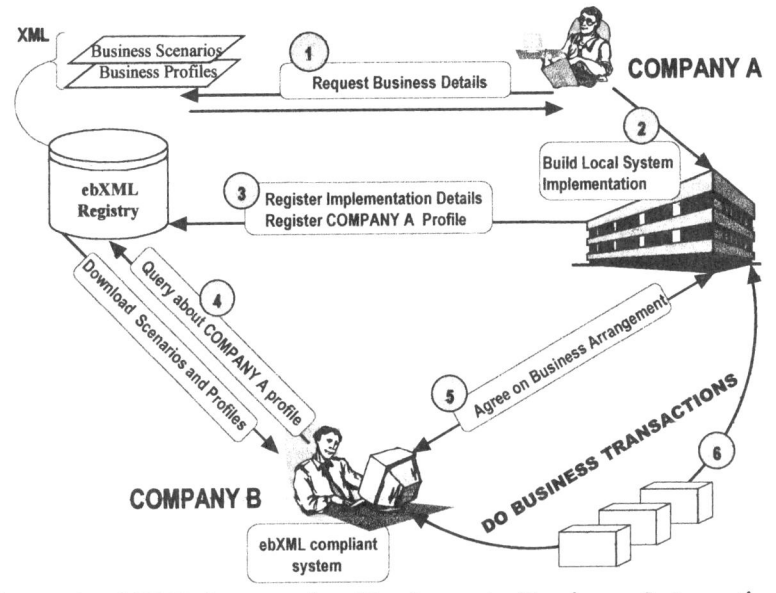

Appendix D - Understanding ebXML, UDDI and XML/edi 301

Figure 1. ebXML Automating Business-to-Business Interactions

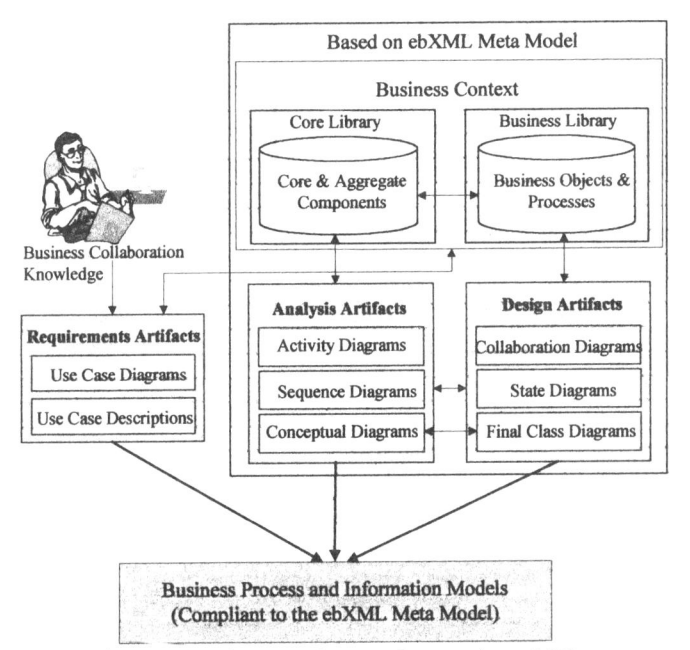

Figure 2. The Business Operational View

Second is the Functional Service View (FSV), which addresses the supporting services and meeting the deployment needs of ebXML. The implementation of the FSV of ebXML has three major phases; implementation, discovery and deployment and then the runtime phase. The implementation phase deals specifically with procedures for creating an application of the ebXML infrastructure. Then the discovery and deployment phase that covers all aspects of the actual discovery of ebXML related resources and self-enabled into the ebXML infrastructure. And after that, the run time phase that addresses the execution of an ebXML scenario with the actual associated ebXML transactions.

FSV focuses on the information technology aspects of functional capabilities, service interfaces and protocols including the following:
- Capabilities for implementation, discovery, deployment and run time scenarios;
- User application interfaces;
- Data transfer infrastructure interfaces;
- Protocols for interoperation of XML vocabulary deployments from different organizations.

In order to deliver on the BOV and FSV, integral to the ebXML architecture is the Registry System. An ebXML Registry provides a set of distributed services that enable the sharing of information between interested parties for the purpose of enabling business process integration between such parties by utilizing the ebXML specifications.

The shared information is maintained as objects in an ebXML Registry that is managed by ebXML Registry Services. Access to an ebXML Registry is provided by the interfaces (APIs) exposed by Registry Services. The Registry provides the access services interfacing, the information model and reference system implementation and the physical backend information store. For example, an ebXML Registry may provide a Collaboration Protocol Profile (CPP) in response to a query; or an ebXML Registry may contain reference DTD's or Schemas that are retrieved by the Registry as a result of searching a metadata classification of the DTD's or Schemas. Figure 4 provides an overview of this configuration.

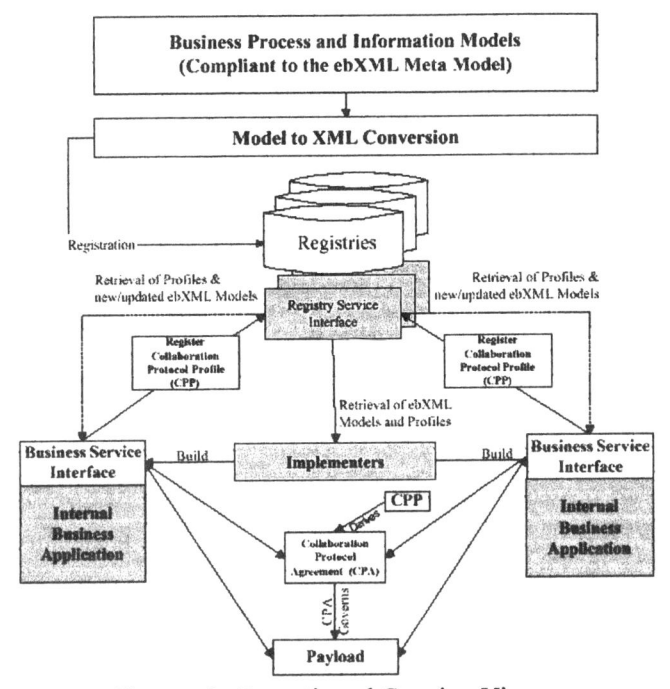

Figure 3. Functional Service View

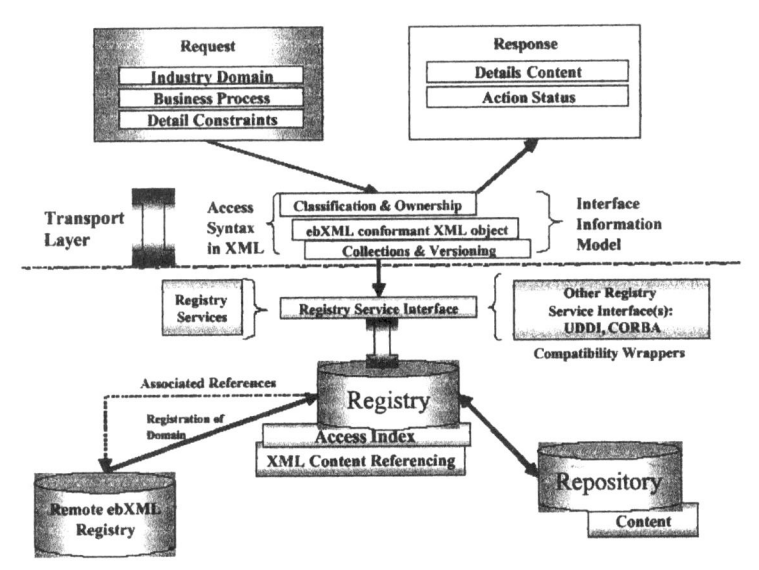

Figure 4. Registry Interaction Overview

UDDI

Hot on the heals of the OASIS sponsored ebXML initiative comes the Universal Description, Discovery and Integration Project co-sponsored by IBM, Microsoft and Ariba and announced only in September, 2000. In addition to the sponsors, a selection of other companies has signed on since September including particularly those focused on directory services and enterprise system integration. Interestingly, IBM, Sun and several others involved with the UDDI project are also already committed to delivering ebXML solutions, and to working with the associated groups, most notably OASIS, CEFACT and the W3C.

The fundamental difference between UDDI and ebXML is that UDDI is aiming to create a standard registry for companies that will accelerate the integration of systems around Net Marketplaces, while ebXML is working to standardize how XML is used in general business-to-business (B2B) integration. The core of the UDDI model is therefore focused particularly on middleware connectivity, and using XML itself to describe the systems that companies use to interface with one another. UDDI plans to do this by storing information about companies' integration profiles and capabilities in a shared directory that other companies can access via a set of XML standards currently being worked on.

The initial UDDI registry system contains three types of information that are being referred to as the white, yellow, and green pages. The white pages directory will allow companies to register their names and the key services they provide, and will allow other companies to search the directory by company name. The yellow pages component of the directory will categorize companies in three ways: by NAICS industry standards codes set by the U.S. government, by United Nations/SPSC codes and finally by geographical location. The final element of UDDI is the green pages, which is where companies will be able to interface with other companies in the registry using XML. Because it will be clear from their search which formats are being supported, the companies can then communicate and send documents based on a specific XML format.

Therefore it is also apparent that ebXML systems will be able to also integrate to UDDI systems at this level, since ebXML also provides all these same capabilities. So why was the UDDI initiative work launched at all? Mostly internal time-to-market pressures on the three principles, who had simply decided they could not wait for ebXML to complete its work.

The UDDI project aims to expand the number of categories and add more complete features to help smooth the searching capabilities of the Net Marketplaces effort. Suggestions include customizing the categorization features and accommodating the needs of large corporations with a variety of business units focused on different goals. In addition, a number of vendors expressed interest in building upon the standard as it progresses and developing registries with customized features that lie on top of UDDI. All this work could potentially cause potential confusion with major work by organizations such as GCI, AIAG and RosettaNet that are already committed to work with the ebXML initiative in these areas. However there are encouraging signs that the principals in UDDI are now looking to work within the ebXML initiative to align and leverage each other's work to create interoperability in the medium term. Of particular note in this area is the recent decision by ebXML Transport Packaging and Routing (TRP) to formally embrace the W3C XML Protocol (XP) specification of the SOAP (Simple Object Access Protocol), and following this both Microsoft and IBM have endorsed the licensing of SOAP technology to the ebXML participants, as and where this might be necessary to allow utilizing of the work.[6] This means that both UDDI registries and ebXML registries could potentially interact via SOAP based messaging at some future point.

XML/edi

While traditional EDI had proved the feasibility and efficiencies possible when using electronic business transactions the limitations were found to be the cost of integration and deployment to the smaller business partners. The vision for XML/edi, therefore, was to build a system that would allow organizations to deploy smarter, cheaper and more maintainable systems to a global audience. XML/edi approached the problem by developing a system that allowed each trading partner to quickly synchronize their systems by exchanging not just the old structures of EDI data, but also process control templates and business rules as well.

The central idea to XML/edi is to add enough intelligence to the electronic documents so that they (and the document-centric tools that handle them) become the framework for electronic business commerce. By combining the five components together, XML/edi provides a system that delivers not just data, but more importantly, information accompanied by the necessary processing logic. Thus not only is data exchanged but also the enabling underlying processing information.

Examining the critical business parameters, as opposed to the technology, history has shown that traditional EDI failed to create a broad based acceptance for a number of reasons. To deliver a next generation global EDI solution, the following capabilities must be addressed as the "Business Top Ten" requirements list:
1. Reduce the cost of doing business.
2. Reduce cost of entry into e-business.
3. Provide an easy to use tool-set.
4. Improve data integrity and accessibility.
5. Provide appropriate security and control.
6. Provide extendable and controllable technology.
7. Integrate with today's systems.
8. Utilizes open standards.
9. Provide a successor to X12/EDIFACT and interoperability for XML syntaxes.
10. Globally deployable and maintainable.

So far ebXML is proving that it has the components to come closest to these goals. However simply redefining the old EDI message formats in XML, to make them Web deployable is not enough. The ebXML initiative has concentrated on modeling tools to capture the business processes, not just the transactions, and storing standard definitions in globally accessible registries (repositories). Done correctly the small businesses can avoid the need to do costly and complex modeling, while still able to quickly and easily tap into existing process models and off-the-shelf application solutions. Whereas the XML/edi guidelines have added two additional key components: Process Templates and Software Agents to assist in this. The idea is to provide truly dynamic software processes based off XML representations by using the ability of XML to define not just the data but also processing scripting systems. The ebXML work sees this as a second phase need; with the first phase being based on simpler rigid well understood more static interfaces.

Within the integrated XML/edi system (Figure 5), XML itself provides the foundation, whereby XML tokens and frameworks are the syntax that transports the other components across the network. XML tokens replace or supplement existing e-business transactions, and thereby enrich the capabilities and transport layers of the Internet in general. Process Templates built using XML are the glue that holds the whole XML/edi system together. Without them you could not use the XML syntax exclusively to express all of the needed work requirements. The templates are globally referenced, or travel along inside the XML as a special section and set of tokens where they can be easily read and interpreted. They also control and define the business context and process definitions that allow users to locate the correct components that they need. The ebXML classification work and ebXML Business Process Metamodel are also now moving to implement these same capabilities within the Registry indexing system, but as yet without the Template and business token focus. This may change as the XML/edi GUIDE[7] work matures and provides synergy with the ebXML metamodel.

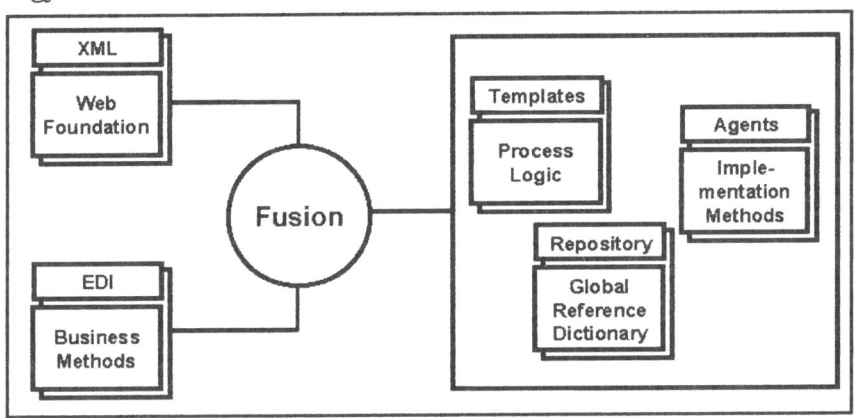

Figure 5. The Power of Five – The Components of XML/edi

XML/edi Internet Repositories (referred to as Registry/Repository systems in ebXML) allow users to manually look up the meaning and definition of e-business elements. Additionally the concept takes this to the next level and provides automatic lookup interfaces, much like an advanced Internet search engine.[8] This XML/edi repository component of the system provides the semantic foundation for global business transactions and at the same time the underpinnings needed by the software agents to correctly cross-reference entities.

Thus the software agents serve several functions. First, they interpret the Process Templates for performing the work needed.

Second, they interact with the e-business transaction data definitions and the user business applications to integrate each specific task. Third, they look up and attach the right template for existing jobs by accessing the Global Repository. An example would be an agent that can take an e-business transaction and examine the underlying global repository definitions and construct and determine display characteristics for forms to display the information to users.

Conclusion

We are facing a very interesting moment in the development of e-business and the Internet. The Internet itself has shaped our ability to develop open public standards across diverse groups of people who are geographically located on all the major continents. The emergence of pervasive networking and small personal computing devices are challenging previously understood limits of information delivery and utilization. While the United States continues, for now, to dominate the development of business standards, this is based mostly on the fact that the US economy constitutes over 30% of the world economy. Within the software industry itself countries such as India and the Eastern European countries are already making significant in-roads into this domination as the labor pool for cost-effective development resources are stretched to the limit worldwide. Consequently over the next five years we can foresee that the industry is moving to an open global economy where new and profoundly different metrics will emerge. The measure of ebXML, UDDI and XML/edi will be how well they are able to provide and satisfy these needs.

The ebXML initiative is planning to release its first version of the specifications following the plenary meetings to be held in May in Vienna, Austria. Vendors can be expected to deliver product shortly thereafter. While there has been a slow-down in Internet related business development funding, the use of the Internet for business information interchanging is forging ahead driven by the simple economics of automating dynamic business processes through the use of XML. The ebXML specifications remain an unproven entity for now and with a block of technical issues undetermined, nevertheless the underpinning for the overall architecture is being delivered on. Clearly the specifications will mature, as implementations are able to provide direct feedback from fielded experience.

Also encouraging is the early preparations being done by government departments to support ebXML. Government institutions rely heavily on open public specifications to provide consistency and to avoid dependence on vendor proprietary technology. Also the ebXML work provides an excellent methodology whereby large organizations can begin to migrate their existing business processes to an Internet and real-time business model. One of the other key drivers will be the creation and adoption by industry bodies and associations of registries of business semantic information that will allow their members to build consistent application software system. Particularly important is how well legacy EDI formats can be migrated to and based around the ebXML registry and associated core component business information definition guidelines.

While all these technical factors are important, perhaps the most important factor is one of mindshare, the will to succeed and the confidence to inspire businesses around the world to commit to utilizing the ebXML specifications and to step from the current paradigm to a new world and a new age in the chapter of world trade and human endeavor.

References

[1] http://www.ebXML.org
[2] www.oasis-open.org
[3] www.uddi.org
[4] www.xmledi-group.org
[5] www.ebxml.org/specdrafts/approved_specs.htm
[6] www.ebxml.org/news/pr_20010308.htm
[7] www.xmlguide.org
[8] www.goxml.com

Appendix E:
Web Resources

Comprehensive sources of information are available on the Web, but there are so many that they can be overwhelming. We maintain our favorite links as a quick reference to help us in our continuing research. These links include:

- Analysts' Research Reports

- Online Publications

- B2B Information Portals

- XML Initiatives and Applications

- Providers of Commerce Resource Platform Software

Classroom Presentation Materials for the Book

Professors and corporate trainers who use the book for teaching will find the figures for the book located at the book's companion Web site.

http://geocities.com/m_kpress

If you experience any difficulty with the Web site or require further information, please e-mail: mkpress@tampabay.rr.com

Bibliography

The number of books on the business and technology aspects of e-commerce and the digital economy is large and growing. We have made every attempt to include those titles that would be of the greatest interest at the time we went to press with this book. To keep abreast of the latest titles or to obtain reviews of these books, visit *The Essential Library for the Digital Economy* –it's on the Web at http://home1.gte.net/pfingar

ABA Professional Education, *A Commercial Lawyer's Take on the Electronic Purse: An Analysis of Commercial Law Issues Associated With Stored-Value Cards.* ABA Professional Education, 1998.

Abell, Howard, *The Electronic Trading of Options: Maximizing Online Profits,* Dearborn Trade, 2000.

Adam, Nabil R. and Yelena Yesha, *Electronic Commerce: Current Research Issues and Applications,* Springer Verlag, 1996.

Adam, Nabil R., *Electronic Commerce: Technical, Business and Legal Issues (With CDROM),* Prentice Hall, 1998.

Ahuja, Vijay, *Secure Commerce on the Internet,* AP Professional, 1996.

Aldrich, Douglas F., *Mastering the Digital Marketplace: Practical Strategies for Competitiveness in the New Economy,* John Wiley, 1999.

Allen, Cliff, Deborah, Kania and Beth, Yaeckel, *Internet World Guide to One-To-One Web Marketing,* Wiley, 1998.

Amor, Daniel, *The E-business (R)evolution,* Prentice Hall, 1999.

Austin,Thomas E., *New Retail Power and Muscle,* BRG, 2000.

Baker, Abercrombie Stewart, *The Limits of Trust: Cryptography,Governments, and Electronic Commerce,* Kluwer Law International, 1998.

Baker, Mike, *Strike It Rich On eBay* (The World's Largest Online Internet Auction Site), Mike Baker Publishing, 1999.

Barefoot, Coy, *The Quixtar Revolution: Discover the New High-Tech, High-Touch World of Marketing,* Prima Publishing, 1999.

Barnes, Stuart and Brian Hunt, *E-Commerce and V-Business: An International Money Making Machine,* Butterworth, 2000.

Barrett, Neil, *Advertising on the Internet: How to Get Your Message Across on the World Wide Web*, Kogan Page Ltd, 2000.

Bayne, Kim M., *The Internet Marketing Plan*, John Wiley, 2000.

Bekkers, J. J. M., Bert-Jaap Koops and Sjaak Nouwt (Editors), *Emerging Electronic Highways: New Challenges for Politics and Law*, Kluwer Law International, 1996.

Benesko, Gary G., *Inter-Corporate Business Engineering: Streamlining the Business Cycle from End to End*, Research Triangle Consultants, 1996.

Bernstein, Jake, *Strategies for the Electronic Futures Trader*, McGraw-Hill, 1999.

Berry, J. A. and Gordon Linoff, *Data Mining Techniques: For Marketing, Sales, and Customer Support*, Wiley, 1997.

Berst, Jesse, *The Magnet Effect: Attracting and Retaining an Audience on the Internet*, McGraw-Hill, 2000.

Betancourt, Marian, *The Best Internet Businesses You Can Start*, Adams Media Corporation, 1999.

Bhatia, Hamir and Deborah L. Bayles, *E-Commerce Logistics and Fulfillment: Delivering the Goods*, Prentice Hall, 2000.

Bickerton, Pauline and Matthew Bickerton, *Cybermarketing: How to Use the Internet to Market Your Goods and Services*, Butterworth Heinemann, 2000.

Bickerton, Pauline, Jonathan Glasspool and Matthew Bickerton, *Cyberknowledge: Internet Technology and Eservice*, Butterworth Heinemann, 2000.

Bishop, William, *Strategic Marketing for the Digital Age*, NTC Business Books, 1998.

Bloor, Robin, *The Electronic B Zaar: From the Silk Road to the Eroad*, Nicholas Brealey, 2000.

Boettcher, Thomas Charles, *The Infolocus Manifesto*, Gutenberg Press, 2000.

Bollier, David, *Future of Electronic Commerce*, Aspen Inst., 1996.

Bollier, David, *Sustainable Competition in Global Telecommunications: From Principle to Practice*, Aspen, Inst., 1998.

Bollier, David, *The Globalization of Electronic Commerce*, Aspen Inst., 1998.

Bonnett, Kendra, *The IBM Guide to Doing Business on the Internet: A Complete Blueprint for E-Business Success*, McGraw-Hill, 2000.

Botto, Francis, *Dictionary of E-Commerce: A Definitive Guide to Technology and Business Terms*, John Wiley, 2000.

Bovet, David, Joseph Martha, and Adrian J. Slywotsky, *Value Nets: Breaking the Supply Chain to Unlock Hidden Profits*, John Wiley, 2000.

Boyson, Sandor el al (Editors), *Logistics and the Extended Enterprise: Benchmarks and Best Practices for the Manufacturing Professional*, Wiley, 1999.

Breier, Mark and Armin A. Brott, *The 10 Second Internet Manager*, Crown Publishing, 2000.

Bressler, Stacey E. and Charles E. Grantham, *Communities of Commerce: Building Internet Business Communities to Accelerate Growth, Minimize Risk, and Increase Customer Loyalty*, McGraw-H, 2000.

Brinson, Dianne, Benay Dara-Abrams and Jennifer D. Masek, *Exploring E Commerce, Site Management, and Internet Law*, Prentice Hall, 2001.

Brondmo, Hans Peter, *Eng@ged: The New Rules of Internet Direct Marketing*, Harperbusiness, 2000.

Buffam, William J., *E-Business and IS Solutions: An Architectural Approach to Business Problems and Opportunities*, A-W, 2000.

Bruner, Rick E., *Cybernautics and USweb Corporation*, Net Results: Web Marketing that Works, Hayden Books, 1998.

Bullis, Douglas, *Preparing for Electronic Commerce in Asia*, Quorum Books, 1999.

Burnham, Bill, *The Electronic Commerce Report*, McGraw-H, 1998.

Cairncross, Frances, *The Death of Distance: How the Communications Revolution Will Change Our Lives*, Harvard Business School Press, 1997.

Callaway, Erin, *ERP—The Next Generation: ERP Is Web Enabled for E-Business*, 2000.

Cameron, Debra, *E-Commerce Security Strategies: Protecting the Enterprise*, Computer Technology Research Corporation, 1998.

Cameron, Debra, *Electronic Commerce: The New Business Platform for the Internet*, Computer Technology Research, 1997.

Cameron, Debra, *Implementing Next-Generation E-Business Strategies*, Computer Technology Research Corporation, 1999.

Cameron, Debra, *Reengineering Business for Success in the Internet Age Business*, Computer Technology Research Corporation, 2000.

Camp, L. Jean, *Trust and Risk in Internet Commerce*, MIT, 2000.

Cannon, Jeff, *Make Your Website Work for You: How to Convert Online Content Into Profits (CommerceNet)*, McGraw-Hill, 1999.

Carpenter, Phil, *eBrands: Building an Internet Business at Breakneck Speed*, Harvard Business School Press, 2000.

Carrick, Rob and Guy Anderson, *E-Investing: How to Choose and Use a Discount Broker*, John Wiley & Sons, 2000.

Cashin, Jerry, *E-Commerce Success: Building a Global Business Architecture*, Computer Technology Research Corporation, 1999.

Cashin, Jerry, *Web Commerce: Developing and Implementing Effective Business Solutions*, Computer Technology Research, 1998.

Cataudella, Joe, Dave Greely and Ben Sawyer, *Creating Stores on the Web: Insider's Guide to Setting Up a Profitable Cybershop*, Peachtree Press 1998.

Caves, Richard E., Jeffrey A. Frankel and Ronald Jones, *World Trade and Payments: An Introduction*, Addison-Wesley, 1999.

Chan, Sally, Hal Stern, Peter Keen and Craigg Balance, *Gaining Control of Electronic Commerce*, John Wiley, 1998.

Charles, Ann Carol, Christopher P. Foss and Shamita R. Dewan, *Globalizing Electronic Commerce: Report on the International Forum on Electronic Commerce*, Center for Strategic & Int'l Studies, 1996.

Chase Larry, *Essential Business Tactics for the Net*, Wiley, 1998.

Chesher, Chesher and Rukesh Kaura, *Electronic Commerce and Business Communications*, Springer Verlag, 1998.

Chinoy, Hussain, Tyna Hull and Robi Sen, *XML for EDI: Making E-Commerce a Reality*, Morgan Kaufmann Publishers, 2000.

Chissick, Michael and Alistair, Kelman, *E Commerce*, Sweet & Maxwell, 1998.

Clemente, Peter, *State of the Net: The New Frontier*, McGraw-Hill, 1998.

Cobb, Stephen, and Michael Cobb, *Implementing SET: A Guide to the Visa/MasterCard Secure Electronic Transaction Specification*, Computing McGraw-Hill, 1997.

Cohan, Peter S., *E-Profit: High-Payoff Strategies for Capturing the E-Commerce Edge*, AMACOM, 2000.

Cohan, Peter S., *Net Profit: How to Invest and Compete in the Real World of Internet Business*, Jossey-Bass Publishers, 1999.

Collin, Simon, *The Virgin Internet Shopping Guide: Version 1.0*, Globe Pequot Press, 2000.

Columbus, Louis, *Deploying Electronic Commerce Solutions with Microsoft BackOffice*, Microsoft Press, 1999.

Coyle, Diane, *The Weightless World: Strategies for Managing the Digital Economy*, MIT Press, 1998.

Cox, Barbara G. and William Koelzer, *Internet Marketing in Real Estate*, Prentice Hall, 2000.

Crouch, Matt J., *Web Programming with ASP and COM*, Addison-Wesley, 1999.

Crowder, David A. and Rhonda Crowder, *Cliff Notes Shopping On-line Safely*, Idg Books-Cliffs Notes, 1999.

Cunningham, Mike, *Smart Things to Know About E-Commerce*, Capstone Ltd, 2000.

Cunningham, Peter and Friedrich Froschl, *Electronic Business Revolution*, Springer-Verlag New York, 1999.

Dalgleish, Jodie, *Customer-Effective Web Sites*, Prentice Hall Computer Books, 2000.

Danish, Sherif and Patrick Gannon, *Building Database-Driven Web Catalogs*, McGraw-Hill, 1998.

Dart, Susan, *Configuration Management: The Missing Link in Web Engineering*, 2000.

Daum, Berthold and Markus Scheller, *Success with Electronic Business: Design, Architecture, and Technology of Electronic Busi-*

ness Systems, Addison-Wesley, 2000.

Davidow, William H. and Michael S. Malone. *The Virtual Corporation: Structuring and Revitalizing the Corporation for the 21st Century,* Harper Collins, 1992.

Davis, Stan and Christopher Meyer, *Blur: The Speed of Change in the Connected Economy,* Hardcover, 1998.

De Kare-Silver, Michael, *Electronic Shock: How Retailers and Manufacturers Can Shape the Coming Shopping Revolution,* AMACOM, 1999.

De Kare-Silver, Michael, *Strategy in Crisis: Why Business Urgently Needs a Completely New Approach,* New York University, 1998.

Deise, Martin V., Conrad Nowikow, Patrick King, and Amy Wright, *Executive's Guide to E-Business: From Tactics to Strategy,* John Wiley, 2000.

Deitel and Associates, *The Complete e-Business and e-Commerce Training Course,* Prentice Hall, 2000.

Deitel, Harvey, Paul Deitel and Kate Steinbuhler, *e-Business & e-Commerce for Managers,* Prentice Hall, 2001.

Denning, Dorothy E. and Peter J. Denning, *Internet Besieged: Countering Cyberspace Scofflaws,* Addison-Wesley, 1997.

Department of Defense, *Introduction to Department of Defense Electronic Commerce: A Handbook for Business,* Version 2. Diane Publishing Co., 1997.

Downes, Larry, and Chunka Mui, *Unleashing the Killer App: Digital Strategies for Market Dominance,* Harvard Business School, 1998.

Drew, Grady N., *Using Set for Secure Electronic Commerce,* Prentice Hall, 1999.

Drucker, Peter Ferdinand, *Management Challenges for the 21st Century,* HarperBusiness, 1999.

Eager, Bill, *Complete Idiot's Guide to Marketing Online,* Que, 1999.

Earle, Nick and Peter G. W. Keen, *From .Com to .Profit: Inventing Business Models That Deliver Value and Profit,* Jossey-Bass, 2000.

Easton Jaclyn, *Strikingitrich.com: Profiles of 23 Incredibly Successful Web Sites You've Probably Never Heard Of,* McGraw-Hill, 1998.

Edwards, Paul, Sarah, Edwards and Linda Rohrbough, *Making Money in Cyberspace*, J. P. Tarcher, 1998.

Elliott, Alan C., *Getting Started in Internet Auctions*, John Wiley, 2000.

Ellsworth, Jill H., and Matthew V. Ellsworth, *The New Internet Business Book*, John Wiley & Sons, 1996.

Emerick, Donald, Kimberlee Round, Kim Round and Karen McLean (Editor), *Exploring Web Marketing and Project Management*, Prentice Hall, 1999.

Emmerson, Bob and David Greetham, *Computer Telephony and Wireless Technologies: Future Directions in Communications Computer*, Technology Research Corporation, 1997.

Emshwiller John R., *Scam Dogs and Mo-Mo Mamas: Inside the Wild and Woolly World of Internet Stock Trading*, Harper, 2000.

Evans, David S., and Richard Schmalensee, *Paying With Plastic: The Digital Revolution in Buying and Borrowing*, MIT Press, 1999.

Ezor, Jonathan I., *Clicking Through: A Survival Guide for Bringing Your Company Online*, Bloomberg Press, 1999.

Feather, Frank, *FutureConsumer.Com: The Webolution of Shopping to 2010*, Warwick Pub, 2000.

Fellenstein, Craig and Ron Wood, *Exploring E-Commerce, Global E-Business and E-Society*, Prentice Hall, 1999.

Ferris, David, *Building an Intelligent E-Business*, Prima, 2000.

Figallo, Cliff, *Hosting Web Communities: Building Relationships, Increasing Customer Loyalty, and Maintaining a Competitive Edge*, Wiley, 1998.

Fingar, Peter, Harsha Kumar and Tarum Sharma. *Enterprise E-Commerce*, Meghan-Kiffer Press, 2000.

Fiore, Frank and Jim Cope, *Complete Idiot's Guide to Starting an Online Business*, Que, 2000.

Fischer, Layna, *New Tools for New Times: Electronic Commerce.* Future Strategies. 1996.

First International Workshop on Agent-Mediated Electronic Trading, *International Workshop on Agent-Mediated Electronic Trading*, Springer Verlag, 1999.

Flor, Nick V., *Web Business Engineering: Using Offline Activities to Drive Internet Strategies*, Addison-Wesley, 2001.

Fontanills, George A., *Trade Options Online*, John Wiley, 1999.

Ford, Warwick and Michael S. Baum, *Secure Electronic Commerce: Building the Infrastructure for Digital Signatures and Encryption*, Prentice Hall, 1997.

Frankel, Rob, *The Revenge of Brand X: How to Build A Big Time Brand - on the Web or Anywhere Else*, Frankel & Anderson, 2000.

Franklin, Matthew (Editor), *Financial Cryptography: Third International Conference*, Springer Verlag, 1999.

Frye, Curtis D., *Privacy-Enhanced Business: Adapting to the Online Environment*, 2000.

Galloway, Paul, *E-Commerce Made E-Z Guide*, Made EZ, 2000.

Galon, Derek, *The Savvy Way to Successful Website Promotion*, Trafford Publishing, 1999.

Garfinkel, Simson and Gene Spafford, *Web Security & Commerce (Nutshell Handbook)*, O'Reilly & Associates, 1997.

Gates, Bill, *Business at the Speed of Thought: Succeeding in the Digital Economy*, Warner Books, 2000.

Gerlach, Douglas, *The Complete Idiot's Guide to Online Investing*, Macmillan Publishing Company, 1999.

Ghosh, Anup A., *E-Commerce Security: Weak Links, Best Defenses*, John Wiley, 1998.

Gibson, Rowan. *Rethinking the Future: Rethinking Business, Principles, Competition, Control & Complexity, Leadership, Markets and the World*, Nicholas Brealey, 1997.

Gielgun, Ron E, *How to Succeed in Internet Business by Employing Real-World Strategies; Business Approaches*, Actium, 1998.

Gilbert, Jill, *Cliffs Notes Getting Started in Online Investing*, IDG Books Worldwide, 2000.

Glazier, Stephen C., *e-Patent Strategies for Software, e-Commerce, the Internet, Telecom Services, Financial Services, and Business Methods*, LBI Law & Business Institute, 2000.

Gloor, Peter A., *Making the E-Business Transformation: How to Succeed in the E-Commerce Economy*, Springer Verlag, 2000.

Glover, Steven M., Stephen W. Liddle, and Douglas F. Prawitt, *E-Business: Principles and Strategies for Accountants*, P-H, 2000.

Godin, Seth and Don Peppers, *Permission Marketing: Turning Strangers Into Friends, and Friends into Customers*, Simon & Schuster, 1999.

Godin, Seth and Malcolm Gladwell, *Unleashing the Ideavirus*, Do You Zoom, Inc., 2000.

Gold, LauraMaery, *J. K. Lasser's Invest Online*, John Wiley, 2000.

Goldman, S. L., R. N. Nagel, and K. Preiss. *Agile Competitors and Virtual Organizations: Strategies for Enriching the Customer*, Van Nostrand Reinhold, 1994.

Goralski, Walter, *Virtual Private Networks: Achieving Secure Internet Commerce and Enterprisewide Communications*, Computer Technology Research Corporation, 1999.

Gosling, Paul, *Changing Money: How the Digital Age Is Transforming Financial Services*, Capital Books Inc., 2000.

Grady, Drew, *Using Set for Secure Electronic Transactions*, Prentice Hall, 1998.

Graf, Annette E., *How To Sell On Ebay and Other On-Line Auctions*, Graf Publishing, 1999.

Gralla, Preston, *The Complete Idiot's Guide to Online Shopping*, MacMillan Computer, 1999.

Grant, Gail, *Understanding Set: Visa International's Official Guide to Secure Electronic Transactions*, McGraw-Hill, 2000.

Gray, Daniel, *The Complete Guide to Associate & Affiliate Programs on the Net*, McGraw-Hill, 1999.

Greenstein Marilyn and Todd M. Feinman. *Electronic Commerce: Security, Risk Management and Control*, McGraw-Hill, 1999.

Grewlich, Klaus W., *Governance in 'Cyberspace: Access and Public Interest in Global Communications*, Kluwer Law Intnl., 1999.

Grossnickle, Joshua and Oliver Raskin, *The Handbook of Online Marketing Research*, McGraw-Hill, 2000.

Giunipero, Larry C. and Chris Sawchuk, *ePurchasingplus*, JGC Enterprises, 2000.

Gulliver, Randolph, *The Net User's Guide to Buying, Selling, and Trading Collectibles,* Stoddart Publications, 2000.

Gurian, Phil H., *E-Mail Business Strategies,* Grand National, 2000.

Gutterman, Alan S., *The Professional's Guide to Doing Business on the Internet,* Harcourt Brace Professional Publishers, 1999.

Hackathorn, Richard D., *Web Farming for the Data Warehouse,* Morgan Kaufman Publishers, 1998.

Hagel, John and Arthur, G Armstrong, *Net Gain: Expanding Markets through Virtual Communities,* Harvard Business School, 1997.

Halvey, John K. and Barbara Murphy Melby. *Business Process Outsourcing: Process, Strategies, and Contracts,* Wiley, 2000.

Hamel, Gary, and C. K. Prahalad. *Competing for the Future: Breakthrough Strategies for Seizing Control of Your Industry and Creating the Markets of Tomorrow,* Harvard Business School, 1994.

Hamel, Gary, *Leading the Revolution,* Harvard Business School Press, 2000.

Hance, Olivier and Suzanne Dionne Balz, *Business & Law on the Internet,* McGraw-Hill, 1997.

Hansmann, Uwe, Thomas Schack, Frank Seliger, Thomas Schaeck and Martin Scott Nicklous, *Smart Card Application Development Using Java,* Springer Verlag, 1999.

Hanson, Ward, *Principles of Internet Marketing,* South-Western, 1999.

Hardesty, David E., *Electronic Commerce: Taxation and Planning,* Warren Gorham & Lamont, 1999.

Harris, Wayne, *Cybertools for Business,* Warner Books, 1997.

Hartman, Amir, John Kador and John Sifonis, *Net Ready,* McGraw-Hill, 2000.

Hsu, Cheng and Somendra Pant, *Innovative Planning for Electronic Commerce and Enterprises - A Reference Model,* Kluwer Academic Publishers, 1999.

Hawthorne, Fran, *Teach Yourself Investing Online Visually,* IDG Books Worldwide, 2000.

Haylock, Christina Ford, Len Muscarella and Steve Case, *Net Success: 24 Leaders in Web Commerce Show You How to Put the Web to Work for Your Business*, Adams Media Corporation, 1999.

Haynes, Ted, *Electronic Commerce Dictionary: The Definitive Terms for Doing Business on the Information Superhighway*, Robleda, 1995.

Helmstetter, Greg and Pamela Metivier, *Affiliate Selling: Building Revenue on the Web*, John Wiley, 2000.

Hinkelman, Edward G and Molly, Thurmond, *A Short Course in International Payments: How to Use Letters of Credit, D/P and D/A Terms, Prepayment, Credit and Cyberpayments in International Transactions*, World Trade Press, 1998.

Hitt, Michael A., Joan E. Ricart I Costa and Robert D. Nixon (Editors), *Managing Strategically in an Interconnected World.* John Wiley, 1999.

Hix, Nancy L., *Collector's Guide to Buying, Selling, and Trading on the Internet*, Collector Books, 2000.

Holder, Greg, Frank, Catalano and Bud E. Smith, *Online Business Kit for Dummies*, With CDROM, IDG Books Worldwide, 1999.

Holden, Greg, *Small Business Internet for Dummies*, IDG Books Worldwide, 1998.

Holden, Greg, *Starting an Online Business for Dummies*, 2nd Edition, IDG Books, , 2000.

Holden, Greg, Frank Catalano, Bud E. Smith, *Online Business Kit for Dummies*, IDG Books Worldwide, 1999.

Hoque, Faisal, *E-Enterprise: Business Models, Architecture and Components*, Cambridege University Press, 2000.

Hoskin, Jim and Vincent Lupiano, *Exploring IBM's Bold Internet Strategy*, 2nd Edition, Maximum Press, 1997.

Huff, Sidney Laurence (Editor), *Cases in Electronic Commerce*, Irwin Professional Pub, 1999.

Imparato, Nicholas (Editor), *Public Policy and the Internet: Privacy, Taxes, and Contract*, Hoover Inst Press, 2000.

James, Geoffrey, *Business Wisdom of the Electronic Elite: 34 Winning Management Strategies from CEOs at Microsoft, Compaq, Sun, and Other Top Companies*, Random House, 1996.

Jamison, Brian, Josh Gold and Warren, Jamison, *Electronic Selling: Twenty-Three Steps to E-Selling Profits*, McGraw-Hill, 1997.

Javed, Naseem, *Domain Wars*, Linkbridge Publications, 1999.

Jenkins, Glenn P., *Information Technology and Innovation in Tax Administration*, Kluwer Law International, 1996.

Jilovec, Nahid, *The A to Z of EDI: And Its Role in E-Commerce*, Duke Communications, 1998.

Jones, John W., Ph.D., *The Virtual Entrepreneur: Electronic Commerce in the 21st Century*, Business Psychology Research, 1999.

Judson, Bruce and Kate Kelly, *Hyperwars: Eleven Rules for Surviving & Profiting in the Age of On-LineBusiness*, Scribner, 1999.

Kaiser, William S., *The Art of Electronic Futures Trading: Building a Winning System by Avoiding Psychological Pitfalls*, McGraw-Hill, 2000.

Kalakota, Ravi and Andrew B. Whinston, *Electronic Commerce: A Manager's Guide*, Addison-Wesley, 1996.

Kalakota, Ravi and Marcia, Robinson, *E-Business: Roadmap for Success*,Addison-Wesley, 1999. 2nd Edition, 2000.

Kalakota, Ravi and Andrew, B. Whinston, *Readings in Electronic Commerce*, Addison-Wesley, 1996.

Kaplan, Robert S. and David P. Norton. *The Balanced Scorecard: Translating Strategy into Action*, Harvard Business School, 1996.

Keen, Peter and Mark McDonald, *The eProcess Edge: Creating Customer Value and Business Wealth in the Internet Era*, Computing McGraw-Hill, 2000.

Keen, Peter G. W. and Craigg Ballance, *On-Line Profits: A Manager's Guide to Electronic Commerce*, Harvard Business School Press, 1997.

Keen, Peter G. W. (Editor), Craigg Ballance, Sally Chan and Steve Schrump, *Electronic Commerce Relationships: Trust By Design*, Prentice Hall, 1999.

Kelly, Kevin, *New Rules for the New Economy: 10 Radical Strategies for a Connected World*, Viking Press, 1998.

Kelly, Kevin. *Out of Control: The Rise of Neo-biological Civilization*, Addison-Wesley, 1994.

Kelly, Jason, *The Neatest Little Guide to Making Money Online*, Plume, 2000.

Kent, Peter and Tara, Calishain, *Poor Richard's Internet Marketing and Promotions: How to Promote Yourself, Your Business, Your Ideas Online,* Top Floor, 1999.

Kienan, Brenda, *Small Business Solutions for E-Commerce,* Microsoft Press, 2000.

Kilmer, William E., *Getting Your Business Wired: Using Computer Networking & the Internet to Grow Your Business,* AMACOM, 1999.

King, Janice M., Paul Knight and James H. Mason, *Web Marketing Cookbook,* John Wiley, 1997.

Kirchoff, Steve and Stephen Mendonca, *Instant Advantage.com, Winning Strategies for the Online Economy,* Prentice Hall, 2000.

Klusch, Matthias and Gerhard Weiss, *Cooperative Information Agents II: Learning, Mobility, and Electronic Commerce for Information Discovery on the Internet:* Second International works by CIA '9, Springer Verlag, 1998.

Kosiur, David R., *Understanding Electronic Commerce,* Microsoft Press, 1997.

Kou, Weidong and Yelena Yesha, *Electronic Commerce Technology Trends,* IIR Publications, 2000.

Kuegler, Thomas J., *Web Advertising and Marketing,* 3rd Ed., Prima Publishing, 2000.

Lamersdorf, Winfried, Michael Merz and J. Hartmanis, *Trends in Distributed Systems for Electronic Commerce,* Springer, 1998.

Larsson, Mats and David Lundberg, *The Transparent Market: Management Challenges in the Electronic Age,* St Martins, 1998.

Leebaert, Derek, *The Future of the Electronic Marketplace,* MIT Press, 1998.

Lessard, Bill and Steve Bald, *Net Slaves: Tales of Working the Web,* McGraw-Hill, 1999.

Levine Young, Margaret and John R. Levine, *Poor Richard's Building Online Communities: Create a Web Community for Your Business, Organization, Club, or Family,* Top Floor, 2000.

Liflander, Robert, *The Everything Online Business Book,* Adams Media Corporation, 2000.

Litan, Robert and William A. Niskanen, *Going Digital: A Guide to Policy in the Digital Age,* Brookings Inst., 1998.

Litan, Robert E. and Peter P. Swire, *None of Your Business: World Data Flows, Electronic Commerce, & the European Privacy Directive*, Brookings Institute, 1998.

Locke, Christopher, Rick Levine, Doc Searls and David Weinberger, *The Cluetrain Manifesto: The End of Business As Usual*, Perseus Books, 2000.

Loeb, Larry, *Secure Electronic Transactions: Introduction and Technical Reference*, Artech House, 1998.

Lomas, Mark, *Security Protocols: International Workshop, Cambridge, United Kingdom April 10-12, 1996: Proceedings*, Springer Verlag, 1997.

Loshin, Pete, John Vacca and Paul A. Murphy, *Electronic Commerce: Online Ordering and Digital Money*, 3rd Ed., Charles River Media, 2000.

Lowery, Joseph, *Buying Online for Dummies*, IDG Books, 1998.

Lundquist, Heeter Leslie, *Selling Online for Dummies*, IDG Books Worldwide, 1998.

Lynch, Daniel C and Leslie Heeter Lundquist, *Digital Money: The New Era of Internet Commerce*, John Wiley & Sons, 1995.

Maddox, Kate, and Dana Blankenhorn, *Web Commerce: Building a Digital Business*, Wiley, 1998.

Magretta, Joan (Editor), *Managing in the New Economy*, Harvard Business School Press, 1999.

Markman, Jon D., *Online Investing (Independent)*, Microsoft, 1999.

Marks, Steven, *EDI Purchasing: The Electronic Gateway to the Future*, Pt Pubns, 1997.

Martin, Chuck, *Net Future: The 7 Cybertrends That Will Drive Your Business, Create New Wealth, and Define Your Future*, McGraw-Hill, 1998.

Martin, James, *The Great Transition: Using the Seven Disciplines of Enterprise Engineering to Align People, Technology, and Strartegy*, AMACOM, 1995.

Martin, James, *Cybercorp: The New Business Revolution*, Amacom Book Division, 1996.

Mathiesen, Michael, Jan Zimmerman and Jerry Yang, *Marketing on the Internet: A Proven 12-Step Plan for Selling Your Products and Services to Millions over the Information Superhighway*, Maximum Press, 1998.

Matranga, John, Stephen Tranchida and Bart Preecs,*Understanding BizTalk*, Sams, 2000.

Matthews, Jack, *Time And Money.com: Create Wealth by Profiting from the Explosive Growth of E-Commerce*, Possibility Press, 2000.

Matthijssen, Luuk, *Interfacing Between Lawyers and Computers: An Architecture for Knowledge-Based Interfaces to Legal Databases*, Kluwer Academic Publishers, 1999.

Maxwell, John C., *John C. Maxwell's Electronic Leadership Library*, Thomas Nelson, 1999.

May, Paul Richard, *The Business of E-Commerce: From Corporate Strategy to Technology*, Cambridge University Press, 2000.

McKenna, Regis, *Relationship Marketing: Successful Strategies for the Age of the Customer*, Addison-Wesley, 1993.

McKenna, Regis, *Real Time: Preparing for the Age of the Never Satisfied Customer*, Harvard Business School Press, 1997.

McKeown, Patrick G. and Richard T. Watson, *Metamorphosis: A Guide to the World Wide Web & Electronic Commerce:* Version 2.0, John Wiley, 1997.

Means, Grady (Editor), *E-Business Revolution and the Design of 21st Century Companies and Markets*, John Wiley, 2000.

Mears, Christine, *Business Intelligence With Cold Fusion*, Prima Publishing, 2000.

Melin, Mark, *Computer Inselligence*, Chandler House Press, 2000.

Menasce, Daniel A. and Virgilio A. F. Almeida, *Scaling for E-Business: Technologies, Models, Performance, and Capacity Planning*, Prentice Hall, 2000.

Mendonca, Stephen, *Instant Advantage.com: Winning Strategies for the Online Economy*, Prentice Hall, 2000.

Merkow, Mark S. and Ken L. Wheeler, *Building SET Applications for Secure Transactions*, John Wiley, 1998.

Milley, Don, *The eMarketplace: Strategies for Success in B2B eCommerce*, McGraw-Hill, 2000.

Minik, Phyllis Davis, *EDI QuickStart ebook*, Advanced EDI and Barcoding Corp., 1999.

Minoli, Daniel and Andrew Schmidt, *Internet Architectures*, Wiley, 1999.

Minoli, Daniel and Emma Minoli, *Web Commerce Technology Handbook*, McGraw-Hill, 1997.

Mitrakas, Andreas, *Open EDI and Law in Europe: A Regulatory Framework*, Kluwer Law Intl., 1997.

Mitter, Swasti and Maria Ines Bastos, *Europe and Developing Countries in the Globalised Information Economy: Employment and Distance Education*, Routledge, 1999.

Modahl, Mary, *Now or Never: How Companies Must Change Today to Win the Battle for Internet Consumers*, Harperbusiness, 1999.

Moore, Geoffrey A., *Inside the Tornado: Marketing Strategies from Silicon Valley's Cutting Edge*, HarperBusiness, 1995.

Moore, Geoffrey A., *Living on the Fault Line: Managing for Shareholder Value in the Age of the Internet*, HarperBusiness, 2000.

Moore, Geoffrey A. and Regis McKenna, *Crossing the Chasm: Marketing and Selling High-Tech Products to Mainstream Customers*, Revised Edition, HarperBusiness, 1999.

Moore, James F. *The Death of Competition: Leadership and Strategy in the Age of Business Ecosystems*, HarperBusiness, 1996.

Mott, Geoff, Dirk Schneider, Philipp Gerbet, Alex Birch and Pillip Gerbert, *The Age of E Tail: Conquering the New World of Electronic Shopping*, LPC, 2000.

Mougayar, Walid, *Opening Digital Markets: Battle Plans and Business Strategies for Internet Commerce*, McGraw-Hill, 1997.

Moynihan, James J. and Marcia L. McLure, *EDI: A Guide to Electronic Data Interchange and Electronic Commerce Applications in the Healthcare Industry*, Irwin Professional, 1996.

Murphy, Tom, *Web Rules: How the Internet Is Changing the Way Consumers Make Choices*, Dearborn Trade, 2000.

Nagel, Karl D. and Glen Gray, *2000 Miller Electronic Commerce Assurance Services,* Harcourt Brace, 2000.

Nash, Tom and the Institute of Directors, *E Commerce,* Kogan Page Ltd., 1999.

Nelson, Katherine (Editor), *Websights: The Future of Business and Designs on the Internet,* North Light Books, 2000.

Nemzow, Martin, *Building Cyberstores: Installation, Transaction Processing, and Management.* McGraw-Hill, 1997.

Newcombe, Tod, *Electronic Commerce: A Guide for Public Officials,* Government Technology Press, 1998.

Newell, Frederick, *Loyalty.com: Customer Relationship Management in the New Era of Internet Marketing,* McGraw-Hill, 2000.

Newell, Frederick, *The New Rules of Marketing: How to Use One-To-One Relationship Marketing to Be the Leader in Your Industry,* Irwin, 1997.

Nielsen, Jakob, *Designing Web Usability: The Practice of Simplicity,* New Riders Publishing, 1999.

Nobrega, John and Peter Alexander, *Internet Marketing Tips For Busy Executives,* WinWinWeb Internet Strategy, 1999.

Norman Donald A., *The Design of Everyday Things,* Currency/Doubleday, 1990.

Norris, Mark, Steve West and Kevin Gaughn, *E -Business Essentials: Technology and Network for the Electronic Marketplace,* John Wiley, 2000.

O'Connell, Brian, *B2B.Com,* Adams Media Corporation, 2000.

O'Dell, Susan M. and Joan A. Pajunen, *The Butterfly Customer: Capturing the Loyalty of Today's Elusive Consumer,* Wiley, 1997.

OECD, *Electronic Commerce: Opportunities and Challenges for Government.* ISBN: 9264155120, OECD, 1997.

OECD, *Gateways to the Global Market: Consumers and Electronic Commerce,* OECD, 1998.

O'Leary, Daniel Edmund, *Enterprise Resource Planning Systems: Systems, Life Cycles, Electronic Commerce, and Risk,* Cambridge University Press, 2000.

Oleksy, Walter G., *Web Entrepreneur,* Rosen Publishing, 2000.

Olfman, Lorne, *Organizational Memory Systems: A Special Double Issue of the Journal of Organizational Computing and Electronic Commerce,* Lawrence Erlbaum Assoc., 1999.

Paley, Russell and Michael Craig, *Russ Paley's Ultimate Guide to Network Marketing,* Career Press, 2000.

Pallot, Marc and Victor Sandoval, *Concurrent Enterprising: Toward the Concurrent Enterprise in the Era of the Internet and Electronic Commerce,* Kluwer International, 1998.

Papows, Jeff and David Moschella, *Enterprise.Com: Market Leadership in the Information Age,* Perseus Books, 1998.

Parker, Roger C., *Streetwise Relationship Marketing On The Internet,* Adams Media Corporation, 2000.

Patel, Keyur, Mary Pat McCarthy and John Chambers, *Digital Transformation: The Essentials of e-Business Leadership,* McGraw-Hill, 2000.

Payne, Judith E., *Electronic Data Interchange (EDI: Using Electronic Commerce to Enhance Defense Logistics),* Rand Corporation, 1991.

Peppers, Don and Martha Rogers, *Enterprise One to One: Tools for Competing in the Interactive Age.* Currency/Doubleday, 1997.

Peppers, Don and Martha Rogers, *The One-To-One Future: Building Relationships One Customer at a Time,* Currency/Doubleday, 1997.

Perry, James T. and Gary Schneider, *Electronic Commerce,* Course Technology, 1999.

Phillips, Nicola and Nicky Phillips, *E-Motional Business: Wired World, Real Relationships,* Prentice Hall, 2000.

Phillips Publishing, *Phillips Who's Who in Electronic Commerce,* Phillips Publishing Company, 1996.

Pickering, Chris, *E-Business Success Strategies: Achieving Business and It Alignment,* Computer Technology Research, 2000.

Picot, A., Axel Zerdick, Ulrich T. Lange and Alexander Artope, *Funding the Future of Communications: Markets, Users, Economics, Ecc Report 1998 (European Communication Council Report),* Springer Verlag, 2000.

Pine, B. Joseph and Stan Davis, *Mass Customization: The New Frontier in Business Competition,* Harvard Business School, 1999.

Plant, Robert T., *eCommerce: Formulation of Strategy,* Prentice Hall, 2000.

Plunkett, Jack W. (Editor), *Plunkett's E-Commerce & Internet Business Almanac,* Plunkett Research Ltd, 2000.

Porter, Michael E. , *Competitive Advantage: Creating and Sustaining Superior Performance,* Free Press, 1998.

Porter, Michael E., *On Competition,* Harvard Business School, 1998.

Pottruck, David S. and Terry Pearce, *Clicks and Mortar,* Jossey-Bass, 2000.

Power, Thomas, *E-Business to the Power of 12: The Principles of .Competition,* Prentice Hall, 2001.

Powers, Mike, *How to Start a Business Website,* Avon Books, 1999.

Preiss, Kenneth, Rogel N. Nagel and Steven L. Goldman, *Cooperate to Compete: Building Agile Business Relationships,* Wiley, 1997.

Price, Susan and Maria Langer, *Online Investing With Quicken 2000,* Osborne McGraw-Hill, 2000.

Prince, Dennis L., *Auction This!: Your Complete Guide to the World of Online Auctions,* Prima Publishing, 1999.

Prince, Dennis, *Auctionwatch.Com Advanced Auction,* Prima Publishing, 2000.

Prince, Dennis L., *Online Auctions at eBay,* Prima Publishing, 2nd Edition, 1999.

Rahman, Syed Mahbubur and Mahesh Raisinghani, *Electronic Commerce: Opportunities and Challenges,* Idea Group, 2000.

Rajput, Wasim, *E-Commerce Systems Architecture and Applications,* Artech House, 2000.

Reid-Smith, Ellen, *Eloyalty,* Harperbusiness, 2000.

Rich, Jason R., *The Unofficial Guide to Starting a Business Online,* IDG Books Worldwide, 1999.

Richards, Sally, *Ask Jeeves: How to Build a Successful .Com Business,* Osborne McGraw-Hill, 2000.

Ries, Al and Laura Ries, *The 11 Immutable Laws of Internet Branding,* Harperbusiness, 2000.

Rifkin, Jeremy, *The Age of Access: The New Culture of Hypercapitalism*, J P Tarcher, 2000.

Robinson, Gerald and Charlie Jones, *E-Made Easy*, Executive Books, 1999.

Romm, Celia T. and Fay Sudweeks, *Doing Business Electronically: A Global Perspective of Electronic Commerce*, Springer Verlag, 1998.

Romm, Celia T. and Fay Sudweeks, *Doing Business on the Internet: Forms and Analysis*. Intellectual Property Series. Law Journal Seminars-Press. Springer Verlag, 1998.

Romm, Celia T. and Fay Sudweeks, *Doing Business on the Internet: Opportunities and Pitfalls*, Springer-Verlag, 1999.

Rosen, Anita. The E-Commerce Question and Answer Book: A Survival Guide for Business Managers, AMACOM, 1999.

Rosenfeld, Louis and Peter Morville, *Information Architecture for the World Wide Web*, O'Reilly & Associates, 1998.

Rosenoer, Jonathan and Douglas Armstrong, *The Clickable Corporation: Using Innovative Ideas to Profit from the Internet*, Free Press, 1999.

Ross, Manning L., *businessplan.com: how to write a web-woven strategic business plan*, Oasis Press, 1998.

Rounds, Michael F., *Fishin With a Net*. 5th Edition, C P M, 1998.

Sakaiya, Taichi, *The Knowledge-Value Revolution, or A History of the Future*, Kodabsha International, 1991.

Savage, Charles M., *Fifth Generation Management: Co-Creating Through Virtual Enterprising, Dynamic Teaming, and Knowledge Networking*, Butterworth-Heinemann, 1996.

Sawyer, Ben, Dave Greely and Joe Cataudella, *Creating Stores on the Web*, Peachpit Press, 1999.

Schiller, Dan, *Digital Capitalism: Networking the Global Market System*, MIT Press, 1999.

Schmied, Gerhard E., *High Quality Messaging and Electronic Commerce: Technical Foundations, Standards, and Protocols*, Springer Verlag, 1999.

Schutzer, Dan, *Electronic Commerce: The Wired Corporation*, Morgan Kaufmann Publishers, 2005.

Schwartz, Evan I., *Digital Darwinism: Seven Breakthrough Business Strategies for Surviving in the Cutthroat Web Economy,* Broadway Books, 1999.

Schwartz, Evan I., *Webonomics: Nine Essential Principles for Growing Your Business on the World Wide Web,* Broadway Books, 1997.

Schweighofer, Erich, *Legal Knowledge Representation: Automatic Text Analysis in Public International and European Law,* 1999.

Sehrouchni, Ahmed and Mostafa Hashem Sherif, *Protocols for Secure Electronic Commerce,* CRC Press, 2000.

Selzer, Richard, *Shop Online the Lazy Way,* Macmillan General Reference, 1999.

Senge, Peter M., *The Fifth Discipline: The Art and Practice of the Learning Organization,* Doubleday/Currency, 1990.

Senge, Peter M., Art Kleiner, Charlotte Roberts, George Roth and Rick Ross (Editors), *The Dance of Change,* Doubleday, 1999.

Sexton, Conor, *E Commerce and Security,* Butterworth-Heinemann, 1999.

Seybold, Patricia B and Ronni T Marshak, *Customers.Com: How to Create a Profitable Business Strategy for the Internet and Beyond,* Times Books, 1998.

Shakun, Melvin F., *Negotiation Processes: Modeling Frameworks and Information,* Kluwer Academic,1996.

Shapiro, Carl and Hal, R Varian, *Information Rules: A Strategic Guide to the Network Economy,* Harvard Business School, 1998.

Shaw, Michael, Robert Blanning, Troy Strader (Editor) and Andrew B. Whinston (Editors), *Handbook on Electronic Commerce,* Springer Verlag, 2000,

Shim, Jae K., Anique A. Qureshi, Joel G. Siegel, and Roberta M. Siegel, *The International Handbook of Electronic Commerce,* Fitzroy Dearborn Publishers, 2000.

Shim Jae K., Anique A. Qureshi, Joel G. Siegel, Roberta M. Siegel and Joel Siegal, *The International Handbook of Electronic Commerce,* AMACOM, 2000.

Shurety, Samantha, *E-Business with Net Commerce,* Prentice Hall, 1999.

Siebel, Thomas M., Pat House and Charles R. Schwab, *Cyber Rules: Strategies for Excelling at E-Business*, Doubleday, 1999.

Siegel, David, *Futurize Your Enterprise: Business Strategy in the Age of the E-customer*, John Wiley, 1999.

Siegel, Joel, *The International Handbook of Electronic Commerce*, Glenlake Publishing Company, 2000.

Silverstein, Barry, *Business-To-Business Internet Marketing*, Maximum Press, 1998.

Silverstein, Barry, *Internet Marketing for Information Technology Companies*, Maximum Press, 2000.

Simensky, Melvin, Neil J. Wilkof and Lanning G. Bryer, *Intellectual Property in the International Marketplace: Valuation, Protection, Exploitation, and Electronic Commerce*, John Wiley, 1999.

Sindell, Kathleen, *Investing Online for Dummies*, IDG Books Worldwide, 2000.

Slutsky, Scott and Darrell R. Jobman, *The Complete Guide to Electronic Trading Futures*, McGraw-Hill, 1999.

Small, Peter, *The Entrepreneurial Web: First, Think Like an E-Business*, Financial Times, 2000.

Smith, Bud E. and Frank Catalano, *Marketing Online for Dummies*, IDG Books Worldwide, 1998.

Smith, Dayle M, *The E-Business Book: A Step-by-Step Guide to E-Commerce and Beyond*, Bloomberg Press, 2001.

Smith, Emily (Editor) and Gabriel Smith (Editor), *An Introduction to the Internet for Investors*, Knowledge Systems Institute, 2000.

Smith, Rob, Mark Speaker and Mark Thompson, *Complete Idiot's Guide to e-Commerce*, Que, 2000.

Sobel, Glen, Rick Bier and Beth Driscoll, *Poor Richard's Affiliate Marketing: Using Internet Affiliate and Associate Programs to Make Money and Sell Products*, Top Floor Publishing, 2000.

Sokol, Phyllis K., *From EDI to Electronic Commerce: A Business Initiative*, McGraw Hill Text, 1995.

Spector, Robert, *amazon.com Get Big Fast*, Harperbusiness, 2000.

Spooner, Nick, *The Wizard of E: Notes from the Digital Warzone*, Capstone, 1999.

Standing Committee on Procurement and Federal Facilities Council, *Electronic Commerce for the Procurement of Construction and Architect-Engineer Services: Implementing the Federal Acquisition Streamlining Act*, National Academy Press, 1997.

Standing, Craig, *Internet Commerce Development*, Artech, 2000.

Sterne, Jim, *Advertising on The Web*, Que, 1997.

Sterne, Jim, *Customer Service on the Internet: Building Relationships, Increasing Loyalty, and Staying Competitive*, Wiley, 1996.

Sterne, Jim, *World Wide Web Marketing: Integrating the Web into Your Marketing Strategy*, 2nd Edition, Wiley, 1998.

Strauss, Judy and Raymond D. Frost, *Marketing on the Internet: Principles of Online Marketing*, Prentice Hall, 1999.

Sweeney, Susan, *Internet Marketing for Your Tourism Business*, Maximum Press, 2000.

Sudweeks, Fay and Celia T. Romm, *Doing Business on the Internet: Opportunities and Pitfalls*, Springer-Verlag, 1999.

Sullivan, Robert L., *Electronic Commerce with EDI*, Twain, 1998.

Sutton, Steve G. and Deepak Khazanchi, *Electronic Commerce Control and Assurance*, South-Western College Publishing, 2002.

Sweeney, Susan, *101 Ways to Promote Your Web Site*, Maximum Press, 2000.

Szuprowicz, Bohdan, *Supply Chain Management for E-Business Infrastructures*, Computer Technology Research Corporation, 2000.

Szuprowicz, Bohdan O., *E-Commerce: Implementing Global Marketing Strategies*, Computer Technology Research Corporation, 1999.

Szuprowicz, Bohdan O., *Extranets and Intranets: E-Commerce Business Strategies for the Future*, Computer Technology Research Corporation, 1998.

Szuprowicz, Bohdan O., *Webcasting Strategies: Effective Push Technologies for Intranets and Extranets*, Computer Technology Research Corporation, 1998.

Szydlik, Sherry and Lamont Wood, *E-trepreneur: A Radically Simple and Inexpensive Plan for a Profitable Internet Store in 7 Days*, John Wiley & Sons, 2000.

Tan, Felix B., Scott P., Corbett and Yuk-Yong Wong, *Information Technology Diffusion in the Asia Pacific: Perspectives on Policy, Electronic Commerce and Education*, Idea Group Publishing, 1998.

Tapscott, Don, *The Digital Economy: Promise and Peril in the Age of Networked Intelligence*. McGraw-Hill, 1995.

Tapscott, Don, et al. *Blueprint to the Digital Economy: Wealth Creation in the Era of E-Business*. McGraw-Hill, 1998.

Tapscott, Don (Editor), *Creating Value in the Network Economy*, Harvard Business School Press, 1999.

Tapscott, Don, David Ticoll and Alex Lowy, *Digital Capital: Harnessing the Power of Business Webs*, Harvard Business School Press, 2000.

Targowski, Andrew S., *Global Information Infrastructure: The Birth, Vision, and Architecture*, Idea Group, 1996.

Taylor, Dave and Susan M. Cooney, *The E-Auction Insider: How to Get the Most Out of Your Online Auction*, Osborne McGraw-Hill, 2000.

Taylor, David and Alyse Terhune, *Doing eBusiness: Strategies for Thriving in an Electronic Marketplace*, John Wiley, 2000.

Taylor, Jim, Watts Wacker and Howard Means, *The 500-Year Delta: What Happens After What Comes Next*, HarperBusiness, 1977.

Testerman, Joshua O., *Web Advertising and Marketing*, Prima Publishing, 1998.

Thurow, Lester C., *The Future of Capitalism: How Today's Economic Forces Shape Tomorrow's World*, William Morrow, 1996.

Thurow, Lester C., *Building Wealth: The New Rules for Individuals, Companies and Nations*. Harpercollins, 1999.

Tiernan, Bernadette, *E-Tailing*, Dearborn Trade, 1999.
Timmers, Paul and J. J. Timmers, *Electronic Commerce: Strategies and Models for Business-to-Business Trading*, John Wiley, 2000.

Tomsen, Mai-lan, *Killer Content: Strategies for Web Content and E-Commerce*, Addison-Wesley, 2000.

Treese, Winfield G. and Lawrence C. Stewart, *Designing Systems for Internet Commerce*, Addison-Wesley, 1998.

Trepper, Charles H., *E-Commerce Strategies*, Microsoft Press, 2000.

Troy, Carol, *Understanding Electronic Day Trading*, McGraw-Hill, 1999.

Turban, Efraim, Jae Kyu Lee and David King, *Electronic Commerce: A Global Perspective*, Prentice Hall, 1999.

Turban, Efraim, Jae Kyu Lee and David King and H. Michael Chung, *Electronic Commerce: A Managerial Perspective*, Prentice Hall, 1999.

Underhill, Rod, Nat Gertler and Stan Lee, *Complete Idiot's Guide to Making Millions on the Internet*, Que, 2000.

U.S. House of Representatives, *Electronic commerce andinteroperability in the national information infrastructure: hearing before the Subcommittee on Technology, Environment, and Aviation of the Committee on Science, Space, and Technology*, U.S. House of Representatives, One Hundred Third Congress, second session, 1994.

Vartanian, Thomas, H., Robert Ledig and Thoman P. Ledig and Lynn Bruneau, *21st Century Money, Banking & Commerce*, Fried, Frank, Harris, Shriver & Jacobson, 1998.

Vassos, Tom, *Strategic Internet Marketing*, Que, 1996.

Vine, David, *Internet Business Intelligence: How to Build a Big Company System on a Small Company Budget*, Independent Pub Group, 2000.

Ware, James, Judith Gebauer, Amir Hartman and Malu Roldan, *Search for Digital Excellence*, McGraw-Hill, 1998.

Wayland, Robert E and Paul Michael Cole, *Customer Connections: New Strategies for Growth*, Harvard Business School Press, 1997.

Wayner, Peter, *Digital Cash: Commerce on the Net*, Ap Professional, 1997.

Weinzimer, Philip, *Getting It Right!: Creating Customer Value for Market Leadership*, Wiley, 1998.

Welsh, Kate Shoup, *Bargain Shopping Online*, McGraw-Hill, 1999.

Westland, J. Christopher and Theodore, H. K. Clark, *Global Electronic Commerce: Theory and Cases*, MIT Press 1999.

Whinston, Andrew B., Dale O. Stahl and Soon-Yong Choi, *The Economics of Electronic Commerce*, Macmillan Technical Publishing, 1997.

Whiteley, David, *Electronic Commerce*, McGraw-Hill Book Co Ltd. (UK), 2000.

Wiegran, Dr. Gaby and Hardy Koth, *Custom Enterprise.Com: Every Product, Every Price,* Every Message, Prentice Hall, 2000.

Wind, Jerry and Vijay Mahajan, *Digital Marketing: Global Strategies from the World's Leading Experts,* 2001.

Windham, Laurie, Jon Samsel (Contributor) and Kenneth J. Orton, *Dead Ahead: The Web Dilemma and the New Rules of Business,* Allworth Press, 1999.

Wooten Terry, *The Almanac of Online Trading,* McGraw-Hill, 2000.

Wright, Benjamin and Jane K. Winn, *The Law of Electronic Commerce,* Aspen Publishers, 1998.

Wright, Benjamin, *Law of Electronic Commerce EDI, Fax, and E-Mail: Technology, Proof, and Liability,* Aspen Publishers Inc., 1994.

Wyckoff, Richard D., Andrew Wyckoff and Alessandra Colecchia, *Economic and Social Impacts of Electronic Commerce,* Brookings Institution Press/Inter-American Development Bank, 2000.

Yannopoulos, Georgios N., *Modelling the Legal Decision Process for Information Technology Applications in Law* (Law and Electronic Commerce, Vol 4), Kluwer Law International, 1998.

Yesil, Magdalena, *Creating the Virtual Store: Taking Your Web Site from Browsing to Buying,* John Wiley, 1996.

Zeff, Robbin and Brad Aronson, *Advertising on the Internet,* Lee, John Wiley, 1999.

Zoellick, Bill, *Web Engagement: Connecting to Customers in e-Business,* Addison-Wesley, 2000.

Index

.net, 99, 110, 191, 193
@Home, 253
1-to-1 marketing, 266, 272
7x24, 290
Aberdeen Group, 76, 222
ability to change, 131
access control, 92, 93
accountability, 235
active content, 159
ActiveWorlds, 272
activity-based analysis, 143
Adams, Harkness & Hill, 257
Adexa, 78
agent technology, 118, 119, 169, 175, 182, 183
agenthood, 120
aggregated solution, 181
aggregation, 75, 182, 289
aggregator, 139, 178
Agile Software Corporation, 78
agility, 92, 135, 189, 268
Akamai, 291
Alberthal, Les, 72
aligning technology with business, 115
alliances, 78
Alshuler, David, 222
Altra Energies, 47
Amazon.com, 26, 44, 63, 253, 265
American Express, 119
analytic solutions, 236
Anderson, Bob, 114, 149
Andreessen, Marc, 43
ANSI X12 EDI, 107
antidisintermediation, 65
any-to-any, 43, 62, 223, 226
application components, 105

Application Framework for E-business, 99, 110
application frameworks, 105
application integration, 227
application program interface (API), 111
application servers, 95, 189
application service provider (ASP), 39
apprenticeship, 134
architectural approach, 144
architectural planning, 132
Ariba, 46, 77, 78, 108, 193, 258
ARPAnet, 37, 43
artificial intelligence, 82, 119
Aspect Development Corporation, 78
Association for Electronic Commerce, 277
asynchronous, 95, 103, 113
asynchronous communication, 226
Atanasoff, John Vincent, 37
auctions, 47, 64, 75, 119, 138, 216
audit trails, 228
auditability, 228
Austin Ventures, 221
Australia, 28
authentication, 92, 227
authorization, 93
authorization limits, 94
Auto-by-Tel, 267
Automated Credit Exchange, 47
Automatic Data Processing, 39

autonomous software agents, 273
autonomy, 120
availability, 290
B2B, 63, 257
B2B exchanges, 47, 65, 77
B2B marketplace, 47
B2B marketplaces, 27, 199, 200, 223
B2B trading exchange, 76
B2Bi, 179
B2C, 44, 63, 257
Baan, 41, 91
back office management systems, 222
balance of power, 284
Balanced Scorecard, 143
bandwidth, 287
bankruptcies, 258
Barnes and Noble.com, 71
batch processing, 39
batch transactions, 229
behavior, 209
Berners-Lee, Tim, 43
Best Buy, 292
best practice, 56
Bezos, Jeff, 26, 265
Bina, Eric, 43
Black & Decker, 65
Blackburn, Scott, 221
Borders.com, 42
BPML, 210
BPR, 67, 266
Bradshaw, Jeffrey M., 118
branding, 30
brick and mortar, 278, 290, 291
brochureware, 45
broker model, 74
Building Database-Driven Web Catalogs, 270
build-to-order, 235

business application components, 96
business architecture, 143
business component systems, 117
business conversations, 77, 97
business ecosystems, 48, 62, 86, 103
business engineering, 41, 116
business entity objects, 95
business event management, 224
business intelligence, 97, 118
business models, 98, 47, 139
Business Object Generator, 213
business objects, 212, 214
business process integration, 79, 223
business process modeling, 106
Business Process Modeling Language, 210
business process reengineering(BPR), 55, 67
business processes, 178, 181, 182, 285
business rules, 96, 106, 285
business semantics, 106
business service provider (BSP), 81
business strategy, 87, 131, 144
business strategy formulation, 136
business strategy framework, 132
Business Transaction Protocol, 210

Index 341

business transformation, 49
business ubiquity, 285
business webs, 181
business-to-business, 75, 77, 93, 287, 290
Business-to-Business integration, 179
business-to-consumer, 75
butterfly market, 48, 74
Buy.com, 30
buyer's market, 73
buy-side, 74
C++, 191
call center, 268, 273
cannibalize, 139
Carpoint, 267
Carrefour, 73
Catalina Marketing, 273
catalog management, 95, 104
catalog-transact model, 47
catastrophic data loss, 227
cathedral or a bazaar?, 80
caveat venditor, 284
CDNow, 258
cell phones, 285
center-based systems, 150
Cerf, Vint, 37, 43
change management, 77
channel conflicts, 137
channel replenishment, 245
chat, 112
Chat rooms, 287
checkpoint restart, 227
Chemdex, 170, 258
Cisco, 173, 174, 258
Clark, James, 44
Clarke, Arthur C., 253
click and mortar, 290
click streams, 270
click-throughs, 30

client-server computing model, 111
closed markets, 276
Coase, Ronald, 150
Coca Cola, 293
Colbert, Philip, 115
collaboration, 66, 76, 77, 103, 111, 158, 161, 170, 171, 172, 174, 175, 177, 178, 179, 181, 182, 287
collaboration boards, 77
collaborative commerce, 111, 112, 114, 169, 173, 176, 177
collaborative information filtering, 272
collaborative marketplaces, 77
COM+, 95
commerce lifecycle, 95
Commerce One, 46, 108, 258
commerce process rengineering (CPR), 58
commerce resource platform (CRP), 80, 91, 96, 97, 98, 103, 104, 140, 294
CommerceNet, 108, 274, 277
commodities, 47
commodity markets, 119
Common Business Library (CBL), 108
Common Object Request Broker Architecture, 109
Common Warehouse Metamodel Interchange (CWMI), 97, 118
communities-of-interest, 72, 287
community builder, 92, 98
community management, 104
compelling value, 290

competitive advantage, 145, 230
competitive capabilities, 54
complete solutions, 289
complex adaptive systems, 166
complexity, 105, 119
component architectures, 105
component frameworks, 105
component-based architecture, 104
component-based software development, 106, 116
components, 191
composite applications, 190, 191
CompUSA, 292
Computer Telephony Integration (CTI), 273
concept to code, 135
configurators, 287
Connection Age, 149, 151
connectionless communication, 226
consortium business models, 73
constellations, 191
content syndication, 98
context, 83, 87
contextualized spaces, 163
continuing process improvement, 72
convenience goods, 278
convergence, 37
cookies, 270
coordination, 276
CORBA, 98, 109, 191
Corba Component Model, 95
core competencies, 67, 236
Covisint, 47, 59, 68, 73, 108
CPFR, 67

critical success factors, 145
CRM, 94, 273
cross-selling, 66
CRUD, 214
customer care, 72
customer experience, 278
customer relationship management, 71, 83, 97, 103, 110, 273
customer relationship systems, 68
customer retention, 30
customer satisfaction, 178, 182
customer self-service, 268
customer service, 267, 286
customer value, 172
customer value analysis, 136, 138
customer-driven value chains, 136
customer-facing process, 56
customers, 171
customization, 30, 285
CWMI, 97
cXML, 108, 225
DaimlerChrysler, 47
Danish, Sherif, 270
data mining, 97, 123
data repository, 97
data warehouse, 97
Davenport, Thomas, 83
DCOM, 98, 109
Deep Blue, 119
defined services, 118
DeGeus, Arie, 145
Dell, 30, 46, 54, 63, 174
Dell, Michael, 288
demand aggregation, 64
Deming, Edwards, 58
Developing Intelligent Agents, 122

digital corporation, 61
digital economy, 62, 267, 288
digital strategy, 131
Direct from Dell, 288
direct procurement, 54, 62
directory services, 104
disaster recovery, 228
discontinuous change, 71
discussion forums, 178
discussion groups, 287
disintermediation, 29, 161, 266
disruptive information technology, 37
distributed access, 39
distributed artificial intelligence (DAI), 119
distributed components, 117
document messaging, 107
document type definition (DTD), 107
document-centered technology, 107
domain experts, 138, 143
domain knowledge, 205, 214
Dongre, Ashok, 22
dot-com crash, 24, 44
dotcomfailures.com, 260
downsizing, 41
Drucker, Peter, 31, 35
Drugstore.com, 279
duplicate processes, 67
Dutch auction, 75
dynamic content, 95
dynamic pricing, 64
dynamic pricing strategies, 293
dynamic relationships, 176
Dynamic Services Framework, 99, 110
dynamic workflows, 96

EAI, 179
eBay, 170
eBreviate, 47
e-business platform, 192
ebXML, 108, 110
eCo Framework, 108
e-commerce, 46, 277
e-commerce applications, 107
edge of the network, 153
edge-based practices, 163
EDI, 62, 66, 107, 108, 179, 223, 226, 227, 244, 274
EDS, 72
electronic business XML, 108
Electronic Commerce Reference Model, 104
electronic data interchange (EDI), 179, 277
Electronic Funds Transfer, 237
electronic trading networks (ETNs), 230
email, 111, 163, 178
e-marketplaces, 47, 48, 62
encounter models, 79, 104
encryption, 227
end-to-end industry value chain, 54
end-to-end recovery, 227
Engelbart, Doug, 111
English auction, 75
Enron, 47
enterprise architecture, 39
Enterprise Java Beans, 95
enterprise marketplace, 46
enterprise portal, 187, 189, 194, 286
enterprise resource planning (ERP), 41, 91, 179, 183, 236, 266

e-procurement, 46, 76
e-services, 59, 62, 71, 78, 79, 81, 97, 99, 105, 108, 110, 136, 138, 192
e-speak, 108
e-tailers, 46, 266
event handling services, 95
exception handling, 165
exchange, 169, 170, 171, 172, 175
eXcite, 253
expert systems, 119
Express Scripts, 279
extended supply chain, 233
eXtensible Markup Language (XML), 97, 106
external actors, 140
external workflows, 96
extranets, 66, 91, 223
fail-safe, 227
fax, 285
Federated Component Systems, 117
federations, 117
FedEx, 59, 288
file transfer protocol (FTP), 45
finite-state machine, 210
First Albany, 113
first generation e-commerce, 103
first mover, 28
First-Price auction, 75
fit, balance and compromise, 87, 104, 131
Ford, 47, 253
Forrester Research, 45, 72, 75, 77, 169, 269, 273
fragmented buyers and sellers, 74
FreeMarkets, 47, 78, 258
friction-free, 285

frictionless commerce, 23
frictionless economy, 151
FTP, 111
fulfillment, 276
fully distributed computing, 41, 105
fully-distributed information-sharing, 113
functional management, 56, 58
functionality, 74
fuzzy systems, 120, 121
Gannon, Patrick, 270
Gantz, John, 113
Gartner Group, 28, 169, 189, 192
Gates, Bill, 31
Gelernter, David, 265
General Electric, 25, 46, 63, 66, 170
general systems thinking, 57, 145
genetic algorithms, 120, 121
Gerstner, Lou, 71
GM, 47
Gnutella, 113, 153
GnutellaNet, 114
goal-driven agents, 120
Gopher, 111
graphical user interface, 271
Gray & Christmas., 258
Great Plains, 91
green pages, 97
Greenspan, Alan, 23
Greenspan, Alan, 257
Gross, Gabriel, 274
groupware, 111
GTE, 39
guaranteed message delivery, 227
GUI, 271
Hammer and Champy, 56

hard coding, 212
Harmon, Tim, 169
hassle factor, 113
Hayward, Bob, 28
Herzum, Peter, 117
Hewlett-Packard, 79, 99, 108, 110
holistic relationship management, 86
Hollander, Dave, 36
Home Depot, 64, 80, 87
horizontal marketplaces, 75
Hot Mail, 44
HTTP, 191
human cognition, 82
human resource systems (HRS), 94
i2, 76, 78
IBM, 39, 71, 99, 109, 110, 117, 119, 193, 277
IBM 360 mainframe, 39
I-commerce, 277
Improving Performance, 67
incremental releases, 142
independent market, 74
independent market-maker, 47
indirect operating costs, 46
indirect procurement, 54, 62
Industrial Age, 284
Industrial Revolution, 53
industry analysis, 136
information filtering, 123
Ingram, 266
instant messaging, 154, 163
intellectual capital, 134
intelligent agent technology, 182
intelligent agents, 121, 123, 175, 183, 273
intelligent software, 103

intelligent software agents, 48, 103, 265
intelligent support, 103
intelligent task management, 103
inter-company workflows, 96
inter-enterprise business processes, 91, 140
inter-enterprise integration, 179
intermediary, 290
internal business processes, 139
International Data Corporation, 113
Internet, 41, 43, 72, 91
Internet expectations, 138
Internet Inter-ORB Protocol (IIOP), 109
Internet Service Provider, 171
interoperate, 276
in-the-Net analytics, 233, 248, 250
intra-enterprise, 179
intranets, 91, 223
IONA, 193
IP telephony, 273
IPR, 67, 266
islands of information, 40, 55
isomorphic, 117
J. D. Edwards, 41, 91
J.C. Penney, 64, 253
J2EE, 190, 193, 210
Jabil Circuit, 174
Java, 190, 194, 210
Johnson, Maryfran, 256
joint product design, 77
Jones, Dennis, 288
Jupiter Research, 162
Jxta, 114

Kahn, Robert, 43
Kaplan, Robert S., 143
Kelly, Kevin, 85, 283
killer application, 267
Kmart, 253
Knapik and Johnson, 122
knowbots, 120
know-how, 82, 83, 85
knowledge, 170
knowledge engine, 209, 214
Knowledge Interchange Format (KIF), 276
knowledge management, 42, 48, 82, 83, 103, 110
knowledge sharing, 79
knowledge transfer, 135
knowledge-based tasks, 119
Kraft Foods, 258
Lands End, 46
layered architecture, 92
Leebaert, Derek, 72
legacy systems, 223
life time value, 84
local area network(LAN), 40
logical components, 104
Loshin, Pete, 109
Lowes, 64
loyalty, 84, 174, 182, 292
Machlis, Sharon, 79
mainframe, 39
Maintenance Repair and Operations (MRO), 46
Malone, Thomas, 276
managed network services, 228
many-to-many business model, 48, 74
many-to-one, 73
margin, 53
market demand, 29
Market Dictionary, 211, 214
market maker, 92, 98, 138

market networks, 181
market research, 136
market segments, 63
marketing, 276
marketing plans, 293
marketing product data management, 270
marketplace models, 217
Marriott, 174
Marzbani, Ramin, 27
mass marketing, 30
matching, 74
Mattel, 258
McCullough, Ross, 79
McKenna, Regis, 284
McKinsey & Company, 27
m-commerce, 48
mediation, 74
mentors, 134
Merck-Medco, 279
message oriented middleware, 224
message passing, 107
message transport, 230
MetalSite, 29, 170
Metcalfe, Bob, 31, 283
Metcalfe's law, 283
metrics, 142
Microsoft, 26, 91, 95, 99, 109, 110, 117, 191, 193, 291
middlemen, 29
Miller, Herman, 171
minicomputers, 39
mission critical, 226
mission-critical infrastructure, 228
mobile commerce, 48, 110
mobshop.com, 64
model driven architecture, 115

Model Driven Architecture (MDA), 117
model driven development, 116
model-based business systems, 116
modeling, 140, 141
monolithic designs, 119
monolithic information systems, 80
Monster.com, 170
Morris, Barry, 187
Mosaic, 44
Mougayar, Walid, 277
MP3, 113
MRO, 75, 76
multi-agent systems, 124, 276
multi-dimensional collaboration, 150
multi-party discovery, 77
multi-platform compression, 227
multiple simultaneous roles, 92, 98
Napster, 113, 153, 154
NASDAQ, 260
natural language processing, 121
negotiation, 77, 165, 276
negotiation facilities, 47
net market makers, 170
net markets, 163
Net Perceptions, 258
Netaction, 99, 110
Netscape, 44, 111
Network Accessible Service Specification (NASSL), 109
network edge, 188
network horizon, 113
network model, 59
networked intelligence, 83
NetZero, 44
neural networks, 121
new economy, 44
newsgroups, 111
Nickless, Sam, 27
non-deterministic system, 119
nonintelligent agent, 122
Norman, Donald, 83
Norton, David P., 143
OAG XML (OAGIS), 108
OASIS, 109
Object Management Group, 97, 104, 109, 117, 191, 274
object model, 98
object Web, 126
object-oriented, 123
Olson, Ken, 31
one-to-one marketing, 284
on-line transaction processing, 39
ontologist, 83
ontology, 206
Open Information Model (OIM), 118
open market processes, 275
Open Profiling Standard, 270
open sourcing, 77
open standards, 104
open technology platform, 95
OPS, 270
Oracle, 73, 99, 108, 110
outsourcing, 236
Ovum, 222
P2P, 113
Pacitti, Chris, 221
page-oriented metaphor, 111
pagers, 285
palm tops, 285
parallel purchasing activities, 247

parametric search, 95
Pascall, Glenn, 23
PCS, 279
peer computing, 153, 157, 158, 165
peer-to-peer, 41, 66, 111, 113, 114, 153, 154, 155
peer-to-peer application platform, 163
peer-to-peer communications, 157
peer-to-Web, 156
people, process and technology, 131
Peoplesoft, 41, 91
permissions, 93
persistent messaging, 227
personalization, 30
personalized content, 94
person-to-person communication, 157
Pets.com, 28, 257
Philips, Wendell, 35
Phoenicians, 37
physical distribution, 288
physical inventories, 288
pipelines, 114
places to spaces, 43
PlanetRX, 279
planning, 134
PlasticsNet, 29, 170
plug-and-play, 96, 285
point solutions, 91, 229
point-to-point connectivity, 229
portal servers, 189
portal strategies, 190
Porter, Michael, 53
prefabricated components, 106
Priceline.com, 258
pricing policy, 292

primary activities, 54, 59
private marketplaces, 72, 199
privileges, 93
problem-solving, 141
process barriers, 67
process engineering, 141
process integration, 179
process management, 58
process objects, 95
procurement, 170, 172, 175
producer-consumer relationship, 284
productivity paradox, 40
profiling, 270
profiling component, 94
Promedix, 258
proof-of-concept, 141
prosumer, 86
proxies, 270
Public Key Infrastructure, 236
public marketplaces, 74
pull, 63
PurchasePro, 258
purchasing, 179
push, 63
Qualcomm, 30
radical reinvention, 56
Rana, S.P., 169
rapid application assembly, 103, 106
rapid integration, 112
reactivity, 120
readiness for process integration, 139
real-time, 67, 174, 183, 285, 287, 293
reason under uncertainty, 120
Rechtin, Eberhardt, 131
redundancy, 228

Reengineering the Corporation, 56
registry, 97, 104
reintermediation, 139, 266
relationships, 85
reliability, 229, 290
repository, 144, 163
request for proposal, 175
requirements, 276, 289
resistance, 135
reuse, 141
reverse auction, 64
reverse value chain engineering, 136
RFQ, 77
role-based task allocation, 94
roles, 94, 183
RosettaNet, 135, 210, 289
Royal Dutch/Shell, 145
RPC, 191
rules of engagement, 65
Rummler and Brache, 67, 140
San Jose Mercury News, 64
SAP, 41, 91
satisfaction stage, 276
Sawhney, Mohan, 257
Saxena, Manoj, 169
scalability, 228, 290
scenarios, 136
Scient, 259
Scotts, 65
sealed-bid auction, 75
searching, 74
Sears, 64, 73, 267
Secure Electronic Transactions (SET), 273
Secure Socket Layer, 236
securities-trading sites, 291
security, 93, 227, 229
see-buy-get transactions, 77

self-service, 287
Selland, Chris, 144
seller's market, 72
sell-side, 46, 74, 77
semantic webs, 163
server-centric, 114
server-less, 113
servers, 285
Service Level Agreement, 242
service-based applications, 187
service-based architectures, 110
service-based Internet, 108
services-based application architecture, 191
service oriented programming, 108
SETI@Home, 154
Seybold, Patricia, 81
shared repository, 141
shared spaces, 111, 112, 114, 155, 158
shared vision, 135
shared whiteboards, 178
SHOP2gether.com, 64
shopping bots, 120
Simple Object Access Protocol (SOAP), 109
Sims, Oliver, 117
Singh, Biri, 199
single sign-on, 93, 94
Skyrme, David, 82
small and medium enterprises (SME), 81, 91
Smith, Adam, 56
SOAP, 191, 192
soft computing, 122
softbots, 120
software agents, 119, 120
software component architecture, 105

software components, 98, 105
software development process, 116
Soley, Richard, 118
Solow, Robert, 40
solution developers, 105,
specialization of labor, 56
specialty goods, 279, 287
speed, 28
spot buying, 47
spot group exchanges, 64
standards, 105, 275
Stebbins, T. L., 256
Steelcase, 171
Steinman, Justin, 233
stickiness, 78, 272
Stone, Chris, 233
stovepipes, 56, 67
strengths, weaknesses, opportunities and threats, 138, 144
structured data, 106
subscribe, 105
Sun Microsystems, 95, 99, 110, 114, 193
Sun One, 99, 110
suppliers, 171, 172
supply and demand planning, 77
supply chain, 77, 139, 173, 233
supply chain analytics, 240
supply chain event management, 235
supply chains, 62, 181
supply-chain collaboration, 78
support activities, 54
synchronization, 182, 184
synchronous, 113
Sysco, 257

Systems Architecting, 131
systems integrators, 91
systems thinking, 58
tacit information, 82, 103
Tambe, Milind, 103
Tapscott, Don, 83
task automation, 81
task coordination, 160
task delegation, 271
task knowledge, 124, 276
taxonomy, 206
Taylor, David, 115
TCP/IP, 43
Tech Data, 289
technology architecture, 143
technology plumbing, 98
Tessler, Joelle, 64
The Digital Economy, 83
the technology question, 57
The Wealth of Nations, 56
thecompost.com, 260
Things That Make Us Smart, 83
thinkgeek.com, 260
Tilburg University, 276
time and distance, 278
timesharing, 39
time-to-market, 28
touch points, 85, 94, 285
Tower of Babel problem, 108
traceability, 141
traction, 138
trading consortia, 27
Trading Process Network (TPN), 63, 290
transaction engine, 214
transaction lifecycle, 216
transactional mechanisms, 215
transaction-based exchanges, 169, 174, 175
transitions, 134

Index

Transora, 29
trust, 85, 292
trust management, 104
trusted third party, 233, 270
Tymkiw, Catherine, 257
UDDI, 108, 110, 114, 165, 193, 225
UML, 117, 135
UN/CEFACT, 109
Unified Modeling Language (UML), 117, 141
uniform second-price auction, 75
unit record concept, 107
United Nations, 109, 182
United Parcel Service of America, 79
Universal Description, Discovery, and Integration (UDDI), 97, 108
UPS, 79, 80
upside-down, 284
USAA, 115, 286
use cases, 141
user intentions, 83
user profiles, 94
Userland, 111
value, 53
value added activities, 62
value added network, 221
value chain analysis, 53
value chain engineering, 136, 140
value chain integrator, 139
value chain optimization, 65, 67
value chains, 53, 59, 62, 71, 76, 85, 87, 97, 117, 133, 135,139, 152, 181, 199, 226, 249
value chains of information, 63

value proposition, 138, 175, 278
value threads, 62, 66
value webs, 60, 85,103
value-added network, 233
value-added services, 163
VAN, 221, 229
vendor managed inventories (VMI), 67
Verde.com, 259
vertical marketplaces, 75
VerticalNet, 258
Vickrey auction, 75
viral marketing, 64
virtual business models, 236
virtual corporations, 58, 151, 266
virtual integration, 174
virtual private network application platform, 152
virtual private networks (VPNs), 112, 221
virtual reality technologies, 287
virtual spaces, 272
visibility, 181, 233, 241
volumebuy.com, 64
Volvo, 253
VPN, 152, 221, 228, 236
Wadhwani, Romesh, 76
Wal-Mart, 26, 46, 62, 170
WAN, 228
WAP, 92
Watson, Thomas, 31
Web bots, 124
Web presence, 45, 269
Web servers, 95
Web services, 108, 192
Web Services Description Language, 109
Web strategy, 79
Web-based EDI, 109

web-commerce, 277
Web-facing platform, 190
WebTV, 285
Welch, Jack, 25, 131
WfMC, 96, 210
Wf-XML, 141
what if analyses, 135
White House, 53
white space, 67, 91
Wilder, Clinton, 30
Winer, Dave, 111
wireless application protocols (WAP), 48
workflow, 96, 103, 106, 141, 160, 190
workflow interoperation, 96
Workflow Management Coalition, 210
Workflow Management Coalition (WfMC), 96
World Wide Web, 41, 43
World Wide Web Consortium (W3C), 106
WSDL, 109
XMI, 117
XML, 65, 96, 97, 104, 106, 107, 193, 194, 210, 212, 225, 227, 237, 276
XML vocabularies, 135
Yahoo, 26, 291
Yankee Group, 144
zero-sum game, 29
Zona Research, 291

About the Authors and Contributors

Special Thanks

In addition to the chapter contributors, many individuals contributed to and influenced this book: Jim Upton, Manager at the DareStep division of Cap Gemini Ernst & Young; Dr. Barbara Belon, Director, Center for Information Technology, Norwalk College; Marc Luvshis, Architect, Information Buiders, Dr. Himanshu Bhatnagar and Dr. James Pepe, eMoxsha, Inc.; Dr. Fahad Almubarak, Chairman of the Advisory Team for E-Commerce at the Ministry of Commerce in Saudi Arabia; Dr. Dan Conway, Graduate Professor, University of Florida; Robert Guttman, Chief Technology Officer, Frictionless Commerce Inc.; Tarun Sharma and Harsha Kumar, eRunway, Dave Hollander, Co-Chair W3C XML Activity, and Chief Technology Officer, Contivo; Shridhar Rangarajan, Architect, Vayda & Herzum, Inc.; Mark Ragel, General Manager, Al Gosaibi Information Systems; Stephen McConnel, OSM sarl; Dr. Gordon Couturier, University of Tampa; Dr. Stanley Birkin, University of South Florida; Lucretia Caryer, Caryer, Caryer and Associates; Demetrios Yannakopoulos, Chief Architect, SeraNova, Inc.; Damien Miller, Chief Technology Officer, Cometway, Inc.; Tony Brown, Editor, eAI Journal, eaijournal.com; and Dan Gillmor, Technology Columnist, San Jose Mercury News.

Authors and Contributors

Bob Anderson is the Business Evangelist for Groove Networks, a Beverly, MA-based company developing peer-to-peer and peer-to-Web software solutions that provide businesses secure, online working relationships with key suppliers, partners and customers. His primary focus has been on articulating the Groove peer-to-peer value proposition in the business context, particularly with regard to trading partner collaboration in areas including Collaborative Planning, Forecasting and Replenishment (CPFR), Supply/Demand (Value) Chain, New Product Design and Net Markets.

Ronald Aronica, President of Greystone Group, Inc., has provided Fortune 500 companies with advice as to how best to use advanced technologies to improve their businesses and profitability. He was a manager with KPMG's IS Strategic Planning and Consulting group and vice-president and president of other IS consulting organizations. In addition to his work with e-commerce, he teaches technologies and the impact of these technologies to IS professionals and their senior managers. Working with the State of Florida, he designed their first Web-based system for providing work and employment opportunities for the State's citizens. When not consulting and traveling, Ron lives in Florida with his wife, Jan, and relaxes gardening and rearchitecting/remodeling vintage houses.

Scott Blackburn is President and CEO CommerceQuest, the company he co-founded in 1992. He fostered the company's rapid growth from a professional services organization to a leading provider of complex business integration software and services. Under his direction, the company gained success in delivering technology solutions to Anheuser Busch, American Express, Ericsson, EDS, ICG Commerce, Tech Data, AAA, Publix Supermarkets, Wal Mart, Ahold, GTE and State Farm. He has spearheaded partnerships with IBM, BMC, Sterling Commerce and Computer Associates. Blackburn led CommerceQuest's participation as an infrastructure services provider with Internet Capital Group's collaborative network of partner companies. Today, Blackburn's CommerceQuest has over 300 employees on four continents and more than 250 customers. Prior to CommerceQuest, Blackburn held posts at Informix and with IBM as a global account executive for large telecommunication providers. Blackburn holds a B.S. degree in Computer Science from the University of Kansas.

Anthony Dutton is Director of Corporate Communications for XML Global Technologies, Inc. Prior to this post Anthony worked with a corporate communications and public relations consultancy where he represented a wide range of high tech firms in the start-up and early stage phases. Independently, Anthony has also worked as a communications consultant, primarily engaged with film, TV and new media companies. He brings a wealth of corporate communications experience to XML Global where he is responsible for a number of initiatives including corporate positioning, media and analyst communications and investor relations. As well as having a Bachelor's Degree in Architecture, Anthony also holds a joint MBA from The Cranfield School of Management in the U.K and the Ecole Supérieure de Commerce in Lyons, France.

Peter Fingar is one of the industry's noted experts in component-based electronic commerce and an internationally recognized author. His recent book, *Enterprise E-Commerce* is a best-seller recognized for its thought leadership and has been adopted by top graduate schools in the U.S. and abroad. Peter is an Executive Partner in the Tampa-based digital strategy firm, the Greystone Group. Peter has served as Technology Advocate for a Boston-based developer of component-based B2B e-commerce for clients including GE TPN, American Express, Master Card and GE Capital. He recently served as a strategy consultant for a $100 million Internet infrastructure start-up in the Middle East. He has held technical and management positions with GTE Data Services, the Arabian American Oil Company, American Software and Computer Services and Perot Systems. He served as Director of Information Technology for the University of Tampa and as an object technology consultant for IBM Global Services. He taught graduate and undergraduate university computing studies in the United States and Saudi Arabia.

Tim Harmon is the vice president of marketing and product strategy at Exterprise. Prior to joining Exterprise, Harmon served as vice president of Retail & Distribution Strategies at META Group, a leading IT research and advisory services firm. Before joining META, Harmon held a number of senior level management positions, including vice president of marketing at Prodea, a leading vendor in the OLAP market that was later acquired by PLATINUM Technology, Inc., and director of product marketing at Sybase. Harmon also founded Datura and served as president and CEO of the DBA utilities vendor, which was acquired by PLATINUM Technology. Harmon earned a B.S. degree in computer science, business administration and math at Iowa State University.

Bryan Maizlish is the Director of Marketing/Business Development for Lockheed Martin Global Telecommunications, and is responsible for identifying market trends, partnerships, acquisition, and new business opportunities centered on integration, pervasive and convergent technologies in the commercial marketplace. Mr. Maizlish served as Executive Vice President, Chief Strategy

Officer, and Chief Financial Officer for Noor Group Ltd. who is building an Arabic portal, data center, and access network infrastructure in Cairo, Egypt, and he served the same role for Magnet Interactive, whose clients included: Nissan, Infiniti, Mayo Clinic, Federal Express, FirstUSA, Kellogg's, Discovery Communications, Crayola, and DuPont. Mr. Maizlish spent nearly a decade working for major Hollywood and independent studios in various strategic and financial roles, and was introduced to both the entertainment and technology industries in 1985 while working for Gene Roddenberry, the creator and producer of *Star Trek*. Mr. Maizlish graduated with an MBA from Wharton in 1988 and currently serves on the Board of Directors for Perfect Data Corporation.

Barry Morris is Chief Executive Officer for IONA Technologies. Mr. Morris has been with IONA since November 1994. Before being named CEO in June 2000, Mr. Morris was Chief Operating Officer for IONA, with responsibility for its day-to-day operations. As COO, he created IONA's iPortal strategy, oversaw the expansion of the company's U.S. headquarters and field offices, and was instrumental in IONA's acquisition of complementary technology companies. Mr. Morris' previous positions within IONA include Executive Vice President, Senior Vice President of Product Development, Vice President of Business Development, and Vice President of Product Management. He joined the company as Channel Manager and Business Development Manager. Before joining IONA, Mr. Morris was a consultant at Digital Equipment Corporation. Before that, he held positions of increasing responsibility at Lotus Development Corporation, Protek Electronics Ltd., and Leading Technology Inc. Mr. Morris earned his Bachelor of Arts from New College, Oxford University.

Dr. S. P. Rana is co-founder, vice chairman and chief technology officer of Exterprise. Prior to founding Exterprise, Rana was with IBM, where he led IBM Global Services' technology strategy development, global program implementations, and vendor alliances for their strategic outsourcing business. He has over 20 years of IT experience and brings a unique combination of enterprise architecture experience that encompass business process collaboration, distributed computing, and customer service issues. Dr. Rana has a Ph.D. in computer sciences from Indian Institute of

Technology (IIT), New Delhi, India, a master's degree in operations research and a bachelor of science in mathematics.

Manoj Saxena is co-founder, president and chief executive officer of Exterprise. Prior to founding Exterprise, Saxena served as business unit manager at 3M, where he had $100 million of P&L responsibility for the Telecom Systems Division. Saxena brings more than 15 years of experience in business development, product marketing, and strategic planning in the telecommunications, medical, and manufacturing industries. Saxena has an MBA from Michigan State University and received an MMS degree from Birla Institute of Technology and Science, Pilani, India.

Biri Singh, President and Chief Executive Officer, co-founded Idapta in February 1999 with the idea of building an enterprise software company to attack the significant opportunity within B2B e-commerce. Previously, Biri was COO of RelevantKnowledge Inc., a pioneering Internet audience measurement and Web-ratings company that merged with MediaMetrix (NASDAQ: MMXI) in October 1998. Prior to joining RelevantKnowledge, Biri served as a consultant for Ernst & Young's communications, media and Internet commerce practice in Atlanta. Before that, Biri worked for several years in product development/management, marketing, and sales positions at Northern Telecom (NORTEL) in Raleigh, NC and Canada. While at NORTEL, Biri successfully brought to market three significant communications products and in 1995, helped NORTEL launch a new technology venture, managing its marketing and sales operations. Biri holds an MBA from the Kenan-Flagler School of Business, University of North Carolina and an undergraduate degree from North Carolina State University.

Justin Steinman serves as Solutions Marketing Manager for Tilion, Inc. In this role, he is responsible for developing Tilion's service and go-to-market strategy, company message, and positioning. Prior to Tilion, Steinman was a consultant with Accenture's Enterprise Business Solutions group. In this capacity, he led a team of consultants responsible for developing strategic and systems solutions through ERP installations for large, multinational clients. Steinman has extensive experience designing and configuring SAP R/3 ERP software, with a particular focus in the supply chain. Steinman is a Phi Beta Kappa graduate of Dartmouth College.

Christopher Stone is the Chief Executive Officer, President, and Founder of Tilion, Inc. Stone founded Tilion to address the unmet business requirement for an on-demand, unified view of the supply chain. Stone is a noted technology visionary, with more than twenty years of experience leading high technology industry innovation. Prior to Tilion, he spent more than two years as executive vice president of corporate strategy and development at Novell. Stone played a key role in the turnaround and resurgence of Novell. Previously, he was the founder of the Object Management Group (OMG), the largest software development standardization group of its kind. While the CEO of OMG, he created CORBA and numerous other object technology standards. He also drove the group's vision, technology teams and the formation of innovative conferences, publications and partnerships. Stone began his technology career at Data General Corporation, where he spent ten years in various roles leading up to his role as the director of software products. Stone has a BS in Computer Science from University of New Hampshire and an Executive MBA from University of Virginia's Darden School of Business.

David R. R. Webber is Vice President of Business Development with XML Global Technologies, Inc. David has over twenty years experience designing and implementing electronic business systems for a broad spectrum of industries. As well he is a US patent holder for advanced EDI software technologies. David is a co-founder of the XML/EDI Group and an acknowledged international authority on XML, EDI, metadata registries and Web-based software engineering. He lectures frequently in the USA, Europe and Asia and has published numerous articles on XML/EDI technology and related business solutions. He is currently involved in an advisory role with a wide variety of industry initiatives including ebXML where he is very involved with the interoperability standards development. His diverse project experience covers government and military logistics, inventory and personnel management, healthcare and telecommunications technologies and has given David a unique and invaluable perspective on the issues surrounding XML and data management. David received his degree in Physics with Computing from the University of Kent, Canterbury in 1976.

Companion Book

ENTERPRISE E-COMMERCE

Peter Fingar
Harsha Kumar
Tarun Sharma

ISBN: 0-929652-11-8

Dr. Bud Tribble, Chief Technology Officer, Sun/Netscape Alliance, Sun Microsystems, Inc. had this to say about the book, *"This book provides an insightful business and technology discussion of how .com changes everything in business -- and what it portends. My advice for the Internet generation of business and technology leaders is -- Just read it!"*

They have -- the book, in its 5th printing in one year, has been adopted by many of the highest ranked graduate and undergraduate programs in the U.S. and abroad; the first printing sold out in 8 weeks; and Japanese, Chinese, Spanish and Korean translations are in print. It may be ordered at online bookstores or from the publisher:

http://geocities.com/m_kpress

New Web Address
www.mkpress.com

The *Real* New Economy
-World Seminar-

In-House Seminars
Board Room Briefings
Workshops
Roundtables

Keynotes

Tailored to the business and technology needs of your company.

"Peter's presentation provided both content and clarity. The content was insightful and visionary, but pragmatic. The clarity allowed Peter to connect with our combined business and technology audience --no small challenge. His presentation was stimulating and his enthusiasm contagious."
-- Gregory D. Tranter, CIO, Allmerica Financial

seminars@mkpress.com
www.mkpress.com/seminars.html